D0983339

THE HEALER'S BENT

RELATIONAL PERSPECTIVES BOOK SERIES

LEWIS ARON AND ADRIENNE HARRIS
Series Editors

THE HEALER'S BENT

Solitude and Dialogue in the Clinical Encounter

James T. McLaughlin

Edited and Introduced By
William F. Cornell

THE ANALYTIC PRESS
2005   Hillsdale, NJ   London

Published by The Analytic Press, Inc.
101 West Street, Hillsdale, NJ 07642
www.analyticpress.com

Typeset in Garamond 11/13 and Zapf Humanist by
Qualitext, Bloomfield, NJ

Earlier versions of the following chapters appeared elsewhere and are
adapted here by permission:

Ch. 4:   Transference, psychic reality, and countertransference (1981),
         Psychoanalytic Quarterly, 50:639–664.
Ch. 5:   The analyst's insights (1988*)*, *Psychoanalytic Quarterly*, 57:370–389.
Ch. 8:   The play of transference: Some reflections on enactment in the
         psychoanalytic situation (1987), *Journal of the American
         Psychoanalytic Association*, 35:557–582.
Ch. 10: Touching limits in the analytic dyad (1995), *Psychoanalytic
         Quarterly*, 64:433–465.
Ch. 11: Dumb, blind or hard: Can an analyst change his spots? (1991),
         Journal of the American Psychoanalytic Association, 39:595–614.
Ch. 12: Power, authority, and influence in the analytic dyad (1996),
         Psychoanalytic Quarterly, 65:201–235.

Library of Congress Cataloging-in-Publication Data

McLaughlin, James Thomas, 1918–
     The healer's bent : solitude and dialogue in the clinical encounter /
James T. McLaughlin ; edited and introduced by William F. Cornell.
     p.   cm. –(Relational perspectives book series ; v. 30)
     Includes bibliographical references and index.
ISBN 0–88163–436–0
1.   Psychoanalysis. 2. Psychotherapist and patient. 3. Self-analysis
     (Psychoanalysis). 4. McLaughlin, James Thomas, 1918–.
     5. Psychoanalysts—United States—Biography. I. Title. II. Series.

     RC501.2.M38 2005
     616.89'17—dc22

Printed in the United States of America
10 9 8 7 6 5 4 3 2 1

CONTENTS

(Continued)

Acknowledgments
Above and Beyond

There is so much I wish to say to those whose caring helped me take shape, and who gave me the sustenance to enliven my words and me.

About this book: I could not have written it without the support and participation of Bill Cornell. From his adjacent perspective in body-centered psychotherapy, he beckoned to me and nudged me to speak out. In the lively and disciplined way that is his signature, he prompted me to be less retiring in my retirement. What he is and how he works show brightly in his generous Introduction, which frames my contribution. I hope that the early chapters, which he pressed me to put together in the past year, reflect the mounting freedom and pleasure I experienced in getting them said in his presence. An unexpected bonus came with my finding fresh pleasure in some of the content of my old papers as we picked and sorted in the ambience of our growing friendship.

About me in this book: what Mary Hagan McLaughlin, my wife and best friend from 1947 to this day, provided for my shaping is beyond my ken to say. Wrestling with her own Irish hauntings and acting on uncanny insights, she helped me explore marriage, sex, and parenting as we learned together. Mary opened our home to beauty and to the joy of friends and relatives and was halfway-house mother to a long succession of their teenagers venturing into college years. She taught me to hug our two Jims, son and nephew, whom I have loved so deeply but with so little experience of knowing how to show it as a father to a son. She respected the privacy of my analytic work and understood my use of solitude. Mary continues to know how to reel me in and give me space, to have that best-friend timing in saying it like it is.

About all those special others, dear to me as family and friends, close to me as colleagues and patients, with whom I have known the wordless touch that heartens our depths: it may be better to name no names lest omission be felt as slight. You have livened my heart, and I thank you all from the bottom of it.

About the quiet chorus of your voices always in me, you my patients and my fellows: you gave me the words to anchor my analytic knowing. Yours was the background music that challenged and beckoned me to find a lilt and phrasing for my own piping.

Your words grow ever more anonymous as memory dims, but still convey strength and sustenance for me.

One ponderous old phrase you taught me I still see in capitals: *AIM-INHIBITED LOVE.*

It is now rarely spoken.

Yet this kind of love infuses what we therapists can be when we are at our best. It lights up what altruism is about: to give that flame not soon spent in the gust of primary passion, but as a steady breathing-on. It is the reliable inspiration that invites the uncertain flicker of the other to grow to a glow of its own when it is ready.

—Jim McLaughlin

* * *

As this project comes to fruition, I look back now over more than a year of almost weekly Sunday afternoon meetings with Jim as we prepared this manuscript. I have been privileged by Jim to be invited, with his whole mind and heart, to work together so closely in the gathering of a lifetime of thinking and writing. Through this opportunity, I have learned and matured as a therapist, as a writer, and as a man.

I also thank Mick Landaiche. It was his none too gentle shove that got me to shift from my quiet, private appreciation of Jim's writings in my own work to the active creation of this book.

—Bill Cornell

EDITOR'S INTRODUCTION

Deep in the Shed—
An Analyst's Mind at Work

In the years after my second analysis, I became accustomed to dwelling in my off-hours on events with patients that had left me uneasy and unsettled. Working on the impediments that befell me—signaled by sleepiness, boredom, excessive intervening, or steering—brought me to moments of self-recognition of the disturbing likeness between patient and analyst and to fresh perspectives on my old history. Such gropings were not deliberate but were arrived at as, immersed in the serenity of accustomed doing, I puttered in garden or workshop.

—James McLaughlin

To step deep into the shed, to devote oneself to serious study and practice, is to come face to face with two things—the imposing magnitude of one's art and the sometimes nearly daunting details of one's own limitations.

—Stanley Crouch

Jazz musicians have long spoken of going "deep in the shed," removing themselves from audience, composers, and predecessors, to play, typically alone, for long periods in a deep search for exploration and mastery of both instrument and musical form. Jazz at its best reflects a level of discipline and mastery that allows both the freedom and the beauty of individual improvisation as well as of ensemble play. The same can be said of the practice of psychoanalysis at its best. Jim McLaughlin is that rare psychoanalytic practitioner who ventures often deep in the shed. To read his work is to have the privilege of being drawn deep into the workings of a master craftsman. The shed in which Jim labors alone to challenge and stretch his analytic vision is

1

often his woodworking shop, where his hands are immersed in one task and his mind absorbed in private reverie and self-reflection.

Jim seems rarely to have written to provide answers or make theoretical pronouncements. He writes to ask and examine questions. Jim's work invites the reader not only into the mind and psychic struggles of his patients but also into his own mind and struggles. We, as readers, are then invited to dwell in our own. This is not why I began reading Jim's papers in the first place, but it is an important part of what I found and is a crucial aspect of Jim's work that I have come to respect and love: a model of relentless, respectful self-questioning.

I was invited to present a paper to our local psychoanalytic society on direct work with the body in psychotherapy (Cornell, 2000). Jim was my discussant, and this is what he said to me after we left the stage: "I hesitate to say this to someone I have just met, but I have the distinct impression that the closer something is to your heart, the quieter you become about it. You have a lot to say, and I think your writing will improve if you deal with why you quiet yourself."

Although we both lived in Pittsburgh and I had read Jim's work for many years, I had not met him. I am not a psychoanalyst but a psychotherapist trained in transactional analysis and neo-Reichian body therapy. I had long found the psychoanalytic community in Pittsburgh to be conservative and elitist, so I held myself at the edges even as I read Jim's articles. There I saw a very different attitude at work. I was unnerved by the observation Jim made after our presentation that evening, but it was the beginning of a rich collaboration—first on my own writing and now on his. As I have struggled to write this introduction to Jim's book, I have yet again revisited my difficulty in speaking forcefully about someone whose work has grown so close to my heart.

For me, the idea for this book germinated in New York in 2002, during the first conference of the International Association for Relational Psychoanalysis and Psychotherapy, when I heard references to Jim's papers over and over again and found myself wondering why Jim had not been invited to present or, if he had been, why he had not accepted. I wondered if Jim had any idea how influential his papers had become. Although I barely knew him at that time, when I returned to Pittsburgh I wrote him a letter and suggested that his papers be brought together in a book, so as to extend their reach beyond the limited readership of the psychoanalytic journals. To my surprise, he seemed to have little sense of how much influence his papers still had within the analytic community. He responded to my proposal warily at first, and, then, after several frank discussions of his history, temperament, and health, and of my motivations for proposing the project, he embraced our collaboration enthusiastically.

Jim writes much more as a clinician—a physician-healer, he would say—than as a theoretician, though his clinical inquiries constantly challenge and enrich theory. Jim rarely writes from a theoretical position; he writes from clinical questioning. He does not tell the reader what to think or what to do but invites the reader into his mind in the consulting room (and in the shed) and offers lessons in *how* to think.

In "The Question of Lay Analysis," Freud (1926c) observed, "After forty-one years of medical activity, my self-knowledge tells me that I have never been a doctor in the proper sense" (p. 253). Freud saw himself more in the role of a distantly observing, objective scientist that he came to idealize and promote in his papers on technique. Jim, on the other hand, identified with his active physician father, who had been felled by influenza contracted from his patients when Jim was but six weeks old. Jim shaped his professional choices in line with the Hippocratic ideals of the self-sacrificing physician-healer (McLaughlin, 1961). Yet, as we see in the papers collected here, Jim struggled for years to meet Freud's standards of restraint and the strictures of the 1950s American-trained psychoanalyst. Still, his personal idiom persisted. Over the course of 40 years, that persistence formed the psychic infrastructure for a brilliant series of papers arising from efforts to tolerate and ultimately embrace the affective intensities of the analytic dyad, to learn from the interplay of his subjectivity and the subjectivities of his patients, and to *heal,* rather than merely observe, his patients and himself.

Writing when many analysts were content to rest on familiar convictions, Jim pushed his practice of psychoanalysis and psychotherapy past accepted orthodoxy. When I first spoke with Jim of the courage I imagined behind his writing, Jim characterized his early ventures into the analytic journals as an asking for keep and comfort from colleagues embroiled in similar struggles. Many, Jim found, were not as forthcoming about their travails as he. The culture of the time did not encourage candor or doubt. Nevertheless, Jim gradually found himself willing to shake things up, to challenge what he had been taught in favor of discovering something that, though less sanctioned, might just prove superior in practice.

Jim's innovations were guided by the belief that we are capable of more strength and integrity in our dealings with one another. Rather than retreating in dismay at the limits of authorized technique or at the complexity of the other's interior, Jim refused to constrict the vitality or range of unconscious expression within the analytic dyad and instead challenged us to open the playing field of psychoanalytic exploration. In his particular way of opening the field, Jim has defined a stance toward the exploration and use of the analyst's unconscious processes that has a certain kinship with contemporary relational and interpersonal models of psychoanalysis, and yet he remains a unique and important voice.

In his effort to extend the quality of help he offered his patients, Jim actively took issue with some of the prevailing writ and ritual of his time and professional milieu, which he found to be too readily and unquestioningly accepted among his peers. In every case, however, his provocations to reconsider clinical practice are framed not as critiques of others but as gifts to the professional community. More than anything, Jim offers himself as a figure who trusts that we can, by relating most honestly and determinedly to ourselves and with one another, come to some better structure of knowing ourselves and others. For Jim, unconscious impulse is not something from which to recoil in shame or despair but is the very material from which we make our lives most rich and meaningful.

Jim's considerable achievement is that his writing inspires not only respect and thoughtful consideration among those who share his psychoanalytic orientation. He also writes with a rare clarity that speaks to other clinical professionals who work with quite different frames of reference. Bridging the rigors of classical analysis and other therapeutic disciplines, Jim's writing captures what must be commonly recognized as the ongoing, creative tension between practicing by the book and moving, sometimes with considerable anxiety, into less certain realms of exploration and experimentation. One can be trained to function as an analyst or other type of psychotherapist, but to become one who facilitates healing requires committed labor, personal loss, and a willingness to be shaped by one's calling.

One can see, in Jim's papers, the voice and influence of classical Freudian theory, ego psychology, object relations, the interpersonal perspective, and the relational tradition—and yet his voice remains unique. On all sides, his synthesis has proved generative. The result is a body of work remarkable in its iconoclasm and generosity.

Had Jim been of the personality type to found a "school" of psycho-analysis, to seek out McLaughlinian followers, his writings might have given genesis to a kind of middle or independent tradition within American psychoanalysis, much like what emerged in Great Britain around Winnicott's work in the midst of the schools formed around Melanie Klein and Anna Freud. Indeed, as I first read Jim's work, I often thought of Winnicott, who carefully and tactfully evolved his own analytic perspective, delicately and diplomatically finding his way between the Freudians and Kleinians. Winnicott, like Jim, carries the reader into an unfolding series of clinical questions and discoveries. This unfolding of ideas is often fragmentary, with a brilliant observation, notion, or turn of phrase popping up in the midst of some theoretical rumination, picked up often years later in some other paper, or left behind to be forgotten or perhaps elaborated by someone else. In contrast, Jim's published papers read very much like the finely wrought, carefully crafted products of his woodworking shop. Their careful polish feels intimate and inviting to the reader.

Although Jim's writings in many ways foreshadowed the emergence of the relational tradition in American psychoanalysis, I do not think Jim can be categorized as a relationalist as the term is most commonly used today. His work differs in significant ways, and in that difference is much for contemporary psychoanalysts and psychotherapists to learn.

I remember well a particularly compelling moment when I was pressing Jim to allow his voice and perspective to register more forcefully and aggressively in his new writing for this volume. Jim dug in with impressive obstinacy and declared that there is nothing particularly unique about his work. "After all," he argued, "we're all writing about the same thing, trying to capture that mutuality, that attunement, of the mother–infant dyad. That's all. There's nothing that new." "Bullshit," I replied, "Reread your articles. Half the time, you weren't even in the room with your patient when you worked something out. You were alone in your workshop. That is *not* what everybody else is writing about. That is *not* simply about reestablishing the attunement of the mother–infant dyad."

What Jim fashioned through the evolution of his thinking is not a model of therapeutic empathy, intersubjectivity, or analytic coconstruction. To the contrary, Jim's perspective is one of the intimate struggle and unfolding of two distinct and often private subjectivities:

It is this private self that provides inner stability and nourishment. Yet it is also the hiding place for those most unwanted and troublesome aspects of what we fear we are and wish we were not. It is this aggregate that we zealously protect, keep mostly hidden, and cling to as our essence. It is what we bring to the other when we engage in the analytic dyad [chap. 10, this volume].

In a lifetime devoted to an inevitably and unrelentingly interpersonal profession, Jim often sought privacy in his woodshop. He recognized that others in this profession did something similar, that many colleagues had "some private haven . . . discovered without conscious intent, selected for personal dynamic reasons that are vital to the self-analytic enterprise." These were nearly sacred places:

In the familiar safety of these known places and rituals, these "transference sanctuaries," we draw on transitional phenomena akin to those experienced in the analytic situation, yet richer in basic sensory qualities. We tap into traces of our positive experiences with one or both parental figures, and draw once more on their nurturing and releasing aspects which had helped us find our earlier way, to gain affirmation and strength to face our present and assimilate our unwanted, conflictual past [McLaughlin, 1993a, p. 79].

As Jim described it to me, his woodworking shop was a "place of lifelong tactile, olfactory richness . . . a place that said to me, 'You're *here*, you *belong* here,' a place of phantasy carried out with tools that were releasing, crafting, freeing." One finds in this element of Jim's writing a profound regard for, truly a love of, solitude. It becomes resolutely clear that Jim's relation to his work and to his patients has, at its base, the experience of the analytic endeavor as a fundamentally solitary undertaking. Although never explicit in his writing, Jim consistently conveys the paradoxical intermingling of profound solitude in the midst of deep relatedness.

The Organization of This Book

At the beginning of this book, Jim invites the reader into his childhood, his analytic training, his consulting room, and the private spaces of his workshop. "What Was Brought" and "What Was Taught" were written for this volume with unusual personal candor. Jim has long felt that analytic writings would be enriched by more revelation of the author/analyst's psyche as well as that of the patient. Such revelation, however, would not necessarily be made to the patient in session but most certainly to colleagues in the service of dialogue and mutual learning.

These two autobiographical chapters are followed by Jim's classic 1981 paper, "Transference, Psychic Reality, and Countertransference," which he wrote in his early 60s. Much of his earlier writing consisted of a series of formal papers, written with his clinical and research colleagues at the Staunton Clinic in Pittsburgh, exploring pregenital factors in the etiology of psychosomatic disorders. But Jim wrote his psychoanalytic papers alone. After years of writing in the accepted dry, distanced clinical style typical of the time, Jim experimented with a more personal voice. This voice emerged tentatively in the papers he wrote alone (1961, 1973, 1975, 1978) and finally and forcefully broke through, in 1981, by declaring, "If the past 50 years of analyst watching have clarified anything about the nature of the analyst's experience, it is that transference is a matter of equal rights, both on and behind the couch" (see chap. 4, this volume).

With this paper, Jim began to articulate his own vision. He issued an invitation and a challenge to his American colleagues as he unraveled his own training as the objective, all-knowing analyst. The term *psychic reality,* as defined by Freud (1915), was understood as the "internal, subjective reality of the patient's infantile beginnings and early psychic organization cast in the mode of primary process" (see chap. 4), which was, of course, to be held in distant contrast to the objective (external) reality to be seen and put forth by the analyst. Psychoanalysis did not yet have a theory of subjectivity or intersubjectivity, but Jim became intrigued (as well as threatened) by the interface of the patient's *and the analyst's* psychic realities. He argued for recognition of a "resonant and affectively immersed participant observer in a powerfully evocative intimacy touching on all issues of the developmental past of both parties, from the earliest preoedipal through adolescence to current adulthood" (p. 647). With any luck at all, the analyst's ego "would generally keep intact his experiencing, observing, and ordering functions" (p. 647), but, even when those functions collapsed, as Jim came to amply illustrate in subsequent writings and talks, there was much for both parties in the analytic dyad to learn from each other. He saw this learning as the essence of the psychoanalytic project.

The 1981 paper was unusual for Jim in that he did not include any case examples (these were to become a hallmark of his subsequent writing). Instead, it was a carefully crafted work of scholarship. One can see Jim's struggle to define his own voice. He paid homage to his predecessors and colleagues and then, after this brief genuflection to the altar of psychoanalytic dogma, challenged authority and set in motion a set of ideas he would explore for the next 20 years. Britton (1998), in a fascinating account of the politics of psychoanalytic publishing in Great Britain, characterized the writer's conflict as "publication anxiety" and noted that a writer often "fears that his or her publication may damage the authority of the guardians of the paradigm and demoralize his or her affiliates (depressive anxiety), or the writer may fear the wrath of the guardians and exile from the affiliates (persecutory anxiety)" (p. 201). With the 1981 paper, Jim seemed increasingly willing to challenge his own tendency to mute his aggression in both the treatment and collegial settings, willing to move outside the familiar realms of maternal depression and reparation, and willing to risk conflict and potential exile.

Jim's writing style began to reflect the evolution of his style as a psychoanalyst: he proposed hypotheses and quietly provocative observations, wonderings, and challenges but left room for the reader to reflect, disagree, and come to his or her own conclusions. Jim left the theoretical field open for the reciprocity of influence between author and reader.

In preparation for this volume, Jim and I read and reread his published papers and a treasure trove of unpublished talks, including several given to analytic societies, that convey a voice more personal, unfinished, and exploratory than that of his published papers. As we read, themes emerged, some clearly conscious to Jim at the time of writing, others less than conscious and intentional, some hinted at in the midst of some other topic, disappearing for years, reemerging again, sometimes like a shard, other times a more fully articulated idea: the healer; muted aggression and sexuality; the use of eyes as well as ears as receptive organs; body signs as well as spoken words as communicative events; shame; transference sanctuaries; enactment; nonverbal behavior; self-analysis; wondering and hypothesizing rather than knowing and interpreting.

Jim had not been conscious of all these recurring concerns. They became clearer to him as we worked together, meeting almost every Sunday for a year and a half. He talked with me of now seeing how he had often hidden behind his papers and of realizing that he could not have written any differently at the time. As he reread his work, he could see what he described to me as the "steady, uncertain, and painful growth" that his papers reflected and could appreciate how beautifully they demonstrated the way clinical thinking unfolds.

It became clear to us that his papers organized themselves around three central and enduring themes: the patient's psychic reality and the analyst's self-analysis; enactment and nonverbal communication; and the dialectics of influence.

What Was Wrought: Self-Analysis

As for the prime importance of the analyst's role in failures: a steady focus on what the analyst brings and does should afford us the clearest appreciation of how his mixture of dumb, blind, and hard spots shapes, limits, and determines his potential for the task [chap. 5, this volume, p. 75].

As Jim began to write increasingly in his own voice, he presented case material, often of error, impasse, or outright failure. Amazingly, he did not blame the patient but questioned himself and his approach, as evidenced in these powerfully searching papers on self-analysis.

I first began reading Jim's papers, among others, in the early 1990s, when I was searching for psychoanalysts other than Reich who wrote about the role of the body in psychodynamic change and those who drew on infant observation research. Jim was on that dismayingly short list. It was quite by accident that I discovered his papers on self-analysis, which I found compelling and deeply moving. Here was a powerful resonance with Reich's arguments made half a century earlier in the Vienna Seminar for Psycho-analytic Therapy, an ongoing clinical case discussion group that Reich led from 1924 to 1930. Reich argued that participants should be presenting treatment failures, not successes, as a means of questioning the efficacy of both the technique and the character of the analyst. More than 50 years later, this argument was being taken up anew in a series of papers by Jim McLaughlin, who demonstrated a capacity for self-analysis and scrutiny that Reich sought but certainly never personally achieved. I had found something that linked two important strands of my own training as a psychotherapist.

Jim elucidated, without apology, the stresses the analytic encounter placed on the analyst's work ego as well as the multiplicity of factors (including but not limited to the pressures of the patients' transferences) that evoke transference vulnerabilities in the analyst. Jim focused on the "insights that the analyst shapes about himself in the course of his efforts to understand his patient" (see chap. 6, this volume) and offered an observation about these insights that was remarkable in its modest and poetic tone:

> They have been as fireflies: elusive on the wing and enigmatic in the grasp—illuminating in the moment seen, rather dull and diminished when closely scrutinized. Was the guiding glow really there, or imagined in my head? Once in hand, how to keep it glowing?

Jim came to prefer the description of the "interplay of dyadic transferences" (1994a) to that of the more customary conceptualization of the transference–countertransference matrix. "Dyadic interplay" levels the analytic playing field, as Jim urges us to "look on an analytic impasse as a period of breakdown or disruption of the analytic context occasioned by the interplay of defensive behaviors in both members of the dyad, driven by regressive transferences in both." He tended to greet these occasions with honesty, grace, and, when possible, humor:

> The word "impasse" has come to mean many things in our current analytic jargon. It is an unfortunate and daunting term: "an impassable road or way; a blind alley, cul-de-sac; hence, a position or predicament allowing no escape" (Webster's, 1953). . . . Still, it has usually been possible to back out or muddle our way to an escape route. At times this last word might more accurately be pronounced "rout."

One gets the impression at times that Jim never met an analytic impasse that he didn't come to love. This section on self-analysis opens with one written in 1991 for an American Psychoanalytic Association panel and included here as chapter 5. Jim's contribution was "A Perspective on Psychoanalytic Failures," an account of a 1950s abortive analysis with "Ms. Q" that "came upon a faltering termination" in an impasse that Jim could not understand at the time and probably did *not* come to love:

Ms. Q let me know that she had immersed herself in reading Freud. After rather little exploration I asserted, with what I presumed to be quiet tact and "physicianly" firmness, that this wouldn't do, and laid the usual array of good reasons why she should desist. With a quick nod, Ms. Q filled the rest of the hour with increasingly ambiguous allusions to an unsatisfying past liaison with an insecure man. She slept in through the time of her next appointment.

It is perhaps not surprising that, setting aside whatever of Ms. Q's characterologic and temperamental proclivities may have entered the picture, Ms. Q more often felt enraged than engaged by her analyst's positioning.

With characteristic candor, Jim returned to this case with detailed commentary about 11 instances he identified as pivotal on the road to treatment failure. Jim was less than enthusiastic when I suggested that we open this section with this particular paper. I, on the other hand, had read it with the delight of recognition, with memories of my own therapeutic lapses and collapses wafting back, and with imagining readers' identifications with Jim's tale of a therapist desperately clinging to known technique in the face of a patient who needed something different. I couldn't imagine a more engaging entrance into the shed.

"What Was Wrought" then continues with two of Jim's central papers on self-analysis, both of which I quoted earlier. These papers endeared me personally to Jim's writing in the compelling examples they offer of a clinical mind at work.

What Was Sought: Nonverbal Communication

To think of these small gestures only as autistic or narcissistic may be conceptually correct, yet robs these proclivities of the rich context of old relatings, a context that comes to life when the action, words, and music are brought into unison in the analytic work [McLaughlin, 1989, p. 122].

Jim's papers on nonverbal behavior grew out his interest in bodily expression and activity within the analytic hour. During a period in the 1970s, he experimented with making quick sketches and notations of patients' postures and movements on the couch in an attempt to identify correlates of speech and action. His observations bore the mark of subtle and disciplined looking.

These papers first drew me to Jim's work, as I sought to find analytic writings that bridged the gap between mind and body and that I could use as a bridge between psychoanalysis and my neo-Reichian, body-centered perspective. I had learned a great deal from my reading of psychoanalysis and had just entered a personal analysis after two other extended periods of therapeutic analysis and body-centered psychotherapy. I wanted to challenge my therapeutic analysis and body-centered colleagues with contemporary psychoanalytic writings that were both rigorous and creative. I immersed myself in British object relations theory and discovered that American psychoanalysis had finally begun to turn away from ego psychology as its primary orientation. I was particularly excited and moved by the writing of three analysts: Christopher Bollas, Emmanuel Ghent, and Jim.

I had long felt that psychoanalysis had impoverished itself in its turn away from the body. Freud (1931) never seemed able to grasp fully and use maternal and preoedipal functions: "Everything in the sphere of this first attachment to the mother seemed to me difficult to grasp in analysis, so grey with age and shadowy and almost impossible to revivify, that it was as if it had succumbed to an especially inexorable repression" (p. 228). It was to this grey and shadowy sphere that Jim turned his gaze, at first in his papers with his Staunton Clinic colleagues investigating the early developmental underpinnings of psychosomatic disorders (reading Melanie Klein on the sly in the 1950s) and subsequently in his papers on the relevance of infant studies to his observations of nonverbal behavior and enactments in adult analysis.

This shadowy realm has, in fact, been a part of the unconscious text and texture of psychoanalysis from its beginnings. Even as Freud turned his attention from his early experiments with physical interventions and developed his talking cure, the arrangement of Freud's consulting room must have evoked an unusual physical intimacy, especially within the times and culture of fin de siècle Vienna. Although Freud's chair was positioned at a right angle to the patient, the arm of the chair was directly against the back of the couch, which meant that Freud's shoulder was but inches from the patient's head. The patient would have felt Freud's voice resonating from behind, with a kind of closeness we usually associate with being held, the odor of cigars drifting in from the doctor sitting out of sight. Freud could have easily turned slightly, be it in moments of reverie or with conscious intent, to cast his gaze over the patient's body. If Freud turned to look at his patient, could the patient sense this shift from being heard to also being seen? Even as Freud looked away from his patient, enveloped in his own associative processes, his gaze would have fallen on hundreds of antique representations of the human body, filling every available surface and cranny (Engelman, 1976). Everywhere in Freud's consulting room were images, artifacts, and human forms.

Jim consciously and systematically looked as well as listened, and he turned his gaze directly toward the patient. Jim's chair, unlike Freud's, was positioned so that he could more fully see his patients (though they still could not see him). I was excited to discover an analyst who was trying to link the early beginnings of mother–infant research with what he was observing in his adult patients; he suggested that much of the "kinesic-postural components of adult behavior takes its base in this concept of the primacy and durability of this early mode of psychomotor thought" (McLaughlin, 1989, p. 112). A phrase like "mode of psychomotor thought" would be readily recognized by my body-centered colleagues. Here I had indeed found an important bridge to my body-centered community.

As a therapist well familiar with how to work directly with body activity and expression (my own as well as that of the patient), I also found the papers of this era, written by Jim and his analytic colleagues (Jacobs, 1986; Johan, 1989; Chused, 1991; Aron, 1996), to be a theoretical and technical mess. Nonetheless, what engaged me is that Jim's papers on enactment and unspoken communication were alive with his efforts to make sense of and find a way through a welter of ill-defined and rather pejorative analytic concepts: enactment, acting-out, acting-in, counter-transference acting-out, projection, projective identification, primitive modes of expression. All these concepts were then, and in many ways still are, subject to heated debate. For Jim, it was as though his identification as an analyst would not permit him to figure out in a systematic way what to *do* with what he *saw*. Could one *do* something and still be an analyst?

In these papers, Jim writes with his typical honesty. His cases vividly illustrate his struggles to comprehend the body and its means and meanings in the analytic process. As he describes his modest success in gradually getting a patient to reflect on the meaning of a repeated hand movement, he writes with grace that "gradually she dealt with the gesture as she had grown accustomed to work on dreams, gingerly, but with some safety in viewing dream and gesture as being a happening slightly removed from her" (McLaughlin, 1989, p. 120). A page later, he presents a vignette in which the same patient calls him a "bastard" and a "po're jackass" as she stumbles into the vitality of her own fury with him and her consequent individuation.

These papers demonstrate a determination to find one's way anew (for both analyst and patient) and to risk error and accusation in the service of exploration, freedom, and understanding. The last paper in this section, "Touching Limits in the Analytic Dyad," is one of the last published before Jim's retirement and is one of the most compelling examples of his style. Without ever telling the reader what to do, he relates story after story of his own grappling with what to do about touching and being touched physically and psychically in the course of analytic work. He describes his gradual reckonings with "iatrogenically shaped deflections and injuries." In learning to respect the deeply subjective realities of his patients and open up to his own emotional resonances, he forces himself "to see and wrestle with how one's own needs, one's own preferred ways of seeing and coping, inevitably become imposed on the patient's space and freedom." Jim does not encroach on the reader's space and freedom by offering prescription or proscription. He simply provides a model and opportunity for reflection and reconsideration.

I had become tired of the all-too-common attitude in the neo-Reichian therapies of attributing treatment difficulties to the client's character defenses—an amazing contradiction to what Reich himself originally set out to accomplish. I had begun to criticize my body-centered colleagues for thinking that they knew too much, that an attitude that might be a comfort to the therapist was a cost to the client. What I found in Jim's papers was a model of constantly questioning what one knows and how one works.

What I found exciting in these papers was not a new way of working with the body but a refreshing and candid model of how to think about one's work.

What Was Thought: The Dialectics of Influence

I stress here the working of two separate minds in order to make clear that the central focus on the patient's reality view does not mean the seeking of unbroken agreement and oneness in the dyad. . . . It is a dedicated effort and struggle on the part of two separate and different minds to seek information, not to provide empathic responses.

The final two papers vividly portray the transformative potential of analytic work for both analyst and patient. Each paper includes a vivid case portrayal in which Jim relates not only the conflicts and struggles of his patients but his own conflict and struggle within himself—journeys into his own interiority, propelled by recurrent errors with these two clients in the face of their persistent destructive behaviors. He offers us vivid accounts of how his self-reckonings were necessary in his being able to work effectively within these two powerfully cathected analytic dyads.

Jim offers a model of self-analysis that is an effort to hold his mind distinct and differentiated from that of his patient. His mind, consciously and unconsciously, is to be influenced by the patient, but not conjoined with it. His self-analyses did, on occasion, result in self-disclosures, but by and large they resulted in the clearing and opening of his mind and the unconscious field with his patients. Quite likely, his patients did not know the specifics of *what* had changed in Jim, but they would feel and respond to the *experience* that *something* had changed.

Jim's is not so much a model of mutuality in the analytic dyad as a model of a dialectic within which his attention is to the ever present possibilities of tension, of differentness, of conflict, and of unexpected and often unwelcomed disturbance. Clearly, this experience is in sharp contrast to the stance of certitude in which Jim was originally trained and which he had sought to bring to his patients. I read these papers as a return to the searching spirit of Freud, so often evident in Freud's writing but so frequently lost in the codification and transmission of technique. These papers can be construed as a telling of the tale of one analyst's movement from distant observation to dialectical engagement.

The second of the papers in this section presents Jim's last published case material, his work with Mr. F. Here we see the work of a seasoned analyst, almost 40 years after the failed analysis of Ms. Q, with Jim yet again up against the walls of his psychic limits. As Mr. F, deeply engaged in his analysis with Jim, persists in high-risk homosexual and heterosexual encounters during the early years of the AIDS epidemic in the United States, Jim is pushed over the edge of his analytic, moral, and personal tolerance. This time, though, he tells a story of compelling self-analytic and interpersonal encounters. The contrast with his earlier case is stunning:

> For myself, I know that Mr. F challenged me to confront old het-
> erosexual issues anew, to find new levels of comfort with my om-
> nipresent dynamics of aggression and bisexuality. Especially did
> he challenge me to sample and assimilate immediacies of overt
> homosexuality at intensities I had not consciously known before.

By and large, Jim did not bring the content of his self-analytic confrontations and realizations back to Mr. F. What he brought back was a
wiser, more vital sense of self and interpersonal possibility. His self-
analyses reopened the analytic space and granted Mr. F his psychic and
sexual freedom.

When I first began reading Jim's work, now almost 15 years ago, I was
reminded of the tradition of jazz musicians to take periods of time alone
to confront their selves and their work, as Stanley Crouch (1990) so eloquently captured it in the epigraph that opens this introduction.

The internal and private confrontation of stepping deep in the shed
must then generate a stepping back out into the world at large. It is the
stepping out into the world again that creates the encounters that shape
musician and audience alike and that move a tradition to new ground.
Jim's work in solitude had that same transforming effect on me because
he generously made the fruits of his solitary labors public.

My proposal for this book began as an expression of my gratitude for
the essential place of Jim's writing in a fundamental reshaping of my
work as a psychotherapist. My hope, in turn, is that this book will do
more than bring to a new generation of clinical practitioners the an-
guish, pleasures, and discoveries of stepping deep in the shed. I hope it
will also encourage more of us to share our work in Jim's dogged and
compassionate spirit.

CHAPTER 1

To the Reader

The hope behind this book is the same one that impelled my first psycho-analytic publication. Years ago, there was much loneliness in the learning, largely imposed by the rituals clustered around what was then taught as classical psychoanalysis in these United States. I needed to reach out for companions with whom to talk, to compare our seeing, to walk and share the stumble, to find and give the support of the knowing smile.

Now that my walking nears its end, I am grateful for having found such companionship, with colleagues and gradually with patients, as our paths merged and separated. I can still be warmed by what we shared and angered by the failure of intimacies to develop. I cherish the challenges I encountered in trying to grow as a therapist. Early on, I was dimly aware that what I was trying to do as an analyst involved a mix of at least two people: the patient and me. I have long since come to regard my patients as mirror, stimulus, and fellow traveler.

So, I wonder how it is for you as you seek your way along the twisting paths of our calling in this new century. Little in the external field is the same for us, as analyst and psychotherapist, as it was when I began almost 60 years ago. But in our inner ways, basic likenesses surely persist that can let us make common cause.

After more than 50 years in psychoanalysis, I still feel that this occupation of ours is a bit odd. Have you wondered how you have come willingly to spend much of your life subject to the peculiar constraints our work demands? Day after day you sit still, containing your own needs, fears, and passions so that others may be freer, while offering your presence as necessary target and evocative witness to the emotional intensities of others who need your help.

Some of you may have come to realize that you did not just stumble into the role of psychoanalyst or psychotherapist. You surely did not seek the role for its monetary gain or for the placidity of sedentary living. There ought to be compellingly personal reasons why you are taking this path.

I have come to know some of my reasons as these became evident in the heat and light of working with my patients. I hope to nudge you in the search for your own answers, to involve you more deeply in the pleasure and travail of a self-inquiry that can last a lifetime.

In my own growth and search for expanding competence, there have always been more questions and few conclusions. I have learned much from others, but never easily, as I always needed to try the new, to experience it for myself before I could own it. It may be this way for you, and perhaps our need for experiential knowing is a reason why the work itself with each patient carries such potential to affect us and challenge us to change.

For a lead-in to a paper on self-analysis, I used the words of a South American shaman: "You may learn from me. But you cannot follow me. You will but see a man walking through the brush." What I meant then, and do still, is that, as we walk side by side, you alone must learn to know your own feel of your feet. I hope we find the time and pace that allow you to know the feel of you, the man and the brush.

In my earliest papers, my intent was to shed light on what was going on in my patients. I was trained to see impediments as lodged in the patient's psyche. Instead, as my own experience evolved, I grappled with how it often was also the analyst who impeded progress. In my tripping over my own feet in what I was told was countertransference, I could see how our conflicts and defenses merged and clashed, and the question arose: who, in the moment, is the patient? I could not fairly take refuge in seeing my stumbling as counterreaction to the patient's tripping. So I followed the prescription that would surely expunge countertransference. I had a second analysis. This time, a woman helped me to the vast relief and challenge of acknowledging that I would always be grappling with my own conflicts in entwinement with patients. This woman helped me to be more open to my male–female resonances, which I realized I would always have to balance. Only then did I begin to experience the spontaneous sorties of self-inquiry that to this day can light up fresh vistas on old links to my current tensions of relating.

And so it was that I found ways to keep an eye on both my patient and myself. I grew to have some confidence in the validity of some of these fresh sights that the patient and I, both together and separately, were able to discover about ourselves in the course of work often therapeutic for both.

I hope that you, too, will find and learn from your own rich resonances between you and your patient, particularly in the dissonances you must inevitably share.

Most especially, for the sake of our excursions together through the pages of this book, do I hope that you and I will find we have some similar internal dynamics, perhaps even comparable developmental vicissitudes and conflicts, that have helped shape our coping and our character.

Character traits that determined my preference for helping rather then hurting are common enough to our culture. Traditionally, these nurturant tendencies have often been considered womanly virtues, and so they show more conspicuously in male psychotherapists. An overriding inclination to *primum non nocere,* to heal rather than to harm, can alone identify a man as a healer.

Yet there is much more than curbed aggressiveness that contributes to the shaping of the committed therapist. I hope that together we can hold in our hands many of the strands of being that both patient and therapist bring to the work—strands that, in their interweaving, eventually can allow us to witness the prevailing benevolence shaped by the pairing. For both patient and therapist must bring to the interweaving their ambivalence toward self and other; each must experience it in the fullness of their relationship and somehow help each other grow in the knowing.

Here is the heartbeat of healing. It lies in the experience of mutual acceptance, gained through exploring and acknowledging the best and worst that are its core. This is so for the patient who may never have surely known it. It is so for the therapist who may have known it but uncertainly, so always must give of himself again, so that he may once more find the healing it can bring to both. This is at the heart of what I have tried to speak about in the past, and hope to sum up in the words of now.

In most of what I have written, I have counted heavily on clinical material to speak for and about both the patient and me. These data are occasionally verbatim words familiar to both of us, but more often paraphrases by me, with an ear for the idiom and images we shared. With luck, it can be that, in this melange, some oddities of phrasing, of antithesis and paradox, or chance poetics, will catch you up, and you will, at least for that moment, feel and know what you, as the other in the dyad, were about.

You who have read some of my papers already know that I began to provide in them glimpses of my own dynamics and history, in interface with those detailed about my patient. I saw early on the value in detailing both sides of the relationship but could see no straightforward way to use data about my fellow therapists. I was slow to find the courage to use my own data, to stand up to the scorn that surely would be heaped on me were I to show off so egregiously. I had been trained to look on such personal disclosure as irrelevant or, worse, as personal pathology to be hidden until excised.

These pieces and glimpses of my development emerged in the context of work with specific patient-dynamics and often as a consequence of my stumbling on self-analytic insights. I offered these to the reader as possible insights into a deeper understanding of the ways the patient and I were entwined in the dyad—an understanding that might carry beyond what I knew to tell.

Now, in more open times, and to the extent that the purpose of this book is to bring into the foreground the dynamics and motivations of the psychotherapist who needs to be a healer, I ask you to walk longer with me. There is more I need to say about the other patient in the room: me.

And I suspect that, in the altruism that propels so many of us in this profession, you too will often be that other patient. You have plenty of company, of course, among those who give of themselves to teaching, nursing, and other helping endeavors, and you very likely share traits centered in the Golden Rule. But few in these helping professions expect and accept being regularly taken into the emotional world of the other. Nor are they so likely to put themselves at the disposal of that other as do we in the practice of psychotherapy and psychoanalysis.

In the earlier tradition of our craft, analysts dismissed this trait as masochism. I prefer the view of a colleague who years ago summed up this giving of oneself as a valued "regression in the service of another," necessary to therapeutic understanding (Olinick, 1980).

I do not wish to suggest that all psychotherapists and psychoanalysts are cut of like cloth. The motives sometimes accurately attributed to us by others cut a wide swath, from the self-centered concerns of the conquistador, denounced and envied, to the martyr, praised but rarely emulated.

I do wish to suggest that the attributes at the martyr end of the swath are more likely to show up among us therapists. I hold that these reflect the extent to which we had to go to ward off our infantile aggressive destructiveness toward mother and necessary others who, for whatever reason, failed us in our vital need for acceptance and recognition. To ward off our worst, we needed to hold on to character traits that would assert our goodness.

In what I have come to see about the analyst's part in shaping impasses in treatment, I began half-humorously to sort these as dumb spots, blind spots, and hard spots. *Dumb spots* are the inevitable shortfall of not yet knowing enough yet remaining open to an unfolding potential to learn. In taking our work just seriously enough, we can remain open to the dismay and pleasure to be had in recognizing our dumb spots as we push deeper into our discipline and ourselves. *Blind spots* lie in those areas of our psychic functioning that are warped by the vicissitudes of early living and that skew our capacities to be open to the diversity of our patients. These I explore in the next chapter, "What Was Brought."

The subsequent chapter, "What Was Taught," is the tale of my medical schooling and, in particular, my analytic training and the *hard spots* of the assured knowing set in place by that training. Some of the content of the papers that make up the rest of this book reflects my efforts to deal with and lessen the limits set by these lacunae on the range of seeing possible for the patient and me. I hope that in them you may experience stirrings that send you on your own search.

CHAPTER 2

What Was Brought

There are some crucial parts of my personal history that I need to point to here and elaborate on as we go along so that you know me better. They also add relevance to the title and shape of this book.

All three are centered in traumata complicating child–mother beginnings: parent loss, maternal depression and dominance, and, particularly, the overarching impact of the mother's rejection that shames her child. These skewings all loomed large in shaping my development, mostly outside my knowing awareness until I was well into my second analysis. Each in its own right is recognized in analytic lore as a powerful shaper of character development. But it took finding them in me, as I worked with a woman analyst in the deeper reaches of my early involvements with my mother, to free me to recognize their resonance in others. These depths had not been touched in my brief first analysis with an elderly gentleman and proper Freudian in whose benign presence and tacit support I cautiously basked and foraged on my own in fresh oedipal fields.

If it were truly possible to weigh and separate the three confluent traumata, I would point to having experienced maternal rejection as the worst. As I now assess the power and ubiquity of the chilling shame that rejection brings into the lives of each of us, I think of it as the bond that binds us all, the low chord that causes dissonance that strikes most deeply at any age.

Parent loss and maternal mourning or depression in infancy surely inflict abandonment and rejection. Later shunning, as punishment deliberately imposed on a child grown more capable of getting the point, can indeed pierce the deepest and last the longest.

Many times in my early boyhood, my mother, driven to her limits in raising the four of us on her own, packed her bag and threatened to leave

23

on the next boat for Ireland. Even though we knew the steamboat only circled our small lake, her threat brought us to heel in a hurry. Far worse were the times when she literally turned her back on just me, and for days would not speak. I had been bad, of course, and the token switching was not enough. There truly were no words for the nowhere misery and "goneness" that soon had me on my knees in abject pleading for a making up that would not happen until mother broke her silence. Lucky for me these desolations had been preceded by our first two years of closeness, the benefits of which had already given me some confidence in her caring. These present shunnings did not cripple, but crimp they did.

Sometimes I could not be sure what I needed to be sorry about: my big mouth? my playing with myself? my bed-wetting? In extremis, I would tug at my sisters to find out. Their list got longer as I grew taller, and melded into the typical cataloguing a small boy could go to confession to feel guilty about. Feeling guilty about the bad that had a name and a penance was doable. The feelings connected with mother's silence, and imagining the deeds that provoked it, were not. I grew up phobic and fearful, bedeviled in latency years by a full-blown skunk phobia and nighttime fears of a stovepipe fire burning the cottage down. For years I averted my gaze and saw vaguely, and no one spoke of myopia or shame.

I spent much of my youth seeking the safety of trying to be good, or lying low and out of sight when I wasn't. Years had to go by before I could know that the haunting uncertainty of my worth, and of my right to be seen and heard, probably did not have to do with taints peculiar to little Irish Catholic boys growing up in a family of women.

Years later, I found ways to address matters of shame in my patients, but I spoke in terms that did not grasp the shunning and rejection just touched on here. I do think that this is a blind spot I put in place to avoid confronting old shames of my own.

In recent years, I have grown deeply indebted to a friend and colleague, Herbert Thomas, for helping me to see that shame is the most important affect we must deal with in growing up—for showing us that it is antecedent to what we know to be guilt, and even harder to expunge. We have been pressed to see the damage we inflict when we reject and belittle others who need our acceptance. Herbert slowly made us see how these belittlings, too early begun and too often repeated, inflict terrible and literally physical woundings. We know them now to be assaults that our culture has long called shame. These at their worst are mortal rejections of any one of us by the important Other whose acceptance we need as we need air.

I need to double back to maternal depression as a matter of particular pertinence, not just in reference to my growing up, but for many of us in our field. A child's experience of his or her mother's serious depression is said to deaden the child forever (Green, 1986; Bollas, 1999), but it also is known to motivate a child to become a psychotherapist later in life (Greenson, 1960; Olinick, 1969).

For me, the first warp of these several threads began with the death of my physician father in my sixth week of life, which shaped my mother's silent years of mourning, and her quiet depression that never entirely lifted. For the rest of her life, she idealized him and his heroic exhaustion in caring for his influenza patients. She enshrined him in our summer home until her death, long after we children were grown and gone. There she shaped for her lifetime a lively base for the four of us, plus our summer uncle and his "flu-orphaned son," and gave Irish hospitality to an incessant flow of visiting relatives eager to share our rural lake.

Even as mother breast-fed me during my first two years, her grieving silenced my three older sisters and quieted me. Her commitment to bring us up on her own required the full Irish-Catholic need to proscribe, through shaming and shunning silence, any sexual or aggressive sinning. This dampened but did not drown the liveliness of the summers in our only home and haven over the next 20 years. I wanted to be a man like the only man she loved but about whom she rarely spoke. We children did not ask her to speak of him, as we silently respected her silence. Others idealized him as deeply religious, as doctor and healer. To be saintly like my ghostly father, however, seemed always beyond my grasp, and I settled for whatever I could from my earthy summer uncles.

The actual death of father or mother leaves an enduring hole in the fabric of the developing self and in the fullness of self-esteem, for which growing up in a triangulated family context is optimal. What then has to be put in place are ways of being that both fill the gap in the self and restore the connection to the other.

When the father dies, the mother also is lost, at least for the length and depth of her mourning, and the gap compounded. Even though her grief and depression may eventually dissipate, the impact on children is a comparable loss. At its worst, the effect on a child is a gone mother lost thereafter in her pain, and the child hovering in her shade forever

(Green, 1986). More optimistic for the child is the mourning mother, as in my mother's instance, unpredictably there and not there. In this latter situation of grieving and depression, the mother's ability to be alive enough for the child, at least some of the time, affords him hope, chance, and example to undo the damage and breach he must surely have caused by being bad. Without this infusion of aliveness through the mother, his own resources may evolve only into fixed compulsions and forced altruism, a thumb-in-dike posture of blighted personal fulfillment.

In this context, I need to dwell further on my mother's breast-feeding me during the first two years of her grieving. I believe that her act, stabilizing for both of us in her oscillations between despair and reparative hope, she somehow shaped and I shared. I think it to be an extreme instance of the many fortunate ways the depressed mother and her child may manage to mitigate the repetitive traumata of the mother's withdrawals.

I am sure that she gave me more than milk. I feel that her hanging in there so long, for me and for herself, provided me sample and example of a basic optimism that good could endure and be, no matter what the catastrophe, and that hanging in there and being good were the way to get there. She embodied all this in her doing. I could be part of her, with her, and in her find bits of myself coming to be, while giving us both time to get there.

I think that it is in acts like this that we lucky ones surmount common disasters and learn ways and willingness to share self with other so that both may prosper. By *lucky,* I mean to connote the imponderables that determine whether the enhancements of positive experience will outweigh the negative. The need to cling and restore at any cost, as the only alternative to rageful destructiveness or giving up, becomes sustainable only as long as hope of acceptance outweighs the certainty of rejection.

The positive sustenance of these almost preverbal years may have helped to get me through the later miserable occasions when she held us in check with her major weapons: threats of actual desertion, and shunning silences that could go on for days. I knew I was bad, for I was a biter who would not quit until she bit me back. But her not talking to or seeing me brought me to my latency knees in lost despair. At the same time, I always hoped that she loved me, even when she did not approve of me, and that these bad times could pass.

These expiative dynamics have been known to psychoanalysts since Ferenczi in the 1920s. In my first analytic paper (late 1950s), I dwelt on their embodiment in the Hippocratic oath and the myth of Aesculapius. I hoped to show how oath and myth together imposed binding constraints on the aggressive and narcissistic sexuality of their guild, extending across the centuries to include Western physicians from Greco-Roman times even into the modern era. I wanted to relate the likenesses of the crimes and punishments of those ancient healers to those I had encountered in my own psychosexual history, and in that of my physician-analysands, most of them men.

In my early years as a fledgling psychoanalyst, I was immersed in the world of academic medicine at the University of Pittsburgh medical school. I tried to get medical students and psychiatrists interested in psychosomatic medicine, to train analytic candidates in our new institute, and to do analytic therapy with other physicians.

Not surprisingly, I found that some of us doctors, particularly those in analytic training, had traits in common, particularly traits centered on a willingness to dampen one's own sexual thrust and narcissistic claims for reward and recognition, so that others might be enhanced. In my first analytic paper, I made much of the strong similarities between these traits, which I was encountering in myself and these others, and I linked descriptions of Asklepian priest-healers with the lot of us through the shaping consequences of their Hippocratic oath and traditions on medical practitioners well into the waning of the 20th century.

With the passing of years, fewer physicians are entering the field of psychoanalysis and the dynamic psychotherapies. The cultural image of the Old Family Doctor is nearly extinct. Our work is increasingly in the capable hands of non-MD therapists.

Women, for so long prominent participants in psychoanalysis, will soon outnumber men as psychotherapists.

However, what I have to say about the healer dynamics in us is likely to remain valid for many women therapists, given that the base of these dynamics lies largely in old libidinal attachments to and aggressive conflicts with our mothers. Male or female, each of us was impelled into struggles of reparation and defense around early maternal identifications that shaped our character style and signature in the blending mix of our bisexual nature.

I have come to refer to this discernible cluster of character traits as the *healer's bent. Bent* underscores both the persistent internal shaping of character and behavior wrought by these reparative necessities and their external social thrust into the healer's world. It acknowledges also a slang reference to overt homosexuality. Together with *healer,* the word acknowledges some aspects of feminine identifications common to the homosexual and the healer—a link long accepted in American Hopi and Navajo shamans.

The colloquial allusion anchors the ubiquity in all cultures of the damage inflicted at any age through shaming by stronger males pointing to inadequacy of genital size or stature as the manifest of effeminacy in lesser males, or through shunning of lesser females by other females held to be socially superior.

For a long time, psychoanalysts restricted formulations about exhibitionism and shame as simply narcissistic urgencies based in infantile concerns over genital and sphincter inadequacy. Most of us were all too familiar with the fear of this level of shaming in our own childhood. We were slow to see the full power of shaming to inflict damage on the vital narcissistic needs of optimal human development. Slowly, we have become more aware of how these belittlings, too early begun and too often repeated, involve more serious hazards. We know them now to be assaults that our culture has long called shame. These at their worst are mortal rejections of any one of us by the important Other whose acceptance we need as we need air. Spurnings that ignore, mock, or belittle the best that we know to offer, when we are young and literally at the mercy of our caretakers, are truly equivalent to physical traumata that can kill us. They trigger an aftermath of crippled self-esteem that can last a lifetime. When rage, despair, and the impulse to get rid of self or other are helplessly experienced—are not discharged in rage that can destroy self or other—their cumulative weight can truly bend, distort, or destroy. Extreme measures of expiation and undoing, often withdrawal from living itself, must be set permanently in place so that the shamed one is allowed to try to live—to deny or master the rage, despair, and need.

There is strong evidence that this pattern of shattering or deforming, when the best self is spurned by a significant other, is first set in place in infancy by too severe or too prolonged threat or fact of rejection or abandonment by the mother.

These affect states persist over a lifetime as the core of shame. I am belatedly persuaded that the fear of abandonment and the shame of rejection as its realization are the core experience of life, and antecedent to guilt (Thomas, 1997; McLaughlin, 2002). Guilt, however burdensome, is held so tightly because, even at its worst, it asserts a connection with the necessary other: better to be linked through guilt than cast off and abandoned to the lostness of shame.

Although the restitutive dynamics in the healer's bent are similar to those of guilt, and can be interwoven with the self-flagellations of guilt, they are almost oppositely displayed. The bent of the healer is toward selfless being exhibited through sustained benign acts pleasurable to self and to others. These acts assert reassurance of own goodness rather than excoriation of the self, with the aggression now a self-inflicted restriction of being and a plea to be saved.

As one shaper of our character, the healer's bent is blessing and bane but not something that can be chosen. For some of us, it has been a steady call for adaptations that have enhanced our prospering and even survival, and yet the primary value of these adaptations is in their benefit to others.

Because this *primum non nocere* has been so for me, and for many therapists I have known as colleagues and patients, I want to dwell on the dynamics of this bent. Let me generalize about what I see as commonalities, and I present my personal and dynamic data to illustrate the general.

These reparative character traits evolve in the larger framework of sex and personality as culturally defined. One specific shaping prominent in men with the healer's bent is a cluster around muted expression of masculine aggression and assertiveness, in combination with strong admixtures of maternally tinged nurturing and receptivity that point to maternal identifications.

I believe that I carry these primary character traits in large measure, consequent to developmental shapings set in place by fairly specific early life circumstances, beginning with early paternal loss magnified by maternal mourning and depression. Counters to these shapings were my mother's qualities of active mastery and never giving up, and my dogged clinging both to her and to an inner self modeled on her and my two uncles. I grew up too fast and too little in a pseudomaturity and bookishness accelerated by myopia and constant changes to new grades, schools, and domiciles.

I had two childhood neurotic syndromes specific to our summer place, and so classically obvious in Freudian lore that I had to laugh when in my training I heard them described. The first was a full-blown skunk phobia; the second consisted of nocturnal panic attacks set off by dreams and phantasies of a stovepipe, like that in the dining room of the cottage, overheating and burning the place down as we slept.

Around beginnings such as these, the therapist-in-the-making can evolve various secondary traits marked initially with avoidance, inhibition, and compulsion. Their mitigation requires compensatory adaptive measures that were at their outset essentially counterphobic.

Therapeutic analysis, twice entered after I returned from World War II, was, for strong personal reasons, truly life enhancing. The first analysis allowed me to get into the never boring pleasures and plights of marriage and work. The longer, second analysis, already mentioned, somehow opened me to drift in times of heightened stress into unwilled and happenstance self-analytic sorties. The quiet and occasionally still surprising happenings in these contexts have been very helpful in all aspects of my life.

I think this is so for a number of therapists with healer propensities. For most therapists, even for well-adapted therapists whose outlook is firmly in the working self, there will be moments when tremors of early concerns are felt when dealing with a patient or with one's own life challenges. Drifting to reflective attention on these moments can, at times outside conscious intending, often illuminate fresh perspectives on the revived traces of old pain.

Within these old papers as originally shaped, you probably will notice two large lacunae. These gaps surprised me when I saw them afresh and together.

My early years were spent in a woman-centered world, and a strongly Irish Catholic home as well. How could I have written so little about the psychology of women and the power and place of women in all that we are about? And how could I claim to speak as an analyst yet say so little about the force of shame, the emotion the Irish have known so deeply for so long, both to endure and to inflict?

One sheepish answer is that I knew a lot of shame but talked about it in the roundabout words of tact and empathy. And women are ever a part of me, informing what I have managed to write. The more compelling answer lies in the sheer power of the taboos and scornful sanctions our mother imposed on the open assertion of aggression and sexuality of all of us, including the banishment (when I was 12) of my summer uncle for his indiscretions. Although mothering us as best she could, she knew well how to shame us. On her own and single-handedly, our mother and her religion, by word and example, held us firmly in place, out of what I dimly held to be her need to dampen her own rage and hunger over lost love.

I also took for granted that the healing impulse in women is more powerful than in men—of course more subtly deployed and less noticeable in the familiar range of mothering prerogatives.

It has become a larger purpose in selecting these papers to dwell on the lifetime power of these dynamics to shape and drive growth and change in the therapist, in my case an analyst, so that my actions might more deeply touch and enhance others and in the doing enhance myself.

CHAPTER 3

What Was Taught

These days, psychotherapists come from diverse training backgrounds. One training component that remains indispensable is extended immersion in insight-seeking personal psychotherapy. This has long been a given of psychoanalytic training, and I remain persuaded of its worth.

Whatever the shortcomings of the two classical analyses I experienced, both provided ways of doing and speaking about the work of psychoanalysis, and for their help I am still grateful. The disciplined restraint of their quiet modes, and the open space they offered me for the exploring, helped me to see better what I kept bringing to the scene. My second analyst, Charlotte Babcock, had lively ways of doing and showing in the second effort that particularly engaged and freed me to act on my familiar inhibiting of anxious self-consciousness. I was able to evolve these liabilities into self-analytic venturing that thereafter nourished my work.

May you have found such enlivening in the personal therapeutic work you have done, or yet will do, with your trusted one. And perhaps you can find resonances of your own in this sketch of what my shaping was like as I floundered to be an analyst.

We know that as analysts we evolve our analytic identity most enduringly from the mixture of the motivations and capacities we bring with us from our developmental past, and then from what we make of these in the course of our personal analysis. We reinforce these through the identifications we make with our analyst and supervisors, bolstered by the loyalty we establish toward them and others central to our training and schooling. From all this, we fashion an initial set of theoretical perspectives and working modes on which we hope to rely. Then off we go.

Once on our way, however, we find that what we have shaped is liable to new twists and bends under the influence of the work. No two of us respond alike to this forging. Years of showing and being shown, of working and searching with my fellows to see what it is that we do, have allowed me to watch them and me changing and settling, evolving and congealing, coming on mixes of our own unique blending as our years have gone on.

Each of us hits on his particular ways to enjoy and endure the expansions and constraints of our very strange calling, the cave-dweller existence of restricted mobility and muted affective outlet to which we sentenced ourselves, so that others might find, in just these dimensions, an openness and freedom that they previously had not experienced.

I have been taught a lot by my fellow analysts. Like one's family, one's colleagues are positioned for maximum impact. Those whom I have been privileged to know as my analysands and supervisees have especially provided depth and detail to what I have learned about how analysts grow. They have given me riches on which I cannot draw, except the comfort I derive from noting the likenesses and differences among us, whereby I know that we indeed are fellows, and knowing that what I shall have to say about my own shaping need not be entirely idiosyncratic.

So I have structured this account of my own beginnings as an analyst around two ideas that I see as central to getting our bearings. First, the maturing analyst gradually builds his theoretical and technical preferences out of what was provided him in his training, selectively shaping the lot on the basis of his clinical experience, itself a reflection of his view of reality and of himself. He built this view out of his particular amalgam of strivings and defensive adaptations. These preferences are thus susceptible to modification through experience over time. Second, analytic work with patients is the major impetus for self-analytic endeavor and adaptive change over an analyst's lifetime. I place it before the shaping power of the analyst's own marriage and family, given their larger license to satisfy basic needs directly. The therapist must always bend to the greater constraints and needs of his discipline as set both within and around him. This is inevitably so to the extent that the analyst is impelled to go on doing what he does as an outgrowth of adaptive and reparative necessities learned in mastering troubled childhood relations to primary others. I am speaking, of course, about transference, and the central organizing place it holds in shaping our view of our reality and place in that reality. I hold to the perspective that carryover from past experience inevitably influences our processing of all subsequent experience throughout life. The analytic relationship that we may be able to offer our patient, or a psychotherapeutic experience of sufficient depth, offers one more and potentially special transference opportunity to expand both participants.

In the 1970s, when I began confronting the knots of hard spots entangled in my classical analytic training, I had to part company with all conceptions of the working psychoanalyst as a neutral and detached observer offering up analytic truths. I gradually came to envision analytic work as best poised for optimal depth and range when carried out from a position that acknowledges the relativism of knowing. Whose knowing gives direction and meaning to the analytic quest—the patient's? the analyst's? both?

For me, the only logical answer was that the patient's reality view must provide this base. This position accepts that analytic knowing must be sought rather than asserted. It must evolve within the dyad through searching interaction and negotiation between two separate realities, both claiming their own validity and both idiosyncratically shaped by separate developmental pasts.

Freud's Paradoxical Recommendations

Freud remarked often about technical matters in his early writings but published only six papers specifically on psychoanalytic technique (1911, 1912a, b, 1913, 1914, 1915a). Although in some respects overtaken by advances in technical knowledge, these papers are still considered our base. Certain of their pronouncements stand the test of time, whereas others do not. What is central to our topic is how Freud in these six papers set forth, in dialectical tension, opposing views of the analytic relationship and of the respective roles of patient and analyst in doing analytic work.

According to the first view, which came to be dominant in classical analytic training, the analyst uses his essential and deeper knowing to guide the patient past unresolved infantilisms to a more mature grasp of reality provided by the analyst through interpretations based in his theory and analytic experience. This view is that of a detached and superior observer that candidates of my era were to emulate.

I discovered the second view only many years later, when I began to speak as an analyst working from a vantage point of close involvement of two parties in a specially shaped relationship wherein the depths of both might be sounded for the ultimate benefit of the patient.

Here is a close paraphrasing of this subordinate perspective, as excerpted from the six papers. Freud asked that the analyst be utterly open to the patient's view. The analyst's stance is exploratory. He does not know what he will find. He is always aware of the surface of the patient's mind and listens without a personal or theoretical bias that might predetermine meaning. Otherwise, the analyst is "in danger of never finding anything but what he already knows; and if he follows his inclinations he will certainly falsify what he may perceive" (Freud, 1912b, p. 112). The analyst sets in motion a process that he can facilitate or vitiate; yet it goes its own way and does not allow direction or prescription. The division of labor is such that the analyst's task is to apprise the patient of his resistances, and the patient's is to respond with his own discoveries of what he had needed to forget. The passionate love of the patient for the analyst is as real as other states of being in love; for the analyst, there is an incomparable fascination in a woman of high principles who confesses her passion. These shared intensities require the perspective that the patient's reality view is the necessary base for what the patient is about and that the analyst's involvements have their own reality as well.

This honest acknowledgment of the reality, the legitimacy, of the feeling states of both participants in the immediacy of the analytic relationship posed a technical problem for Freud (1914). He let us know that he solved it by coming down authoritatively on the side of the safer view afforded by his other perspective: the analyst as the holder of a detached and superior view of what is real or not real in their relationship. This expediency allowed him to impose constraints of conscience and ethics in insisting that the analyst resolutely regard the passionate feelings of the patient as the by-product of the medical-analytical situation. He was to see these only as a transference product of the patient's resistance to discovering the infantile origins of her passion; similarly, he was enjoined to look on his own feeling states as counterfeelings induced by the patient's infantilisms, on both sides without current legitimacy or reality in their own right.

Once assigned to his place behind the couch, the analyst is to view these intensities as both real and unreal but technically to accept them in a way "for which there is no model in real life. He must take care not to steer away from the transference-love, or to repulse it or make it distasteful to the patient; but he must just as resolutely withhold any response to it. He must keep firm hold of the transference, but treat it as something unreal, as a situation that has to be gone through" (Freud, 1914, p. 153). This stratagem would allow the patient to feel safe enough to allow all her pre-conditions for loving, all her desires, to come to light, and "from these she will herself open the way to the infantile roots of her love" (p. 166).

We can hear the promise and challenge to the analyst in this won-derfully evocative and ambiguous prescription for addressing the psy-chic reality of the patient while remaining in touch with one's own perspective. This promise has provided an enduring challenge for sev-eral generations of analysts. For many of us, however, its potential has been overshadowed by Freud's persuasive emphasis on the other per-spective in which I was grounded. I was surprised by my belated recog-nition of Freud's subordinated perspective. I had surely known the words and phrases as part of my accumulated lore. But I could not grasp and appreciate them until some time after I had been through ex-periences with my own patients that pressed me to alter my technical approach (see chap. 4, this volume).

It is evident to me that Freud had grasped this awareness of the pri-macy of the patient's psychic reality in doing our work, as well as the in-herently unresolvable dialectic that must be lived with when we try to bring two different reality views into the working conjunction Isakower defined as the analyzing instrument (Balter, Lothane, and Spencer, 1980).

But Freud skewed the focus of his vision for what must have been many reasons. In my view, as stated by Burris (1990), timely external rea-sons could have included his need to protect his enterprise from the sex-ual impulsivity of some of his followers, and his ever pressing need to assert a more persuasive stance of scientific knowing. In the doing, he let slip from his grasp the full potential of his primary insight into the nature of psychic reality.

The constraining result of the imbalance between the two views that Freud or his translators provided is the liability of a double vision versus a balanced binocularity. I know that my reading of Freud in this manner still puts me at odds with prevailing views—possibly one reason I could not attain its publication in the journals that were my familiar haunts.

The blending of the two perspectives in my own clinical work has been a quiet preoccupation all these years. I have benefited from my Freudian beginnings, and I continue to value the clinical lore and gen-eral mappings. I continue to prefer to keep our focus on the patient, par-ticularly around the extent of personal disclosure of my resonances. Of this knotty topic, more later. To the extent that I have been able to find a comfortable grounding in Freud's other perspective, I shall continue to see myself as Freudian, preferably uncategorized. Although I admire and respect the labors of those who refine the distinctions between single- and multiple-person psychologies, I have long been comfortable in ranging across whatever perspectives the patient and I find most apt at the moment.

My Training as an Analyst

For those of us entering analytic training in Philadelphia in the late 1940s, Freud's technique papers constituted The Word. The perspective that I took from them then, the work identity I believe I was taught to take from them, emphasized Freud's preponderant view of the analyst as the holder of an essential and superior knowing. In condensing the familiar that follows, I have stayed close to Freud's words and metaphors.

I learned that the competent analyst's listening mode is one in which his unconscious is a receiver that reliably picks up all the cues needed to guide him. Encountering these links to the patient's unconscious wishes and fears, he then speaks at the right time to what he has discovered, and he helps the patient to see his resistive ways of wishing not to know what he is now being helped to know. The result satisfies the necessities of the treatment. The analyst can trust his memory about what occurs in the sessions and is confident that he will usually be right in any dispute with the patient.

From this position, the analyst can with assurance define as resistance those behaviors of the patient that interfere with the patient's collaborative participation. Such resistance is known to derive from intrapsychic defenses against the emergence of unwanted and repressed impulses. A major motivational source of both impulse and resistance lies in the patient's transference, the directing onto the analyst of wishes and fears originally experienced in relation to primary persons in the analysand's childhood years. Whatever the turbulence in the analytic relationship, the reasons are sought in connections between these current disturbances and the misapprehensions of infantile sexuality. Helping the patient recognize their anachronistic nature, the analyst contrasts them with a contemporary maturity now possible for the analysand to experience through the disciplined objectivity of the analyst.

To be this kind of analyst, we were to be emotionally as cold as a surgeon—to put aside all feelings, even human sympathy, and to be as opaque as a mirror, showing nothing but what has been shown to us.

To ensure this working stance, Freud required that we be more than approximately normal persons. We had to be free of and intolerant of any resistance in us that would distort our conscious awareness of our unconscious perception of the patient's unconscious and disqualify us as analysts.

The crucial word here, of course, is what we have learned to call *countertransference*. Freud, and now his representatives, our teachers, expected that we would undergo the purification of a training analysis and continue some form of further self-inquiry indefinitely. Lacking this, we would surely lapse into acting on our countertransferences, bringing discredit to psychoanalysis, and leading ourselves astray.

I shared with my fellows a conviction that tracing the footprints of one's training analyst was the sure road to purity. For many years, I followed the designated paths to the working committees of our institute and of the American Psychoanalytic Association and happily hoed the pea patches of both as manifest of my worth. In sweat with the best around the practicalities of helping develop new training programs, I found my measure in the clasp of good and lasting friendships.

Attaining the prescribed ideal of the imperturbable and detached analyst at work was quite a different matter. I tried to wait with reasonable confidence for the correct understanding of the hidden significance of the patient's associations to rise to my awareness. I hoped to put this understanding into a correct interpretation with optimal words and timing. I worried about the liabilities of coming out with an inexact interpretation (Glover, 1931) or blundering into an unintended parameter (Eissler, 1953). I assumed that the patient's responses to my interpretations could be understood in terms of his acceptance or resistance to facing the truth that had been revealed to him through my words. More often than not, such enlightenment was rare, or at best but a glimmer, and I improvised as best I could.

At the same time, the confidence of presuming to command and dispense this powerful knowing from safe detachment was heady stuff. It sustained many of us whose *furor sanandi* had been whetted by the movie *Lady in the Dark* and a spate of similar fictions. It was demonstrated to us that deep layers of unconscious meaning were there to be discerned in the most minute of samples. At any clinical conference, there could be as many illuminating formulations as there were participants, each sure he had captured the essence of the patient's dynamics. Dreams gave us special license to romp in the playpen of psychoanalysis, with dream symbols our toys and tools for tapping the richness and wit of primary process. Ours was the exhilaration of privileged knowing, with entitlement to wordplay and the reach for clever aphorism. We needed but to watch, listen, and learn the ways and words of our betters. With time and luck, we might make it.

Fortunately for my patients and me, there was the sobering of sometimes excellent supervision, as in Robert Waelder's reminder that the truth we had to offer our patients was only analytic truth, not Truth. I was slow to grasp the full significance of his message.

I was equally slow in coming to grips with the second and very different perspective Freud also described in his technique papers. Centering the analysis in the patient's reality was a radical alternative to what I had been taught. I must have registered it in my candidacy readings, but with little attentiveness.

Some in my generation of psychoanalysts, perhaps educated in surroundings more relaxed than those of my training years, may have grasped the rich potential of this alternative view. They may have been freer to play with the implications of Freud's having put these two inherently conflicting viewpoints into enormous dialectic tension. But my overall impression is that what I have sketched was very much the prevailing mode in American psychoanalysis during the last decade of World War II and the first decade afterward, when some refugee analysts from western Europe needed urgently to stake their claim to their exclusive hold on real psychoanalysis.

My training took place at a Philadelphia institute recovering from a recent split, with each side intent on demonstrating its sound grasp of Freudian analysis. Shortly thereafter, the institute began sponsoring a new, academically based training facility at the other end of Pennsylvania. Both the institute and our provisional training program in Pittsburgh were subject to heightened, prolonged scrutiny by the American Psychoanalytic Association and the usual skepticism of American academia toward psychoanalysis. At both ends of the state, we had only to gain from heightened orthodoxy and the claim to sure knowing, in reflection of the national scene.

Only recently home from the European theater of World War II and the exhilaration of holding my own in the military, I much needed to seek analytic answers to the chafing of an Irish Catholic upbringing. Once in analysis, I comfortably exchanged the old orthodoxies for the new. I was happy to share with Freud and his delegates their view of the analyst as possessing a superior hold on reality, and I looked forward to dealing correctively with a patient whose grasp of her real world was hampered by a psychic reality distorted by the consequences of repressed infantile sexuality. I think it fair to see here a resonance between the larger scene and my own primary hitch in my relationship with my mother.

A sampling of casual aphorisms from those times speaks vividly of the power of the analyst and his deliberate silence: "If you don't know just what to say, better to remain silent." "Silence will never get you into trouble. It is our most valuable tool and manifest of our accepting hovering." "Find out what the patient wants. Then don't give it to him." "Frustration of the patient's wishes encourages regression, which leads to the uncovering of infantile ambivalence and the recovery of the original infantile neurosis." "Analysis is basically an exercise in sensory and emotional deprivation."

A burdening aspect of this assumption of superior status is fear of failure. Shortfall carried the shaming stigma of countertransference, self-evident proof of an incomplete analysis. The remedy was single and quickly advised. Even well into the 1950s, to discuss one's countertransferences was to encounter the prescription to seek further analysis.

It was customary, at my new institute as in the American Psychoanalytic Association, to prescribe for newly fledged analysts several years of working on their own in the "independent practice of psychoanalysis" before being brought into the educational processes of the institute.

This constraint imposed less analytic isolation, as I found out only much later, in well-established institutes that had developed out of a preexisting analytic society—for they provided access to ongoing study groups and society-affiliated enterprises that made continuing learning with peers a natural postgraduate sequence. These opportunities were largely lacking in our Pittsburgh community—a void that went unnoticed in the bustle of other sorts of academic pursuits in which all of us were immersed. It would be years before our local group could act on and find comfort in the need for the open and full showing and telling of what we did. We simply paid too little attention to how we might best learn in groups.

It did not help that the prevailing language of both written and spoken clinical analytic discourse in this country was veiled in the generalizations of ego psychology. How senior analysts did true analysis remained unspecified.

The enforced loneliness of independent practice and working in relative isolation added a powerful reinforcement for the vulnerabilities of shame and inadequacy already whispering in many of us. Locally and in many other institutes across our country, the voices of many good hearts and gentle people were muted, some permanently, out of fear that what they had to say would be judged not good enough. Sadly, such dismissive judgments could be too easily made, by us and about us, and too little remediation and support provided. The solitary stress of intensive work went on day in and day out, with patients too often outside our range of expectation. Some of us it shook and shaped. Others seemed to freeze in time and place.

From my perspective today, I see little to be gained from this practice, and I am glad it has left the scene. At the time, however, such a removed status seemed natural, quite in keeping with the other detachments and austerities I had learned to equate with an optimal analytic stance. In my own shame-shaped bent for orthodoxy and acceptability, I contributed my share to the reticence and shielding that were part of our anxieties about countertransference and other inadequacies.

Only later, when accustomed to holding my own in the committees of the American Psychoanalytic Association, did I begin to realize the damage this prescribed isolation had inflicted on our institute and others that I came to know. Overall, we were painfully slow to work on how to enhance one another through the give-and-take of ongoing small group learning. We were even slower to recognize that we needed always to sustain some form of ongoing open clinical seminar as a safe forum for each of us—a forum in which we would wish to show one another what we do not know. We still cannot fully accept the mutual responsibilities we share to give and respond to both praise and criticism fairly given across all stages of our professional development.

One telling instance came in those early years when I attempted a written canvassing of colleagues, both locally and elsewhere, to inquire of their experiencing of dreaming about their patients. Occasionally, I dreamed about certain of my patients, and I hoped to find, if not understanding, at least a fellowship of flounderers. I received just three replies, two affirming. The third came at a cocktail party soon thereafter.

One of my senior colleagues stood ramrod before me and announced with impressive solemnity, "Were I ever to dream about any of my patients, I would feel obliged to return for more analysis."

This proscription of any persisting inner resonances in the analyst about his patients, as the telltale exposure of countertransference, was prevalent—a challenge I had no choice but to meet. Only a very few years at the work made clear to me that it would rarely be my lot to be lacking in countertransference. I came to prefer the broader definition of the concept that would acknowledge the stirring power inherent in the continuing interplay of mutual influence of patient and analyst deeply invested in each other (Tower, 1956; Reich, 1960).

I heeded the injunction to seek more analysis, two years or so after graduation—this time with Charlotte Babcock, whose working style was one of active involvement. I could understand how it was that those writing about mutual involvements in countertransference were women analysts. From her I learned the legitimacy and therapeutic power of the analyst as an articulate participant in the joint analytic quest. This analysis also yielded me the perspective of the work as a never finished quest into one's multiple identifications with both sexes, and the richer possibilities for experiencing reality that these multiple choices open up to us.

I need at this point to stop midstride to touch on a few of the many hazards of shame facing those who sought postwar analytic training. In the eastern United States particularly, where the majority of refugee analysts found haven, it was a given for many that only those schooled in the Old Country could claim to do real analysis; Americans need not apply. Some made difficult to learn from or measure them, because of their preference for the opaque terminology of ego psychology as only they could understand it. Even early Arlow and Brenner had their jousts for the right to be heard. Thankfully, there were notably generous exceptions among those who escaped to our shores, and I was fortunate to be one of those who at times found expansion in their presence.

For us outsiders, attending the annual midwinter meetings at the Waldorf in New York City was at best a pilgrimage (Poland, 1977), a rite of passage carried out in wary silence from side seats not preempted by the advance outriders of the elect. At worst, it involved watching the pecking order wait for acknowledgment to speak. The ultimate worst was having a paper of one's own to present. We saw and came to expect that too often a first offering by some fellow wretch would elicit a lofty dissection of fatal flaws, and the sop of faint possibility that a useful morsel might at the last breath be discovered. This style, known as *true Teutonic,* was powerful in its shaming and belittling. It was often aped by the rest of us in our discussions back then, even by many American-trained peers and teachers initially inclined to the so-called American soft soap: first approval and support, then criticism.

Lest my description of our American scene seem exaggerated, I recommend to you Kirsner's (2000) *Unfree Associations.* It took an Australian academician to amass interview data about what our organized psychoanalysis was like during the years of which I speak, and to hold the mirror for us to see ourselves.

Until well into the 1960s, this style of superior and hierarchical knowing prevailed in too many of our analytic institutes. Its ubiquity, and the part each of us had in it through our claims to sure knowing, surely has provided us all with a demonstration of the hoary analytic concept of identification with the aggressor.

We do become the bad that was done to us. Defending against our shame by shaming others taints any social context. We become masters in passing it on. Even a casual look at any of our training institutions can still show our group skills in pinning the tail elsewhere.

A stance in certain knowing probably always will offer a tempting base from which we can easily dispense our knowing that stains forever: how to inflict shame. Like graffiti on marble.

In the years after the end of my second analysis, I gradually grew accustomed to dwelling in off-hours on patient events of the day that had left me puzzled or uneasy. This scanning was especially apt to occur during time spent in the garden or workshop. There was so much I had not grasped with confidence during the working day, so much seen only through a glass darkly. I learned to welcome these half-reflections not deliberately sought, and came to count on them to illuminate my later work. I continued to dream at times about my patients. When I became comfortable accepting these goings-on as part of my groping ways, I could be open to seeking how to learn from them. The serene grounding of the weeding or wood shaping and crafting gave me the context in which to do these bits of self-analysis better, quite like the quiet foraging I had done on my own during my first analysis. This, too, puzzled me as something that was reliably there for me but not recognizable until later.

It may be a natural maturational sequence for the analyst, in search of identity and competence, first to seek the safety of mimicry of his or her own analyst; then to face, in the mirror of the patient, disturbing likenesses that must be worked through before one can engage these freely; and only then to trust in one's own freedom and resilience to engage and respect the essential differences between self and other—an engagement that I have come to feel is the basis for optimal analysis.

For some, this sequence may have been swift. For me, some years passed before I could comfortably forgo my trained expectation that I function from a position of superior knowing and detachment, before I could accept as idiosyncratic fact that I could not work well with those operational definitions of patient and analyst that placed me at a level of remove that I could not recognize—relating to patients not matchable to the maps issued me in basic training.

This realization was forced on me by the difficulties I kept encountering with patients who simply could not, or would not, tolerate being dealt with from a position of detachment, cool objectivity, and minimal communicative contact. Like the patients Freud (1914) wrote about more than 50 years earlier, some of my patients some of the time, and a few of them all the time, were unable to relate to the usual analytic tasks or to me except through behaviors intended to persuade me about what they could not put into words and to dissuade me from either encroaching on or abandoning them.

In attempting to meet these within the technical modes of my original training, as I then understood them, we at times could make analytic progress. But, far too often, we would become stuck in a Sargasso of quiet misery, becalmed in too much silence and bilateral, wary waiting.

Each of these patients, in many respects so different, had in common a huge sensitivity to and anxious monitoring of my ways of attempting to relate to them. Each was liable to regressive withdrawal, affective distress, and decompensation in the analytic setting. They were prone to disruptive actions outside, in response to my behaviors they experienced as slighting, intrusive, preemptive, or repudiating. Often I was dismayed and puzzled that their reactions seemed so far out of line with my perception of my analytic work. My interventions pointing to the deeper meanings of their behavior struck me as accurate, well articulated, and humanely presented and my silences as benignly accepting of the patient's vulnerability. I spent much time in pressing my insights, and silently amassing irrefutable evidence that was intended to persuade and rectify.

It took me some time, longer than I wish, to be able to hear, in the patients' allusive distress, and even in their direct plaints, that there was more to these negative responses than defensive avoidance and transference-driven repudiation of a truth. I had to learn to hear, instead, that my accustomed ways might realize their worst fears—that how I stated my view could be experienced as a threatening repudiation of the patient's view, and my expectant silences as demand or abandonment.

Looking for ways out of these stalemated states and in contemplating my failures, I put into the background the uses of formal technical theory and fell back to a less knowing attending to the patient and to my own inner workings.

Groping in this fashion, enhanced at times by unsought self-analytic incidents, I was able to see for myself that the analyst, this analyst for sure, was truly a participant-observer resonant to the dynamics of the patient in the ways Racker (1957) did so much to elucidate, and was often as liable to regression as the patient under the impact of the patient's problems and own intercurrent stresses in the rest of his life (McLaughlin, 1975).

Work with these patients drove home to me a recognition of the relativistic nature of the analytic enterprise when perceived from the different reality views of the two participants. I had no choice but to consider the extent to which my holding to a superior knowing could be very much at odds with the analytic aim of understanding the uniqueness of the patient, and to seek alternative ways that might better acknowledge the primacy of the patient's psychic reality (McLaughlin, 1981).

One lesson that early on I grimly pasted in my helmet was that mine was the necessity to acknowledge any mistake or change made by me in our work, so that we might explore its consequences. It was my mistake, mine to rectify, mine to be sorry for. Some patients were casual and supportive, others remorseless for their measure of flesh. But over time the two of us usually found that we survived the discord and that our relationship indeed was often advantaged by what we had discovered about both of us.

For me, the easement of trying to right the wrong quickly erased the grimness. Yet the more enduring therapeutic yield lay in being sure that I or we talked about the breach and did not bury it in silence. In that exposure lay the reliable expectation that we often could reach a stronger therapeutic base and impetus for growth for both in the dyad.

Here for the grasping was an insight as old as Kant and as recent as the contemporary findings of Tronick and Gianino (1988) in child developmental research: that the sociopsychological maturing of the child to adult occurs not solely from the idyllic oneness of initial union but also from the enhancing ebb and flow of likeness and dissonance in all that needs to be said and done in the subsequent pairings. Ergo, there was less mutative magic and support to count on in our analytic silence than we had been schooled to expect. Instead, we could expect shared deadness and inertia, which the therapist must actively mitigate. It may not be too far a reach to read into these dialectics some unsettled technical aspects of intersubjectivity as it currently preoccupies our interest.

Now with reasons and license to speak, where and about what are the therapeutic limits set, and by whom? Is the therapist now freed to reveal whatever occurs to him?

On the basis of what I think I know of analysis, I still prefer to keep our field of observation centered on what the patient brings to its filling. An analyst's aim is to learn and speak about the patient's limits and stretching of his knowing. When his contributions exceed and miscarry in ways evident to one or both, these surely call for the best acknowledgment and reparative efforts that the analyst or any other psychotherapist can learn to use. In the closing years, I learned to say more about the strong feelings I was experiencing in my listening to moving content from patients who were conspicuously flat in their telling. The results were mixed but inconclusive. I take refuge in my expectation that I will hear more with my mouth shut.

That brings me to a technical matter currently brought front and center in our disciplines in the context of intersubjectivity: the pros and cons involved in the extended verbal sharing of the inner mental life of the two parties as they participate in the treatment dyad. I hope I make it evident that I feel that the observational field that we share belongs primarily to the patient and that our focus is best kept on what he brings to it. Without personal experience in the trying and testing of shared intersubjectivity, beyond the reparative necessities I have just outlined, I do not feel qualified to speak.

What I did was return to Freud's more encompassing view, one elegantly captured in Loewald's (1960) statement that "there is neither such a thing as reality or a real relationship, without transference" (p. 32).

Our psychic development and our reality view are formed in a life-long continuum of relationships, each affected by those preceding, and each having the potential to provide new shape and patterning to what is there or to confirm in the here and now the earlier that was. But, as Schwaber has shown repeatedly in her many contributions, and as I am ruefully aware, all of us in our daily work can be noted to have a strong propensity for declaring and steering in directions based on one's own theory or preferred perspective (Schwaber, 1983).

My own acknowledged bias rests in the importance I attribute to the phenomena we subsume under the concept of transference, wherein experience of the past affects our expectancies about the present, as an inevitability of the essentially conservative modes of survival of our psychophysical being.

For me, the analytic quest is more than a story constructed for the comfort of the two participants. It is a quest for the stuff of prior experience in each of us that pumps through and from the roots and trunks of our separate developmental pasts. These insistent pressures give individual shape, color, and vitality to the unique experiential present that patient and analyst shape between us, separate at first but now conjoined.

This same conviction shapes my notion of the fundamental task of the analyst: to use his powers primarily to lead and guide the patient toward *how* rather than to *what*—to help the patient grasp how he can contemplate himself and others—rather than toward what he will find when he does so.

The analyst will do this best insofar as he or she can provide example and base, can serve experientially as a model, flawed but trying, of exploratory openness to reflect, respond, and be informed. In this, the patient can find the comfort and incentive to explore his surface-to-depth personal view of the world and himself through the shared refraction of another's gaze.

My own stance, similar to Gill's (1982) and more closely aligned with Schwaber's (1983) but inevitably not identical with either, can be put so:

I will listen to whatever you may wish to say, with the intent to understand your meaning and viewpoint, and with the least imposition of my own view or meaning as I can manage. As I do not presume to know, I shall need often to question and to ask for illumination. I will be alert to and inquire about your nonverbal behaviors and shifts of affect, particularly as I listen for allusions to how you perceive and react to my behaviors. My aim there and always will be to help you articulate the validity and logic of how you see your world, and me in it. Through looking at how you see me, I will try to help you see yourself, hoping thereby to strengthen your capacities to find even more of yourself to authenticate and own.

This readiness of the analyst to be, like the patient, the object of scrutiny can come only from some temperamental openness in the analyst, spurred by curiosity about exploring within this perspective.

The therapeutic rationale for working like this lies in what experience has taught me to expect: that this authentication of the patient's perceptual powers and viewpoint strengthens the patient's capacities to look further into himself and bring forth conflicted content in his own recovery of developmental antecedents.

This expectation has a venerable history in psychoanalysis, beginning with Freud's (1915a) closing paper in his technique series, "Observations on Transference Love."

Bernfeld's (1941) "Facts of Observation in Psychoanalysis," a neglected classic, was retrieved and amplified by Calef and Weinshel (1985). Bernfeld observed that a patient's divulging of a secret tended to follow an analyst's comment conveying acceptance and thereby diminishing obstacles of internal shame or distrust in the patient. Results from the psychotherapy research of Sampson and Weiss (1986) and their Mount Sinai group independently extended and expanded on Bernfeld's notion. From a very different operational perspective, Schwaber (1983, 1986, 1990) has consistently attested to the therapeutic impetus inherent in the patient's perception and responses to the analyst's persistent seeking to be informed of the patient's perceptual experiences and their inner historical determinants.

This sustained quality of listening, played out and enacted in endless repetitions and variations, offers the patient the fundamental experience of being believed.

"Believing" here connotes multiple levels of meaning. It starts with the commonplace analytic acceptance of the patient's stated view as indeed a reflection of something of himself that he needs to convey. It adds an essential dimension: responding to the need of the patient to know that what he is offering is being received as it is. This is not a listening mode of naive acceptance of received and final truth. It is a face-value acknowledgment of the impact and value of the patient's

view and thus a resonant affirmation of the patient herself. This acknowledgment is lived out through the analyst's sustained commitment to exploring and expanding the further significance that the patient can come
to see in what he has experienced, now in the light of their shared quest.

It is the analyst's effort at forbearing acceptance that in turn fosters
the patient's willingness to gamble on the integrity of the analyst's invitation to attempt the collaborative exploration of the patient's psychic
life to its depths, in the patient's own idiom and from his point of view.

I wish it to be clear that this search for the patient's psychic reality is
not all that I find I must do. I consider the stance essential from the beginning of the analytic relationship, and it needs to be sustained in order to establish the basis for what some think of as the therapeutic
alliance. I consider it primary thereafter as well, to ensure contact with
the patient's surface, before I feel right about bringing in an agenda of
my own.

My justification for assuming the right at times to assert my knowing
derives from a conviction, self-serving or otherwise, that goes like this. I
am convinced that much of the incentive for mutative change, for moving on to new positions, lies, for all of us from childhood on, in the affirming and releasing challenge of the other who has first proved the
reliability of her or his commitment to our cause.

I in no way wish to convey the impression that my use of this mode
invariably surmounted all obstacles. What it did accomplish was a re-
duction in what I came to see as unnecessary burdens that made it more
difficult for the patient to do her work. Placing such high value on psychic reality as being all we have to work with, in or out of analysis, would
seem at first to take more from the analyst than it gives. It places the psychic reality of patient and analyst in an ambiguous and relativistic opposition, far from the claims of the latter to a secured and superior
reality-view. But the yield carries a potential far beyond that of the earlier and more tilted conception of the analytic pair (see chap. 4). I have
no doubt that patients' cues, goading, and encouragement, the bread-
breaking of their companionship in the journey, provide again and again
fine adventure and fulfillment for both parties.

In this core experience is a moving power, by and for the two participants, that for years I did not fully fathom.

A possible clue to a central ingredient may lie in the archaic quality of
the belief, particularly when mutually acknowledged, that one can indeed
be the cause of the behaviors of the other, that one can have such

significance as to evoke the behaviors of the other. This way of experiencing the interplay of mutual influence and power is prominent in the closeness of baby and mother (Stern, 1985). The utter absence of this belief, in early development, can stunt or kill a child or bring a mother to despair. It is a belief that pervades the entwinement of lovers and colors every intense relationship throughout life, including the analytic relationship.

Therapeutic work around basic acceptance can counter and help repair the trauma inflicted by shame. This repair calls on the best efforts of both parties of the dyad so that together they may rekindle the vitality lying at the heart of the shared archaic belief about our mutual power to influence each other. This last phrase itself points to the once-upon-a-time bliss of being affirmed as one with mother, with lover. It is the living antithesis of dead aloneness.

I need to dwell more fully here on the therapist's pair in this repairing, whence comes the energy that must be marshaled to sustain the pair along the way, for often it will fall to the therapist to carry the heavier load when the patient can or will do no more.

It was at such times that I came to seek the comfort and replenishment that might come from runs of self-analytic foraging. These I first chanced on in my second analysis, in times of perplexity and tension around impasses with patients. The experience of these sorties could enlighten old perspectives and restore calm expectancy. Although their occurrence always lay beyond my conscious control, it took some years before I came to see that they often began when I was absorbed in routine chores in the garden or workshop, and they carried over into my sleep and dreaming.

Discovering these furthered an old interest in growing and shaping whatever I could lay my hands on. It had grown to a quiet passion along with marriage, parenting, and homemaking. I was happy in the mid-1960s to bring my analytic work and office into my home, in the manner of my Philadelphia mentors. There, without conscious intent, I brought under one venerable Victorian roof all the vital aspects of my loving and working. I came to think of garden and workshop as "transference sanctuaries." I finally had a winter home for the longings and reveries of my childhood summers. I reveled in this protective immersion until my retirement five years ago. Whatever creativity I could muster first found expression and excuse in restoring and enhancing the fine old structure and its grounds as my hands found their way with tools and dirt.

Gradually, I became freer to speak and write about what I was discovering in my analytic work. I noticed that I usually began a new manual project when starting a new paper. I oscillated between the two, turning out acceptable analytic papers with pen or processor while fashioning wood arbors and benches, larger than I knew to do, that were needed for the garden surround, or hammering and punching sheets of roofing copper into fireplace hoods and screens, or doing the dirty work of scraping, painting, and plastering.

Probably the least utilitarian quirk of applied creativity had to do with chicken eggs. Dye-dipping Easter eggs with our little people, a carryover from my own childhood, got us started, and soon I was hooked. I learned to master emptying the raw egg, and I could turn in my hand that light, perfect shell, in its whiteness inviting but always receding, easy to hold and behold, but fragile to the grasp and never fully seen. Here lay invitation and challenge that no stretched flat canvas or blank paper could offer.

In 1975 and 1976, I sometimes got lost for hours in easy chair and shop, where I enjoyed holding and turning out some 80 lacquered eggs. I learned to master the tools and methods for depicting a bird and its surround in living color around an egg (using felt-tipped pens), or I scratched through oak-dyed dark shells (with a sharp-tipped knife) to the white beneath, in the manner of our forebears. I still have a few of these eggs, and still I experience mild surprise at the beauty I wrought. Over the years, I gave many eggs away, often to women and little girls with whom I shared close family ties. Later, when I realized that I had given many eggs away as casual gifts to senior women analysts with whom I had shared hard work on committees or symposia, I began calling these my "analytic eggs." For a time, I tried to color in the background of an egg while behind the couch and in my silent listening mode. This added nothing and became a deflection from the more active work I now preferred. Gradually, my egg work ceased to fascinate, and I laid it aside.

Only recently, while preparing these pages, did it occur to me to seek out my notebook listing the eggs and what went into their preparation in 1975–1976 and to align those years with data from my curriculum vitae.

In 1975, I published "The Sleepy Analyst," my first clinical paper, completed a year earlier—a paper cautiously detailing an affliction common to analysts, including me. My diffidence showed in my attributing to anonymous others some close clinical detail that belonged to me. I had written it as a fellow flounderer seeking support. It drew the ambiguity of both criticism and laughter, then the usual silence of the times. I do not recall being particularly abashed. I had earlier survived a small storm of published rebuttal to a paper championing a non-reporting stance for training analysts (McLaughlin, 1973). My surmise is that my nonchalance covered the pain of feeling twice rebuffed, for I went back to the familiar respite of lying low in solitary doing.

Coincidence perhaps: 1975 marked the beginning of the bird eggs, and my paper silence lasted until 1978, when I published an applied analytic paper on cerebral lateralization. During these years, I continued the slow loosening of my tethers to my ego-psychological groundings and sought freer ways to do and show my work. In retrospect, I can make much of the obvious imagery enacted in the egg work, but in fact I do not recall giving it any attention at the time of creation. In 1981 came my only extended venture into pure analytic theory (see chap. 4). Although that paper was overdocumented and tedious to read, I still value it for its allusions to the thrust of most of the papers I went on to write. It suggested an alternative to the analyst-centered basis for understanding that instead gave analytic primacy to the patient's own perception of the reality he had learned to know. I knew that this could be seen as an open break with my beginnings, but I needed to say it. No heavens fell, and from then on I averaged about one fresh paper a year until retirement. Aligning the dates helped me to recognize anew the rich tangle of conflicts played out in my hide-and-seek defending, in my avoiding and engaging crucial issues of analytic intimacy. I feel that chapter 4, taken from this old paper, also offers some evidence of inner gains gathered during those years, and some justification to my conviction that self-analysis is not beyond our reach and can make for positive change at whatever age.

What I found behind and essential to these years of busy doing were the relaxation and freedom for contemplation in desultory minding anchored in some routine physical activity, reenforced with familiar sights, sounds, and smells. I had come to know and rely on these specially sought circumstances as transference sanctuaries, havens in which I could be replenished by the most nourishing relationships rooting me to my past.

Aging, illnesses, and the sober satisfaction of surviving for the pleasure of still working and loving—these do temper the temper. The same
old needs to reach out and make contact with the other, for the sake of
healing and enhancing us both, remain alive.

CHAPTER 4

Transference, Psychic Reality, and Countertransference

The concept of countertransference has posed practical and theoretical problems since its beginnings as a derivative concept in early psychoanalysis. Its restriction to the analytic situation reflects the importantly different ways in which Freud (1912a, 1915a) used the concepts of transference and psychic reality as (a) general psychological principles and (b) patient-centered constructs in the analytic situation. His crucial stratagem of designating transference as not-real in the analytic situation afforded the analyst the protected role of detached observer vis-à-vis the intensities on both sides of the couch; but it also created misunderstandings concerning the contributions and capacities of the two parties in the analytic relationship.

Freud emphasized the infantile nature of the patient's psychic reality, itself acquired through transferential processes, and assigned it to the dynamic unconscious of primary process and primitive drives, set off against the rational, objectifying secondary process of scientific thought. When applied to the analytic situation, this perception of the infantile aligned the patient closer to the primitive and overemphasized the neutrality and imperturbability of the analyst.

The literature on countertransference reflects a long struggle to acknowledge the humanity and liabilities of the analyst at work, to recognize his participant-observer role open to countertransference responses and to integrate these aspects into the theory and technique of the psychoanalytic method. The psychoanalytic literature reflects a trend to reject the categorization of both primary process and psychic reality as belonging only at the infantile levels of development and to claim once more for transference and psychic reality their earlier importance as general psychological principles reflecting ubiquitous phenomena.

The literature on follow-up of analysis indicates that improvement and change depend not on obliteration of old structures and conflict, but on their inactivation through internalization of higher level psychic structures built up through processes of transference in the analytic work. In the course of his training analysis, the work ego of the analyst receives significant shaping through these processes of transference and internalization. And, as a relatively new psychic structure with highly specialized functions, it may have impressive durability yet be susceptible to disruption and regression.

Hence, it is useful to put aside the concept of countertransference in favor of the more relativistic view that the analyst's transferences, like the patient's, are central to all he is or does and that they determine the psychic reality he lives in and brings to the analytic task. This view allows the psychoanalytic situation and process to be conceptualized as an experience of shared exploration in which the analyst uses his more developed transferential capacities to sound, with the patient, the latter's depths of transferences, toward the goal of a more evolved psychic reality for the patient authenticated through hard analytic work.

If the past 50 years of analyst watching have clarified anything about the nature of the analyst's experiences, it is that transference is a matter of equal rights, both on and behind the couch. What we have come to know about ourselves and our fellows points toward a conclusion that now seems obvious. All that we were, see ourselves as, or wish to be is caught up in the analytic relationship, as it is for the patient.

The banality of this comment is itself a tribute to the struggles of many to see beyond the constraints imposed by the traditional uses of transference and countertransference. One casualty has been the word *countertransference,* itself so variously defined as to be by now almost unmanageable (Orr, 1954; Kernberg, 1965). For reasons that may become persuasive as this chapter unfolds, I would like to see the word laid to rest, with all appropriate honors, so that we might talk instead of the "analyst's transferences." My position is based in the historical fact that the concept of countertransference has been skewed from its beginnings in being derivative, designating reactions of the analyst to the patient's transference, and confined solely to the patient-centered focus of the analytic situation.

Freud's (1910) comments on the matter were sparse: "We have become aware of the 'counter-transference,' which arises in [the physician] as a result of the patient's influence on his unconscious feelings" (p. 144); "we have noticed that no psycho-analyst goes further than his own complexes and internal resistances permit" (p. 145). A little later, Freud (1915a) spoke of the patient's falling in love with the analyst as a manifestation of transference induced by the psychoanalytic situation—a conquest not to be attributed to the analyst's charms (pp. 168–169). Simultaneously, he acknowledged the power of the transference–countertransference experience: "Sexual love is undoubtedly one of the chief things in life. . . . [I]n spite of neurosis and resistance, there is an incomparable fascination in a woman of high principles who confesses her passion" (pp. 169–170). Freud (1912b) went to far greater lengths to cite the reasons, ethical, scientific, and therapeutic, why the physician should view the patient's behavior and his own erotic stirrings, as infantile or not real; why he should hold firm to his abstinent role as the emotionally cold surgeon (p. 115), opaque like a mirror (p. 118).

Reinforcing this viewpoint, Freud (1905) designated in particular ways the transference experiences of the patient on the couch:

> What are transferences? They are new editions or facsimiles of the impulses and phantasies . . . aroused . . . during the progress of the analysis. . . . [T]hey replace some earlier person by the person of the physician. . . . [A] whole series of psychological experiences are revived, not as belonging to the past, but as applying to the person of the physician at the present moment [p. 116].

Over the years, Freud (1914) enlarged this aspect of transference to make it central to the analytic situation as a process of the patient's living out his infantile relationships via the "transference neurosis."

I argue that Freud also saw transference in a much broader perspective and that the gains of his selective emphasis have been offset by enduring difficulties in conceptualizing the analytic relationship, particularly the role and function of the analyst, and hence the phenomena generally subsumed under "countertransference." As I see it, this emphasis on the infantile origins and aspects of the patient's contributions, in stressed contrast to the mature wisdom and scientific objectivity of the analyst, forced on our analytic concepts of transference and of psychic reality this same infantile and primitive emphasis.

Why I would wish to involve psychic reality in the consideration of countertransference may seem as ambiguous as my opening comment about the ubiquity of transference. A scanning of Freud's broad and narrowed views of transference and of psychic reality may help to relate these to our ways of understanding what we now call countertransference.

Transference and Psychic Reality

At the time Freud (1912a) was developing his views of transference within the analytic situation, he attributed to transference a ubiquity of occurrence in the human relations of all neurotics (p. 101). Earlier (1900), he had given transference the power of a general principle of psychological functioning as a particular mode of displacement:

> An unconscious idea is as such quite incapable of entering the preconscious and . . . it can only exercise any effect there by establishing a connection with an idea which already belongs to the preconscious, by transferring its intensity on to it and by getting itself 'covered' by it. Here we have the fact of 'transference,' which provides an explanation of so many striking phenomena in the mental life of neurotics [pp. 562–563].

Even earlier (1895), he used the concept (not there yet named) to describe the mode by which memory traces of the experiences of the infant in relation to his surround are used and applied (transferred) to later perceptions as expectations that select and organize the latter: "If the perceptual image is not absolutely new, it will now recall and revive a mnemic perceptual image with which it coincides at least partly" (p. 330).

> Let us suppose that the object which furnishes the perception resembles the subject—a fellow human-being. If so, the theoretical interest [taken in it] is also explained by the fact that an object like this was simultaneously the [subject's] first satisfying object and further his first hostile object, as well as his sole helping power. For this reason it is in relation to a fellow human-being that a human-being learns to cognize [p. 331].

The indispensability of transference as a central organizing mode is conveyed in Freud's (1925) reflection: "The first and immediate aim . . . of reality-testing is, not to find an object in real perception which corresponds to the one presented, but to refind such an object, to convince oneself that it still is there" (pp. 237–238); "it is evident that a precondition for the setting up of reality-testing is that objects shall have been lost which once brought real satisfaction" (p. 238).

From this sweeping view of transference, it is possible, indeed inevitable, to claim, with Loewald (1960), "that there is neither such a thing as reality nor a real relationship, without transference" (p. 32)—to assert that all we feel we know or can ever come to know about ourselves and the reality in which we exist can be ours only through psychic structuring shaped by transference, that this psychic reality is what we live with.

Yet within the psychoanalytic situation, the focus on a patient with a psychopathology and a physician with a cure (Freud, 1912b) reinforced the differentiating bent. Both the concept of psychic reality and transference became narrowly perceived as phenomena more particular to the patient and most particular to the analytic situation. "Psychic reality" (Freud, 1915b) became the internal, subjective reality of the patient's infantile beginnings and early psychic organization cast in the modes of primary process; objective reality became the external reality that the patient through analysis could come reasonably to perceive, like the scientist-observer-analyst, in terms of rational discursive thought.

That Freud chose so sharply to separate two realities in this fashion may have been a heuristic device used to emphasize the startling differences he had discovered between the modes of primary and secondary process. It may in part have reflected his abandonment of the seduction theory (an external reality theory) of neurosogenesis for the infantile phantasy theory (internal drive theory).

I emphasize a third factor: that Freud had to make the distinction between two realities to create the unique circumstances of the analytic situation, without which there would be no analytic process. Freud's operational set was that, within the analytic situation, the patient would experience the transferences as real; yet, the analyst (and eventually the patient) would consider them objectively as nonreal anachronisms. This artifice provided an enormously facilitating and constraining therapeutic dialectic for the analyst and patient. It was indeed a stroke of genius to hit on a mode that allowed freedom and protection for both parties in a real–unreal intimacy, a simultaneity of close hovering and distancing from, of seeking of likeness and difference, of cursive merging and discursive objectifying (Freud, 1912a).

That this inspiration had behind it the perspiration of painful clinical experience and self-analysis we can perhaps infer from the Irma dream. As Freud (1900) himself revealed (pp. 107–121), as Erikson (1954) later brilliantly amplified, and as Schur (1966a) subsequently complicated, the Irma dream covered an extraordinary range of conflicts in the dreamer's current and past relations, including his transferences to Fliess. The dream involved the starkest concerns of narcissistic needs and vulnerability: masculine–feminine conflicts caught up in Freud's creativity and relations to Fliess. It reflected the multiple levels of his wishes to penetrate and know his patient and her secrets, his anxiety over discovering his disturbing receptive feminine identifications with her. In his dream, perhaps as in his technical set toward transference in the analytic situation, he pulled back from the affective intensities of transference and countertransference to a refuge and safer perspective in the distancing identity of the detached and objectifying (if not always accurately) physician-scientist.

The Literature on Countertransference

For well more than 30 years after Freud initiated definitions of counter-transference and prescribed the functions of the analyst, the analytic literature reflected the selective emphases implicit in the compound word. It also reflected a struggle, still ongoing, over the uneasy coexistence of two conflicting concepts about the analytic relationship and the contribution of the analyst: (a) the objectifying ideal of the analyst hyperbolized in Freud's surgeon-mirror imagery and in the therapeutic power attributed to the verbal-interpretive function of the analyst; and (b) the subjectifying ideal of the emotionally involved and responsive analyst asserting his analytic powers through all aspects of his affectively intense relationship to the patient, including, yet going far beyond in order to support and actualize, the verbal interpretive mode.

Constraints of space allow but a sampling of the literature to sketch the reflections of these conflicting viewpoints on the theory of counter-transference (for details, see Orr, 1954; Kernberg, 1965).

Early on, there was recognition that the analyst's narcissism (Ferenczi and Rank, 1924), his qualities of character, particularly aggressive propensities (Glover, 1927), plus his necessary regressions for the purpose of understanding (Ferenczi, 1909; Deutsch, 1926), made countertransferential intrusions inevitable and demolished the myth of the analyst's perfectability (Deutsch, 1926; Glover, 1927). Stern (1924) may have been the first to insist that the analyst's reactions had the same infantile and genetic roots as the transferences of the patient.

Yet, emphasis remained on the intrusive and reactive aspects of countertransference, regarded as lapses and shortfalls from the objectifying ideal. This view prevailed well into the 1930s, despite the impact of Freud's theoretical revisions of anxiety (1926a), structure of personality (1923), and aggression (1920), forcing new light on the analyst as reflections of his more illuminated view of his patient. Awareness of the developmental stages of anxiety stimulated attention to the clinical relevance of the pregenital libidinal phases of infant development. The prominence of the ego in determining defense and adaptation focused a keener technical interest on character, on drive organization, and on reality testing and integrative processes (see Lowenstein, 1969). Emphasis on aggression and neutralization processes demanded close attention to the role of the superego in intrapsychic conflict: together, these altered the concepts of the analytic process and of the analyst's place in it. As Benedek (1953) put it, the analyst had to come out from behind the mirror in order to engage and work on the full range of oedipal and preoedipal issues now perceptible in the patient's defensive-adaptive modes. He had to stretch his range of accommodation and experiential understanding of his own preoedipal concerns in order to keep in check his own sadism and masochism (Low, 1935; Fenichel, 1941; Menaker, 1942), his narcissistic claims and oral gratifications in doing his work (Low, 1935).

Yet in counterpoint, the prevailing view in American analysis remained fixed on the liabilities and unmastered infantilisms of countertransference—evidence of an incomplete analysis that had fallen short of the idealization of the objective analyst epitomized by the rational man of ego psychology (Hartmann, 1939). The analyst was, as English and Pearson (1937) put it, ideally to conceal any feeling beyond the desire to help, to mirror, to be inquiring but impartial. His humanity and support were to be conveyed only through his physicianly manner. There must have been sufficient caricaturing of the idealized stance to call for Reich's (1933) protest against blank screens and mummylike attitudes and for Fenichel's (1941) warning that fear of the countertransference could cause the analyst to suppress all human freedom. Yet, at the same time, the power of the idealization made it difficult for matters of countertransference to be freely discussed by analysts in this country even into the mid-1950s (see Weigert, 1952; Tower, 1956).

A gradual counter to this proscriptive attitude emerged in a deepening attention to the inner processes of the analyst's work ego. Fliess (1942) used the vantage point of impeccably classical analysis to build bridges between ego psychology and early object relations theory. He put the concept of empathy into the operational terms of clinical analysis, using concepts of *introjection* and *trial identification* to describe the analyst's inner processes of understanding, and *projection* for his assignment of his perceptions back to the patient in exercising his interpretive functions. He warned of the hazards of this sequence: the analyst's counteridentifications and countertransference, the inevitable mood alterations, fatigue states, and narcissistic vulnerabilities of even the most seasoned analyst.

The enduring theoretical and clinical value of his schema lies in its providing a workable frame of reference, combining structural and object relations concepts, by which to articulate the depths of involvement of the analyst in his own resonances and those of his patient (see extensions by Racker, 1957; Kernberg, 1965).

Object relations analysts, both here and abroad, championed concepts that put the analyst's personality and behavior, and the patient's awareness of these, in the center of the analytic relationship (Balint and Balint, 1939). Countertransference was defined as all that the analyst did or brought to the relationship (Little, 1951), considered positive if facilitating the analyst's commitment and capabilities (Winnicott, 1949) and always potentially a valuable part of the analyst's efforts to understand the patient (Tower, 1956), who was just as intently bent on perceiving and influencing the analyst (Benedek, 1953). The actual affective relationship between the pair was seen to constitute the basic leverage of the therapeutic process (Gitelson, 1952). The analyst would develop, in a deep analysis, something akin to a countertransference neurosis (Tower, 1956) and would in any case need to experience, during termination, his side of the Oedipus complex (Johnson, 1951) and mourn the departing patient (Weigert, 1952).

This strong emphasis on the relationship as the carrier of the analytic process received at least theoretical reinforcement from analysts who stressed the mother–child relationship in which the deeper levels of transference were rooted for both patient and analyst (Spitz, 1956; Stone, 1961; Gitelson, 1962). Stone (1961) particularly emphasized the analyst's diatrophic maternal identifications, freed of infantile ambivalence and raised to sublimatory capabilities, which supported the analyst's benignity and steadiness in carrying out both his nurturing and releasing functions. This emphasis on the reflection, in both patient and analyst, of early mother–child relationship configurations may throw light on the fact that women analysts have been so conspicuously in the vanguard of those seeing the ubiquity of countertransference and in a developmental perspective.

Thus, by the early 1960s, a rather different concept of the nature of the analyst at work seems to have emerged. No longer was the analyst a removed and consistently objective "catalyst" whose occasional perturbations were largely epiphenomena occasioned by the magnitude or special qualities of the behavior of certain patients under very particular circumstances; instead, the analyst was a resonant and affectively immersed participant-observer in a powerfully evocative intimacy touching on all issues of the developmental past of both parties, from the earliest preoedipal period through adolescence to current adulthood. The analyst's ego was to be such that he would generally keep intact his experiencing, observing, and ordering functions. He would use these only to sample the rich intensities of the highly cathected interpersonal field, using all the data, including his countertransference responses, to understand and formulate the intrapsychic processes in himself and in his patient.

It was around this latter point that formidable and still unsettled controversies emerged. These centered on how and how much sound analysis might permit or require the analyst to act on and play out his inner resonances toward the patient (see reviews by Orr, 1954; Kernberg, 1965). Some analysts working with severely regressed patients have emphasized the necessity for the analyst, overtly and explicitly, to use his own inner experiences to clarify, enhance, and supplement the fragmented and faulty ego capacities of the psychotic or borderline patient (Fromm-Reichmann, 1939; Fairbairn, 1954; Searles, 1959). Others, adhering to a more classical position, could agree that diatrophic and anaclitic dynamics echoing the child–mother relationship would be activated in both parties but should be confined to phantasy and should never, certainly by the analyst, be translated into action (Spitz, 1956; Reich, 1960).

These claims and controversies of the early 1960s over what is really central to the psychoanalytic process are with us today in their original as well as altered forms. As Friedman (1978) noted, these reflect enduring differences over the relative significance of the interpretive, relational, and reeducative components of the analytic process. These differences frequently are articulated in debate over what is "real" or "not real" in the analytic relationship (Greenson and Wexler, 1969; Greenson, 1971); over real developmental deficit versus intrapsychic phantasy and conflict (Kohut, 1971; Kernberg, 1976); over what is to be included in real psychoanalytic technique and process (Rangell, 1969; Friedman, 1980; Rothstein, 1980).

Fresh light on this aspect of the controversy has come from contributions of analysts pressing for reconsideration of Freud's (1933) equation of psychic reality with the infantile unconscious—his assignment of primary process to the "cauldron of seething excitement" of the id.

Loewald (1951, 1960, 1962, 1978) interwove structural and object relations theory to trace the progression of primary process and evolving transference in the structuring of psychic reality, seen by him as the sense of self and reality accruing through increasingly refined processes by which object relations are internalized. Beres (1960), Rycroft (1962), and LaPlanche and Pontalis (1968), from quite different viewpoints, detailed the continuing contributions of primary process to the unfolding of the imaginative faculties on which psychic development and the eventual capacities of the individual to engage and perceive reality together depended. The thrust of their contributions, in my reading of them, is that this reality so perceived is identical with and inseparable from the psychic reality of the perceiver—that even the most subtle objectifications of secondary process are related to and interwoven with the contributions of primary process. Schur (1966b), Noy (1969), and I (McLaughlin, 1978), among many others, have opted for the position that both primary and secondary processes be viewed along a developmental continuum rather than in the disjunctive, oppositional mode of Freud's (1933) horse-and-rider imagery of classic ego psychology. Arlow's (1969; Arlow and Beres, 1974) contributions in these areas, from within the formal positionings of structural theory, have illuminated the power and reach of phantasy in determining the form and content of the individual's grasp of reality. Much earlier, Langer (1942) and Cassirer (1946, 1953), from outside our field, offered compelling data and arguments to support this press for revision. Wallerstein (1973) explicitly criticized the views of reality held by classical ego psychology; he saw these as simplifying assumptions of theoretical and heuristic convenience but a man-made way of seeing and giving meaning to nature that limited the field of study. His own preference was for a perspective of "varyingly overlapping and varyingly congruent partial realities" (p. 19). As I see it, Wallerstein was arguing for the primacy of psychic reality as the basis for a consensually validatable view of external reality.

I have dwelt on these several contributions because they direct us to Freud's original and broader vision of psychic reality, and the transferential processes that are its basis, as central to all psychic phenomena. I wish to build the strongest possible case for asserting the relativism, on both sides of the couch, of a perceived reality (psychic reality) and the ubiquity of the transference processes on which these perceptions are organized. I know that my view of "psychic reality" represents a shift, from its narrower meanings traditionally assigned, toward an acceptance of its inclusive connotations and their implications for what we term *countertransference.*

Obviously, I am not clearing new ground in these matters. At the semantic level, Olinick (1969) and Bird (1972), among others, have questioned the continued use of the term *countertransference,* favoring such alternatives as *eccentric responses* in the *psychology of the analyst* (Olinick) or simply the *analyst's transferences* (Bird). Conceptually, Bird's appreciation of the processes of transference as a "major ego function," a "universal mental function which may well be the basis of all human relationships" (p. 267), clearly anticipates the direction and intent of my argument.

New knowledge of the complexity and content of transference has come to adult analysis from the fields of child and adolescent analysis and child development (Kernberg, 1979; Kramer, 1979; Richards, 1980) and from studies of narcissistic and borderline patients. Although these have broken no new theoretical ground for countertransference, they have provided opportunity and challenge to the work ego of the adult analyst to integrate both cognitive and experiential understanding of the range of separation-individuation experiences and the vicissitudes of narcissism in the patient and in himself. Like all the challenges of the past, these have shaken to their primitive transferential roots our deep investment in our working processes and theoretical preferences.

I see as one useful outgrowth of this perturbation the sharper interest and greater openness we have come to in detailing our experiences as analysts and in revealing the vicissitudes of our work ego, as in this sampling: the analyst's drowsiness (Dean, 1957) and shifts in states of consciousness (McLaughlin, 1975); his hypnoid states (Dickes, 1965; Dickes and Papernik, 1977); boredom (Greenson, 1953); postural changes (Jacobs, 1973); visual imagery while listening to dream recital (Ross and Kapp, 1962; Kern, 1978); bizarre somatic sensations in the presence of psychotic patients (Goldberg, 1979); awareness of overidentification with the patient (Shane, 1980); difficulties in conducting interracial analyses (Schachter and Butts, 1968; Ticho et al., 1971). What is central to these contributions is captured in Ticho et al.'s summary, stated in formally structural terms, about the liabilities for the analyst dealing with a patient from an unfamiliar culture:

> When the organizing function is overtaxed, higher ego achievements, like self-concept, identity, value systems, ego interests and skills, are threatened and may result in a reinstinctualization of autonomous functions. If regressive phenomena are observed . . . those ego and superego functions least autonomous would be the first to be subject to reinstinctualization. . . . There is a regressive pull to more primitive defenses [p. 320].

The work-ego concept has gradually come to stand for the aggregate of character traits and ego capabilities especially deployed by the analyst in doing analytic work. The panel (Greenson, 1961) on selection of candidates for analytic training collectively provided such an array of aptitudes to be sought in the budding analyst that to one participant suggested a composite portrait of Pasteur and Thomas Mann. Fliess's (1942) definition was more evocative: "It is not the analyst as an individual who approaches that 'rare and exalted perfection,' but the temporarily built-up person who does so under the circumstances and for the period of his work" (p. 225). According to Olinick et al. (1973), the work ego "manifests a relatively stable autonomy of function . . . [that] operates very effectively in certain instances of interpretation and other therapeutic interventions. . . . It is definable in terms of its functions" (p. 143). Although the classical ideal of the analyst remains that of the "impartial observer at a post equidistant to all psychic instances" (Greenson and Wexler, 1969, p. 38) as reflected in the views of Rangell (1979), the hour-by-hour functioning of his work ego consists of a continuing ebb and flow of regression and mastery (Olinick et al., 1973): "we view the analyst's reactions as a continuum, from trial identification (empathy) at the one end through more regressed phenomena of counter-identification and over-identification. Differentiation is made on the basis of evaluation of the degree of ego discrimination and mastery" (p. 144).

This concept of the analyst's work ego as operating in a far from steady state over a wide range of capacities, from most evolved to most regressed, has stirred interest in the moment-to-moment details of the interactions between patient and analyst. I am not referring to the ever present alternative of interpersonal psychology but to a closer scrutiny of the verbal intervention–response sequence and patterning of classical technique. Langs (1976), Dahl et al. (1978), and Gill (1979), from different operational positions, have provided rich data to demonstrate that both parties are caught up in a communicative field of incredible sensitivity and subtlety, with transferential–countertransferential shadings constantly at play in enormous affective intensities—a field in which the possibility of a neutral or catalytic comment, given or received, is remote indeed.

Exploration of the analyst's character traits and their developmental base has enriched our appreciation of his involvements in the work. In particular, his masochism (Racker, 1958; McLaughlin, 1961), his conflict and comfort with his maternal identifications (Spitz, 1956; McLaughlin, 1961, 1975), his having experienced depression in himself (Greenson, 1967), and his mothering person (Olinick, 1969) have all become recognized as sources of his capacities and liabilities.

One closing perspective on the analyst's transferences, on the shaping of his work ego, has come indirectly from follow-up studies described over the past 20 years (Pfeffer, 1959, 1961, 1963; Schlessinger and Robbins, 1974, 1975; Oremland et al., 1975; Norman et al., 1976). Among their consistent findings was the discovery that the experiences of the analytic relationship remained a living part of the patient's inner life and were revived transitorily in the follow-up interviews—that the transference neurosis was attenuated but not lost and that, in like fashion, traces of the conflicts the patient had brought to treatment could still be detected. Crucially different was that adaptation to these dynamic and object-related issues had, in successful cases, altered for the better through the patient's internalization of aspects of the analyst's ways of looking at things—now a self-analytic function and probably a permanent new intrapsychic representation. Just as significantly, in unsatisfactory outcomes, the internal representation of the analyst had become absorbed into the patient's old transferential difficulties. In all cases, the original conflict patterns were discernible as a "relatively immutable . . . childhood acquisition" (Schlessinger and Robbins, 1975, p. 776), inactivated in successful cases by attitudes and adaptations acquired in the analysis.

Studies of the training analysis (Shapiro, 1976; Baum, 1977) point in the same direction: even in the many satisfactory outcomes, unresolved conflicts and the residual traces of well-attenuated character and symptomatic issues were still apparent. The transference neurosis itself was not entirely obliterated but carried over into the analyst's subsequent attitudes toward and relationships with his patients, institute, and society. Further, many analysts carried over vivid memories of countertransference attitudes and enactments from training analysts, with effects that were enduring.

Discussion

Countertransference, a term that has been part of psychoanalysis almost from its beginnings, is unlikely ever to lose currency. It is, in fact, rather like an old siege coin: crimped, bitten, filed down, worn beyond clear recognition in serving defenders of proud causes. We try to use it, and we know that it is worth something, but we are not sure what it signifies; we may need it in some embattled future.

Unlike transference, which could be applied to any behavior anywhere, countertransference as term and concept has consistently reflected its base in the psychoanalytic situation. Its early and narrow designation of unwanted erotic and egoistic concerns in the analyst, to the exclusion of all else that the analyst brings to his task, deflected for a long time an appreciation of the full implications of Freud's broad concept of transference for the analyst's experiences at work.

It seems likely that Freud's momentous decision to step back from the affective intensities in patient and therapist, which were the undoing of Breuer—to view them as unreal and to dwell instead on their anachronistic (infantile) aspects—had much to do with the restrictive concept of countertransference, for in the doing he also narrowed and gave selective meanings to his otherwise broad and general principles of transference and psychic reality. Freud was working in the objectifying

tradition of Western medical science. His so positioning himself in relation to the patient's intensities, and his own, won for him and the rest of
us the place of the participant-observer in a unique yet replicable experi-
ment of nature. His designation of transference phenomena as real but
not real, plus his enjoining on the analyst an idealistic commitment to
the detached, rational observer, combined in a powerful mix both superego constraints and ego ideal enhancements. For both patient and
analyst, the relationship was shifted from action to reflection, an aim-
inhibited mode crucial for intimate work sustained over time.

The personal importance of this stratagem for Freud may be sur-
mised from the Irma dream (1900) and from the fact that his sparse contributions to the literature on countertransference had to do with erotic
heterosexual impulses toward desirable patients: it is clear that he put
much importance on the necessity for sexual abstinence by both parties
and made the analyst responsible for its preservation, and that he did so
out of reasons moral, pragmatic, and scientific (Szasz, 1963).

Freud's example and directives extended in the literature as a generally wary and repudiative set, notably reflected in an almost total absence
of further exploration of the analyst's erotic propensities. More than 50
years later, Tower (1956) noted as a generally valid instance her considerable difficulty, as a supervisor, in helping a supervisee to be comfortable with acknowledging and learning from his sexual responses to an
attractive patient.

The compound word *countertransference* itself fostered the skewing and
differential attitude. *Counter-* helped to anchor the analyst's phenomena
both to the analytic situation and to the patient. It took on longlasting connotations of "reacting to," a comfort to the analyst claiming rationality,
detachment, and imperturbability in the presence of the "all too human-
ness" of his patient; he could more easily take a pejorative set toward the
untoward behaviors of his patient and an I-was-pushed stance toward
his own. In a more subtle way, the term encouraged the analyst to accept
a cleavage, a kind of splitting, of perception that cut in three planes: how
he saw himself as an analyst, how he saw the rest of the continuum of his
own psychic development; and how he saw what he and his patient
brought to the actuality of the work. This flat-on-back/feet-on-ground
opposition became stereotyped in the early literature: the analyst as the
detached scientist-observer comprehending a truer reality and prepared
to clear the dark glass of neurotic distortion. It lives on in the bleakness

of the removed and inarticulate analyst, in the polarizing debates around how much or how little interaction, even verbal, can be considered true analysis.

Major trends in the analytic literature of the past 50 years have been an increasing knowledge and appreciation of the contribution of all stages of the life cycle to adult psychic organization (Erikson, 1950). Gradual acknowledgment of these in the character and capacities, the humanity and liability, of the analyst at work has fostered an alternative conception of the analyst as a crucially involved participant-observer in a relationship of enormous complexity and interactive sensitivity.

Follow-up studies of therapeutic and training analyses have helped us understand how analysis produces change: through the internalization, as new psychic structures, of attitudes and values experienced in the relationship to the analyst. Yet these studies also make it plain that the shadows and structures of old conflicts, old object relationships, remain potentially revivable. This realization, which should not have surprised anyone, allows analytic outcome to claim a solid base. But it is a far and sobering cry from the sweeping therapeutic claims of a half-century ago.

As supported by these data, the implications for countertransference theory and for understanding the analyst's work ego are that the analyzed analyst functions with his old conflicts now altered (more or less sufficiently) by his training analysis into new psychic structures established through transference processes. He can draw on a new and expanded range of capabilities for all his living, and particularly for the complex functions of his work ego—specialized constructs never intended for bed or barroom. At any given time, these new levels of synthetic and especially discriminative capacities (Hacker, 1962) may be quite sufficient for the work. But, like any psychic structure more recently acquired, the construct may not hold together under inordinate stress, and the inherent instability of its highly evolved and specialized functions requires constant equilibration and monitoring.

The time-honored opposition of transference–countertransference simply cannot encompass all this. The term countertransference particularly cannot accommodate the intrapsychic range and fullness of the analyst's experiences vis-à-vis his patient.

If we use instead Freud's broader view of transference, we can picture our psychic development as formed in a lifelong continuum of transference relationships in which each successive relating shapes and is shaped by the previous, in such fashion that their interplay either fosters our new capabilities and structures or only affirms and fixes the earlier. From this standpoint, there is transference in all our processing of experiences, at all times and in all stages of the life cycle. The analytic experience affords an opportunity for one more transference relationship. Yet it is far more than just one more, in the uniqueness of its aim-inhibited openness, by which the patient can learn, with both head and gut, capacities for more evolved discrimination between, and integration of, the world of differences around him (Matte-Blanco, 1975). Follow-up studies underscore this transferential base of the new capabilities the patient brings to his living and the analyst to his work. The outcome of even quite successful training analysis consists of intrapsychic transformations of old transferences into new and more adaptive transferences organized around a new object, the training analyst.

From this broader view of transference, it is logical and perhaps more fruitful to see that the analyst's transferences, though importantly different in degree, are for the analyst, as they are for the patient, involved in everything he does. This especially includes the functioning of his work ego. As a new transference set that too often shows its identificatory shapings, these highly evolved capabilities are his best and finest tuned assets. Anything that happens in him or his surround can affect these specialized and not invulnerable capabilities, facilitate or impair them, and thus alter regressively or progressively the level of transference at which his work ego is functioning. If it is the patient's behavior or the analyst's efforts at introjective sampling that prompt the alteration, we may or may not choose to dub this countertransference. (It is a telling fact that the term in its narrow definition has yet to be applied to finely adaptive behavior of the analyst facilitated by the patient.)

More important than what we call it is the concept of an unbroken continuum of transference in the workings of the analyst, from his infantile beginnings to his best working behind the couch—a hierarchy of transferential states over which he ranges in empathic resonance with his patient. It seems conceptually clearer to speak of his experiencing of these various states as the "analyst's transferences," to assign them some developmental designation as "regressed" or "evolved," and particularly to designate as specifically as possible the psychosexual or developmental level of the state reflected in the analyst's behavior. One brief example must suffice: we might speak of an analyst's evolved maternal diatrophic transferences in reflecting on his habitual stance of quiet nurturance and facilitation with his patients, and see these as regressed when he behaves with masochistic submission in his experiencing a patient's assaults.

Placing such high value on psychic reality as being all we have to work with, in or out of analysis, would seem at first to take more from the analyst than it gives. It places the psychic reality of patient and analyst in an ambiguous and relativistic opposition, far from the claims of the latter to a secured and superior reality-view. But the yield carries a potential far beyond that of the earlier and more tilted conception of the analytic pair.

The "real person" and the "real relationship" that the analyst may feel confident he brings to the analytic situation (Greenson, 1971) become, in this perspective, only relative to the view the patient brings to the work. What becomes mutually accepted as experientially "real" in the two-party system of privacy and isolation can be only a shared consensus wrung from prolonged testing and verification by both. The "therapeutic alliance" is not then a pregiven for analytic work but a gradually shaped trust that patient and analyst build up about the reliability of their shared views of what goes on between them—a consensus and comfort that allow the deep explorations of psychoanalysis to transpire. In this sense, the outcome of successful analysis reflects an evolving, mutual authentication of the psychic realities of the two parties in the analytic search.

This view more fully apprehends the shared adventure of "doing analysis" and captures the rich implications of the "analyzing instrument," Isakower's imaginative conception (Balter et al., 1980) of the conjoined operation of two minds, patient's and analyst's, working together in a goal-specific intent to reach the infantile depths of the psychic reality of the one, in the course of which both may find themselves affirmed.

WHAT WAS WROUGHT

Self-Analysis

CHAPTER 5

Looking Back At
An Early Case Failure
What There Was Yet to Learn

What are we talking about when we speak of our analytic failures? Or of our analytic successes, for that matter? It is clear that we generally live with both by regarding them with the uncertain comfort of selective inattentiveness.

I come at the matter from a perspective based on three premises, the first echoing our classic lore, the other two more personal reflections from my own struggles to grow as an analyst. First, the analyst's contributions are at least as important to the outcome as are the patient's. Second, we stand to learn more from contemplating our cases of failure or shortfall that have ended not with a bang but with a whimper. Third, the theoretical and technical stance we come to prefer is largely determined by the dynamic forces that shape our character and reality view and that motivate us to persist in therapeutic endeavors.

To dwell briefly on the advantages of dealing with whimpers: an analytic effort that has gone on long enough to provide detailed sequences about the intertwined participation of both parties in the trying and the parting is most likely to inform us of what we did not know or see at the time. As for the prime importance of the analyst's role in failures, a steady focus on what the analyst brings and does should afford us the clearest appreciation of how his mixture of dumb, blind, and hard spots shapes, limits, and determines his potential for the task. Recall that by *dumb spots* I mean true cognitive and experiential gaps in his informed view of the field. *Blind spots* have to do with aspects of experiential knowing that would be available for the analyst's use were it not for constraints set by repression and other defensive avoidances. *Hard spots* lie in the analyst's cherished theoretical sets, by which he views and organizes what he perceives, and which in turn expand as well as limit what he can be free to perceive.

This trio labels some overlapping and mutually influencing components of the work ego that each of us brings to the analytic task. These trained elaborations of the self, which we must acquire, may have much in common with those of our fellow analysts, but each of us shapes these as our unique signature to our analytic outlook and ways of working, no two of us alike.

My third premise requires some elucidation, as it is largely the basis for scanning the clinical samplings I present.

We are accustomed to thinking of our analytic identity as rooted for all time in those identifications and adaptations by which we coped reparatively and defensively with ambivalence toward needed others in our formative years. Our training gives these formations fresh shaping and release through our own analysis and through what we learn from those analysts who are our exemplars and models. Then, under the impact of subsequent life experiences, particularly the necessity of adapting to the needs of patients we are treating, we find the impetus for further development and change in our work ego, in our analytic outlook, and in our reality view itself.

I am aware of having undergone, over 40 years of analytic work, extensive changes in how I see the analytic endeavor and the analytic relationship that supports the quest—changes in what I see as essential to fostering understanding and growth in both patient and analyst. It is from this later and different perspective that I look on some of my viewpoints and technical usages, particularly those in which I steeped myself during my training and formative years, and still catch myself using at times, as having contributed to shortfall or outright failure in my past and present work.

The following might best be characterized as an "attempted" analysis that went on for about two arduous years in the early 1950s until finally we settled, for our quite different and differing reasons, on a faltering termination. The failure of this analysis was one to which I made my own sizable contributions. This case is one of many to which I have returned over the years to discern the ways of working and changing that I have survived. My dumb, blind, and hard spots are the focus of this clinical sample. Most of my remarks are focused on 11 instances of enactment.

Clinical Vignette: Ms. Q. Ms. Q was in her mid-20s when she sought my help for vague discontent in all her relationships and for a sense of drifting in her unsatisfying professional career. She displayed her literacy and high intelligence by condescending flippancies and assertions of scholastic precocity and achievement. I wondered to myself whether these also pointed to a relationship between her actual lack of success, her very evident depression, and the anxious vigilance with which she monitored my every twitch. I felt challenged by the many contradictions posed by her distress and defensiveness and agreed to work with her analytically, despite the implicit reservations I had in assigning to her the tentative diagnosis of chronic depression in a schizoid personality. Today we would probably consider her borderline, with narcissistic predisposition.

Enactment 1. Our early months were spent in an uneasy settling in on her part, as she poured out a torrent of fragmented data from her past history, presented in obvious testing-for-effect fashion. When I remained essentially quiet, she speculated about my sexual desires toward her and the imminence of my raping her but denied what seemed obvious anxiety in the face of my hovering silence. She reported severe headaches and upper-gut distress when I continued asking her to go on. When I held to my silence, she would fall into protracted silences of her own and then break these by increasingly empty or flip intellectualizing or fragmented allusions to withheld thoughts that conveyed enormous grandiosity. I found that she stayed less stressed when I reflected, however superficially, on what she had been relating. Then I could expect to hear a deft ridiculing of my contribution, followed at times by some fresh piece of intellectualized history about her distant and exacting father, or her beautiful and self-absorbed mother and cocky little brother, whom she envied. I concluded from these responses that my reflections were supportive, not contributing to the extent of regression necessary for the emergence of her transference. So I went back to my silent expectancy.

My prevailing silences in this opening phase were consonant with both my training precepts and the mode of my first training analyst. I did not perceive Ms. Q's discomfort to be excessive, and she did not make much of it from her airy position of being above such mundane concerns as her physical state. As I presumed that regression was necessary to the analytic discovery, I stood by as she brought forward what I saw as her various defensive postures, which I hoped to address tactfully through defense analysis. My reflective remarks, which seemed to relax her, I saw as supportive, and best avoided in the interest of regression. Besides, I was mildly put off by her dismissive style and quick erotizations and was not getting any clear sense of what was going on during my efforts to hang in and hover. So I shut up for a while, out of what I came later to see as a defensive withdrawal and retaliation. I missed the potential usefulness of my reflective remarks as facilitating the patient's characteristic and necessary, counterpunching ways of becoming involved in a relationship. This realization, retrospective in this case but affirmed in later work with others, led me for a while to a mode of providing such reflection in the initial portion of most analytic hours, until I could feel that I had the "red thread" for interpretation that several had taught me to seek.

Enactment 2. Two months into the work, we experienced our first surface struggle, much of which I barely registered at the time. Ms. Q let me know that she had immersed herself in reading Freud. After a little exploration, I asserted, with what I presumed to be quiet tact and physicianly firmness, that this would not do, and I laid on the usual array of good reasons why she should desist. With a quick nod, Ms. Q filled the rest of the hour with increasingly ambiguous allusions to an unsatisfying past liaison with an insecure man. She slept in through the time of her next appointment.

Here I had something I could get at, with a conviction borne of basic training and nurtured by my prevailing uncertainties. I laid down the interdiction and reinforced it with irrefutable reasons. I saw the proscription as unassailable as Freud had made it seem, and I did not give it further thought beyond assuming that her absence naturally was her way of protesting. The assumption of superior wisdom, my claim that surely was not being bolstered by any certainty of insights I was generating about Ms. Q, could still be asserted around a set of technical requirements that later would became reified for some of us as "the frame."

Enactment 3. Soon Ms. Q let me know that she had begun reviewing, with her current lover, the content of her analytic hours. Again rising stalwartly to the bait, I uttered another well-reasoned proscription. This time, I followed up by pointing out the possibility that she might be baiting me. This she indignantly denied, and she vented her impatience with people who jumped to conclusions.

Again, my almost conditioned response was to make a correct inter-diction, with the intent of persuading her that much that needed to be analyzed would be drained off into this "outside" relationship. My mo-tives continued to involve the need to get some sense of control of an analysis of a patient who was coming right at me. Her style was familiar to me from prior work with psychotics, but she was not psychotic, and I had not encountered this kind of couch behavior before. I had heard much about the problems of "transference readiness," but I had done psychotherapy with psychosomatic patients, often given to this readi-ness, and was confident that I could prevail now. I think this stance could be looked on as a bona fide dumb spot of technical-experiential ignorance—one that I complicated with my narcissistic claim to more competence than I merited.

Enactment 4. Not long after, Ms. Q casually let me know that she was consciously withholding her "abreactions" to emotional material experienced in the office until she could be alone. I had the good sense this time not to issue another dictum and instead just acknowledged her need for caution. Ms. Q was then able to settle for a while into re-vealing erotized and bisexualized desires and fears toward me: "I got anxious in the last session when you seemed to accept that I have to take my strong stuff elsewhere. I want a strong man to want me very much. But, his wanting me would reflect some serious defect in his makeup. . . . I think sex with me would be good for you and might even enhance my approval of myself."

There was much to be learned from this small stretch of work in which I did not rise to her provocations or provide my own. This time, by my not enacting with her the repetitive mutual affronts that made her life with father so noxious, we were able for a while to get glimpses of that old relationship reflected now toward me: her terror either that she was submitting to her father's power or that she might be the powerful one. I did not see this, or saw it dimly, especially when she stepped up the intensity of her conviction that an actual intimacy was the only solution for us both.

Enactment 5. For a while, we were able to accomplish some bits and pieces of useful work. Ms. Q noted that she was somaticizing less: "I think my father terrified me when I was small. I used to have terrified bowels in coming here, but that's all gone." A little later: "I was beginning to feel that I had the power to make a complete man of you. But, I'd be better off to get back to graduate school. Yet the wish is there, and your need is great!"

Ms. Q began to show increasing hostility and thorny remoteness as I persisted in trying to analyze her various efforts to get from me a response of amorous and loving acceptance of her and her reclamation project. She alternated between extremes of depression and hypomanic grandiosity, cast in terms of phallic prowess and contempt for all men, especially me. "Last time I had that eruption of infantile masturbatory material, you asked if I felt you were reproving me. I had then a little phantasy of being small, sprawled on you the way a man would sprawl after sex, or a child on mother. Yet you don't seem that much of a man to me, and maternal you aren't. I am hung up here and at work, can't sleep, and at night wonder if I should give up trying. And you do nothing to help."

My style of working with Ms. Q at this time often did not help. Distressed by her suffering and feeling limited in my capacity to help her, I clearly became more pressing of my viewpoint. I told her that her distress was a response to my not accepting her offer to save us both. I truly felt that I could help her through her morass if she would just listen to my perspective about her despair over phallic inferiority and frustration rage over my not making make it right. But she could not listen, and I could not stop. We escalated: she toward irritated withdrawal and elaborate boredom and I toward more confrontations about her resistiveness. I remarked specifically about her stated boredom and dissatisfaction as avoidances of dealing with my interpretations She responded with hurt indignation and accentuated what I saw as her favorite obfuscations while alarming me with signs of further regression: fragmented thoughts, sudden bursts of laughter or sobbing, and allusions to messianic feelings.

It is in this stretch that we, I certainly, regressed to an impasse from which I could not extricate us. I fell back on ways of doggedly restating my perspective about what was wrong with her, what she needed to see that could set her right, and how she was stonewalling and dismissing my attempts to have her analyze these. I was by this time angry and distressed with both of us. Although she seemed some of the time able to regroup before leaving the office, her reports of adapting outside portrayed her as alienating others, as either depressed or feeling grandiose. This was in the years when there were few ways of supporting regressed patients short of hospitalizing them. I was feeling increasing doubts about our getting into a better mode, and I was disturbed by my growing ambivalence about persisting. This was the situation when I suggested to Ms. Q that she sit up.

Enactment 6. I suggested that she sit up for the time being, which she did. But she refused to look in my direction as she pedantically poured out a welter of increasingly explicit allusions to visual sexual images, intermixed with yearnings to be fed, suckled, and soothed. I, trying to get her attention in what I felt to be a matter-of-fact and implicitly calming manner, reflected to her what I saw as her obvious conflict: "that she truly did not seem to be able to settle whether she wished to be fed or fucked." She looked at me with blazing anger, denounced me in clear, crisp eloquence for being a stupid, unfeeling bastard, and left the office.

It says much about my transferences to Ms. Q that I was startled by the intensity of her response and had no clear notion of what was so out of line about my remark. My observation seemed accurate enough. She had used the word fucked herself, I was sure, as well as equally pithy language. Briefly, I felt unfairly accused and misunderstood. Then I felt mainly sorry that she was so upset, concerned that she might decompensate, and a strong and familiar sense of guilt. It was this last that alerted me to the fact that I was dealing with a conviction that I had acted hurtfully; here was a familiar state on which I had done a lot of work in my training analysis. I had strong wishes to apologize. But I had been earlier counseled by two of my supervisors that it was unwise to acknowledge any feelings, including guilt, lest doing so confuse the patient and weaken the analyst's optimal position of detachment and authority. In fact, it was conceptually better to assume that I had unconsciously picked up some of the patient's underlying guilt and that it was technically sound to explore for this in the patient's associative stream. When Ms. Q phoned at the close of my office hours, I had not done more with myself about the incident. Her anger was at the same high pitch, and I lost touch with my wish to make amends.

Enactment 7. Ms. Q called late in the day to inform me that she did not want to come to her appointment the next day, as long as she would not be charged. I reminded her of my policy to charge if I could not fill the hour. So she came and refused to talk to me except to tell me that she was so distressed that she wished to cancel all her appointments for at least several weeks. I acknowledged her anger but insisted that this was not a valid reason to interrupt and that, in fact, it was crucial to analyze such a crisis. Ms. Q countered firmly, "I do! I'm getting another analyst," and headed for the door. Feeling both anxious and angry, I came back as firmly, acknowledging that it was her right to leave but reminding her that I would have to charge for all her missed appointments or feel forced to suspend the analysis until she felt ready to resume the work on a steady basis.

In countering her ultimatum with my own, I was adhering to the letter of Freud's technical precepts, as I understood them. I understood that the grim power struggle between us enacted a sadomasochistic happening meaningful to her in the transference. But I had no sense of knowing how it might be resolved at that moment, except to keep on doing what was supposed to work. I came to know that my regressive adherence to the hard spot of learned precept helped to shield me from more anxiety and to justify my anger toward a patient who would not let me realize old reparative necessities of my own.

Ms. Q came back and sat down, and the stalemate went on into the middle of the second year. She openly protested keeping her appointments, and she filled the time by recounting her rejection of me and the analysis and the complexities of her sudden reimmersion in postgraduate studies. I thought it clear enough, from her consistent drift to her failed efforts ever to make satisfying contact with her father, that we were caught up in a sadomasochistic relationship in which I was seen as keeping her in cruel subjection. When I attempted to explore this, she stonewalled the actuality and began what became her prevailing defensive stance until the work ended: to work hard to realize herself in her academic aspirations and to engross herself in phantasies of how she might save me from my misguided ways. Meanwhile, she stopped making payments on her mounting bill.

Enactment 8. Some three months later, Ms. Q accused me of having a character neurosis that allowed me to be comfortable only with her dependence, whereas her rebelliousness caused me to be annoying to her, to "kick her around" when she was vulnerable. Then she voiced a repeated complaint about "my" nail-clicking habit, which chronically irritated her. Often I had watched and heard her nail-clicking as she played with her fingers. This time I denied the validity of her perception, and I pressed her to consider her need for this distortion. She responded by saying that she felt "kicked in the stomach" by my comment. Yet she saw my behavior as testament to my erotic interest in her, and evidence of my essentially beautiful nature, that might be mine to join with hers, were I to let her cure my impairments.

I did not have such a nail-clicking habit, and previously I had tried without gain to explore her belief simply as a phantasy. I do not know why I needed to refute her perception this time. I have been chagrined that here, as in too many other instances, I did not follow up on her sense of being struck in the stomach but instead focused on her rapturous wishes to join us in sexual perfection.

Enactment 9. Ms. Q stepped up her dissection of my character, even as she complained that my behaviors had led her on and then destroyed her. I met her insistent claims on me for a baby, through our genital or cerebral union, with accurate enough, questioning reflections of these wishes. But, when these seemed only to augment her intensity, I fell back on interventions that defined her intentions as aiming for my penis, or my baby in lieu thereof. Her response was a near blissful state of somehow fulfilling her wish to have my baby, now as a recreation of us both, that would bring us forever closer, both to each other and to a realization of the excellence latent in the two of us. She saw herself as now "finished, no longer needing closeness to anyone, nor the need to confide." When I persisted in emphasizing the defensiveness of her phantasies, she became silent, then countered with her insistence that she need tell me no more, for my "unintegrated interpretations were insultingly beneath" her.

Ms. Q soon turned up the heat of her probing phantasies about me, at times surprising me with their accuracy. She picked up my discomfort: "Simbaba—hit him in the head. Throw him in the ditch, and he'll be dead!" I persisted in my often declamatory confrontations, including, "You seem in conflict. You want an analysis but don't want to be analyzed by me," and, "Your idea of this analysis is that you will achieve your aims through perfecting me." To such, Ms. Q simply nodded full agreement.

Ms. Q provided ample data that persuaded me of the primacy of her interest in acquiring my penis or otherwise joining us through our baby. And my reflective explorations seemed mainly to corroborate her grandiose insistence that this was taking place in some undefined way. At moments, these ideas approached delusional intensity. My reactions were in the direction of trying to have her see the powerful and inappropriate nature of these oedipal wishes. Now I would agree with Ms. Q

that these were "unintegrated interpretations" that reflected my concerns over how bad I was doing, but, even now, I have no sureness of a
better way, given the deteriorated state of our relationship by then.

Enactment 10. A few months later, Ms. Q confronted me:

> I feel you resent my curiosity about you. You keep telling me that
> this has to do with my father, but I don't think this to be true. I was
> never curious about my father, for he rejected me. You are very
> odd at times. When in the beginning I grew tired after showing off
> so much to you, you insisted I work harder, and humbled me.
> When I showed myself to you as a little girl ignored by my father,
> you comforted me. When I turned to you and asked questions, you
> got cold. When I tried to get close to you in the only ways I knew,
> you insulted me. When I became a scholar and identified with your
> penis, we did okay for a while. But since I couldn't sustain that ef-
> fort, we have been in constant trouble. And when I try to sort out
> what is going on, you resent it and call it resistance.

I consider these observations to be on-target, especially when I look
at my behaviors from Ms. Q's viewpoint. Hers is a telling summary of a
protracted mismatch in which I could not recognize and make use of the
few occasions when I managed to relate to her in a helpful, recognitive
way that briefly touched her perspective.

Enactment 11. After eight months of waiting for my bill to be paid
and having my variably neutral inquiries ignored, I let Ms. Q know that I
would have to terminate the analysis unless she indicated just where she
stood about the unpaid account. She cried briefly, spoke of her humilia-
tion, flatly announced that she had exhausted her resources, and for-
lornly noted that she "might have to throw [herself] on the mercy of [her]
parents," whom she had long ago identified as wealthy but uninterested
in her well-being. A substantial check, in partial payment, arrived the
next day, along with her scathing denunciations of me, shared with her
family, of my inhumane baseness. To this she associated her uncle's sexual exploitation of her when she was a child. From this point on, she
maintained a stance of cool containment and demonstrated none of the
manifestations of distress I had previously noted.

The stalemate dragged on for another two months. Ms. Q whiled away the time acid-etching the bones of my insufficiencies and contrasting their remains with her own gradual emergence to contentment and satisfaction in having surmounted her hangups about me and everyone else in her past.

Ms. Q, leaving the last hour with an air of great satisfaction, declared that the analytic work she had done on her own was a huge success, though clearly I had much unfinished business of my own. She left me with a small unpaid bill and large residues of chagrin and puzzlement.

I let the unpaid balance go, but in the ensuing years I thought often about this effort so as to learn what I could from Ms. Q as well as other, less striking instances of falling short. Their pressure on me has ever since been an important incentive to keep examining what I do.

By the time we had arrived at our denouement, when I made my pronouncement about the unpaid fee, I was much more aware of my anger toward my patient and of my frustration with my inability to engage her to my satisfaction. I had sought repeated consultation with a friend and peer, who could see better than I the stump I was up, but this friend had no remediation to suggest beyond closing down the work at some opportune point. We both felt that it was important that the patient be the one to call it quits and that she leave on her terms. My colleague's counsel helped me to settle somewhat my ambivalence and freed me to act on the side of my wish to be through with her. The fee issue provided a reason to act toward this end. It also allowed me the comfort of a firm stand on a hard spot of my training—that analysis was hire-by-the-hour, and nonpayment an acting-out that could not long be condoned. I had swung back and forth for months about the mounting fee. I had doubts about any value to what I was still trying to do. What would the actual impact be on Ms. Q? I had managed to like her, some of the time, and had experienced erotic responses of my own, early in the course of this attempt.

Ms. Q's reference to sexual abuse by an uncle was a new piece of data that I registered but did not pursue. I think I was flattened when she steamrollered my previous attempt to reach her from my position, and I had just closed up shop.

I was left with a residue of concern about the outcome, centered more on my own discomfort, and I went into my second analysis. It was very helpful, and it gave me the impetus to go on to self-analytic inquiry ever since.

From where I stand now, I consider my mistakes to be a function of dumb and blind spots magnified by my attempting to work with a patient whose dimensions were often beyond my understanding and whose keen dissection made me defensive in my regressive transferences to her. My discomfort led me to beleagueredly hunker down on the hard spots of my theory, to cling more and more tightly to the conceptual stereotype of the detached, knowing analyst, while applying the major dicta of Freud's papers (and of my training) with an authoritarian insistence that belied my uncertainties. I truly did believe in the therapeutic power of my silences, in my assured pronouncement of my perspective, in my consistent reading of Ms. Q's reactions as resistance to the received truth.

Put most generally, the major skewing of my analytic perspective lay in my denying the patient the validity of her experiences of herself and me, for the sake of a self-protective stance that insisted on my better view and removed position.

Had Kohut (1971) told us of his similar impasses with such as Mr. Z, I might have found an enlightenment that I did not experience through the consultative help I sought at the time. It was agreed that Ms. Q was unanalyzable. But her perspicacious reflections about me, like those of other patients who manage so well to supervise our work, led me to self-analytic searching that has been and continues to be fruitful, illuminated by the insights of many, especially Racker (1957), Kohut (1971), Gill (1983), and Schwaber (1983).

CHAPTER 6

The Analyst's Insights

Insight, as concept, process, and goal, has had an uncertain place in psychoanalysis, as well as in the larger world of discourse from which we borrowed it. In *Webster's* (1952), the word insight is defined as the act or fact of seeing into a situation—or into oneself; of apprehending the inner nature of things immediately, intuitively; of encompassing man's reach to the "mystical contemplation of the ultimate verities" as well as his sad grasp of his own madness.

Within American psychoanalysis, we have formally, even officially, appropriated the word to designate the "subjective experiential knowledge acquired during psychoanalysis of previously unconscious pathogenic content and conflict" (Moore and Fine, 1967, p. 55). Such insight "differs from other cognitive understanding in that it cannot occur without being preceded by dynamic changes" (made through analytic work) that alter resistances and drive energies so as to augment an array of autonomous ego functions that make insight possible.

This emphasis on insight as result and fact throws scant light on how insights are formed in the course of analytic work. Poland (1988) sampled others' contributions regarding insight as process, as part of his searching exploration of how the patient is assisted in forming his insights through the evocative power and subtlety of the verbal dialogue within the analytic dyad.

To that viewpoint, I provide a complementarity focused on the insights that the analyst shapes about himself in the course of his efforts to understand his patient. My emphasis is on the vicissitudes of the work ego as the analyst strives to sustain its optimal functioning in the face of inner turbulence stirred by the patient and by concurrent stresses in the rest of the analyst's personal world.

Such matters are usually designated as countertransference. For reasons I have proposed elsewhere (see chap. 4), I prefer to delete *counter-* and refer to the analyst's vicissitudes as his *regressive transferences,* his falling back from his best evolved analytic functioning. Such lapses are multiply determined by whatever there may be in the analyst's personal life, as well as the manifold impingements of the private worlds of his patients—in particular the one he is with at any given analytic moment. For such reasons of multiple causality, the word countertransference is simply inadequate.

Each party brings to the analytic task a reality view shaped and skewed by the transferential forces from his own developmental past. The analyst's claim to an advantaged perception of reality rests mainly on his trained analytic perspective on human behavior. This achieved perspective, and the analyzing capabilities based on it, are inherently unstable functions, like all the other compromise solutions by which we live—yet developmentally even newer and more vulnerable. These specialized functions of the work ego are subject to fluctuation, regressively and progressively, induced by the work itself, as well as by the stresses and gratifications in the rest of our lives. Although we may strive to bring to our task only our best capacities of knowing self and other, we necessarily stir our own transferential depth as we join with our patient in the shaping of the analyzing instrument (Isakower, 1963).

The insights that I have had in my own analyses, that I have encountered in my patients and in myself in the day-to-day analytic work over the past 40 years, have been fitful happenstance, nothing that I set out deliberately to achieve. They have been as fireflies: elusive on the wing and enigmatic in the grasp; illuminating in the moment seen, rather dull and diminished when closely scrutinized. Was the guiding glow really there, or imagined in my head? Once in hand, how to keep it glowing? Rather than encountering dramatic enlightenment, I learned to expect the insights of my patients, and my own about me, to be small-scale, scattered glimmers, extinguished almost as often as sustained. Those that are mine I often expect to encounter in moments of relaxed immersion in some routine task in garden or shop, when I can drift over unsettled matters between my patients and me, and others of importance to me.

I regard insight, in the broadest sense and however gained, as any fresh perception of oneself. In the specific context of clinical psychoanalysis, I would see mutative insight as that fresh perception of self, conscious or unconscious, that accompanies small or large developmental increments in the patient's psychic organization in consequence of analytic work. And I would describe such mutative analytic work as that in which very real struggles around old issues are replayed in new contexts of high emotional intensity, certainly for the patient and often for the analyst. Without such intensity, whereby intrapsychic conflict in one or both can be "really" brought into the light, there is little psychic growth and structural change—and precious few felt insights. With such intensities, the patient has the chance to experience old matters in new variations, and thereby to see more of himself and his others than he had previously been free to see, given the constraints and skewings of his transferentially derived fears and expectations.

There is an old Chinese proverb (for all I know, begot in Brooklyn): "I heard it and forgot it. I read it and I remembered it. I did it and I understood it." Whatever its origins, this proverb captures the essence of what Strachey (1934) pointed to in his emphasis on the necessity to interpret issues alive in the patient's transference relationship to the analyst. It also echoes Ferenczi and Rank's (1924) earlier insistence on the importance of the patient's living out his transference in relation to the analyst so that the analyst can help the patient to understand both cognitively and experientially how present and past have become convergent in the analytic relationship.

By *struggle,* I mean the heart of the analytic matter: what it takes for the pair to bring about and live through present versions of how the patient shaped and was shaped by his relationships with key others in his developmental past. These moment-to-moment experiences in the analytic dyad become, as Poland (1988) deftly elucidated, the base on which the analytic relationship grows. These are the bits and pieces that affectively and effectively stir the patient, and often the analyst, to experience past and present in a fashion that promotes those fresh recognitions that we call *insight,* along with those capacities for finer discrimination and fuller integration that we link to structural change and psychic growth.

However differently in degree the struggle stirs and sounds both participants, it is the richness and vitality of what goes on in this struggle that must be joined, this match that must be made, that strikes the faint sparks of insight to be fanned in the tinder of relating.

At this point, two related and commonplace observations can be made about how insight takes and makes its shape. They are not thereby the less useful in supporting the importance of the experiences in the dyadic relationship for effecting analytic change and its accompanying insights.

1. No fresh and mutative insight occurs in our work except as some previous and compelling insight. That is, some former understanding of one's self, by which one has lived, is worked over and discounted.

2. In this working-through process of discounting and abandoning older views, the patient, as well as the analyst, is apt to respond to his accretion of fresh awareness not only with pleasure and release but also with anxiety and something akin to mourning.

I look on these paired phenomena as tentative but significant indications that both intrapsychic change and an altered self-perspective (insight) are occurring in the analytic work. Perhaps they can be demonstrated in the clinical data that follow.

Clinical Sample

This vignette reflects a particular instance of analytic stagnation that the patient and I created through the intermeshing of the patient's transferentially shaped behaviors with regressive transferences of my own. A prolonged state of tensional distancing that reflected our shared dynamic concerns was first experienced by both of us until it could be resolved by self-insights stirred in me by a startling moment in the impasse.

Mr. B came to analysis in his late 20s because of chronic anxiety going back some six years, when his father sickened and slowly died from cancer. More recently, Mr. B was troubled with episodes of depression and conscious remorse over bouts of savage inner rage toward his unruly six-year-old son. He also was ashamed and guilty that he had grown distant from his wife and longed for extramarital sex. He held strongly idealized convictions about how good a husband he should be, and how loving a father to his son and cherished infant daughter. During his father's illness, he had fled into early marriage almost consciously bent on escaping closeness with his distraught mother, who had grown even more stickily dependent on him than she was during his boyhood. Then she had openly preferred him over his younger brother and made him her confidant to her emotional and sexual dissatisfactions with his rough-and-ready father. At the father's death, Mr. B resolutely put aside all grieving so that he could provide the strong support his mother and brother sought in him.

Several months into a five-times-per-week analysis, Mr. B began a frequent ritual of lowering himself onto the couch in an unusual fashion. He seated himself with his legs outstretched on the couch and brought both forearms stiffly to a horizontal extension paralleling the legs. Then he slowly lowered himself backward so as to lie for a moment or two with his forearms and hands now pointed to the ceiling. Hands brought gently onto the chest, and legs still rigidly extended, he launched into a circumscribed set of topics in flat repetition: his failed struggles to be a good husband and father, and the distance and frustration imposed on him by his wife's graduate studies and immersion in the children. He dwelt in dull misery on his constricting burdens both at work and at home, where his need to divide his time fairly between the two brought shortfall and dissatisfaction in both. He was pained by his anxious warding off of his too emotional, demanding, intrusive mother and was only dimly aware of his ashamed dependency on her. He made infrequent and flat reference to his deceased father. He always had admired and feared his father and was never close to him or sure of how his father regarded him. When he spoke of either parent in these conflicted terms, he often raised his forearms to vertical, for moments on end—the only motility he allowed himself in the first year or so of our work. At such times, his baritone voice took on an odd quality: as he began or ended speaking, there would be a brief, high-pitched squeak, like the break voice of an adolescent, or a pinched-off cry. Dreams were dutifully and flatly related on the rare occasions of his remembering them. He could do nothing with them associatively, and he became more tense and taciturn when I drew attention to elements of them or tried to interest him in his evident anxiety and distancing.

During the early months of this strained work, I came to have little to say. The silences between us were long. He seemed to me, in his boyishness and skittishness, to be quite vulnerable, someone to be approached carefully, not prodded or challenged. Although I could hear veiled allusions to themes of competitive aggression and passive yearnings, his wariness and fending off made them seem inaccessible and justified my conscious bent to remain hovering and watchful.

From what he did say, I gradually acquired a cautious impression that his constricted content and repetitive kinesics reflected two possible and related phantasy themes: that in settling himself onto my couch, he was lowering himself into his father's grave; and that once there, he felt literally stuck and helpless, even as he felt stuck with and held by his clutching mother through an unresolved and paralyzing sense of likeness to her.

Then came a day when, struggling in the face of my growing boredom and flatness, I drifted into reverie. I had suddenly a powerful visual image, close up, of a stretch of sand or sandy soil broken only by what seemed like a living tube—like a clam siphon perhaps, pulsating slowly in breathing fashion. With the image came feeling tones of immense bleakness, sadness, a little dread. As I pulled back from the phantasy with some mild anxiety, Mr. B broke his silence to speak of a phantasy that had briefly flashed in his head, something about someone buried alive—maybe like torture—maybe something he had read. It left him anxious and bewildered. As he spoke, I had a powerful sense of the uncanny: strong vigilance, the hair on the back of my neck standing on end and tingling, a sense of being in the presence of something powerfully known but not identifiable. As this subsided, I too felt bewildered and fascinated. Words and even images from the epilogue of *Shogun* flashed by.

I wanted to hold on to the close simultaneity of the two sets of images—his and mine—to come to grips with what was in me. But I was aware that the patient, perhaps in acknowledging his bewilderment, seemed to be making an oblique plea for my help, a rare reaching out. I managed to say I could imagine how bleak and painful it could be for him to keep trying to be a good and loving father while he had to go on being aware of his covered-over anger and discontent. He made little response except to resume his recital with somewhat less intensity. As the hour ended, I continued to feel an uneasy need to return to the experience even as it seemed to be receding into relative flatness.

That evening, while doing some mindless woodworking task in my cellar shop—some hand-sanding chore—I returned to thoughts about the hour, my startle and tingle at hearing the patient's "buried alive" imagery so close on the heels of my own. I could not retrieve with clarity the stark visual picture of the breathing protrusion, clam in sand—I do not ordinarily have much visual imaging capacity in the fully awakened state. But the sadness and bleakness came back to me, along with theme fragments from *Shogun:* sons against father, uncles; revolt and parricide, aggrandizement of violence, the sanction of open sadism and destructiveness as casual solution to all problems. How often I had heard the patient's dulled pain over his unwanted aggression toward wife and children—his wish to

be only the loving husband and father, his air of heavy burden, the deadness in me that I felt at times with him. Somehow, in my oscillation between his and mine at that moment, it struck me that I was caught up in
something very difficult for both of us: that from almost the start of his
analysis I had a muted impression of Mr. B as brave and weighted down,
boyish and vulnerable, and that I needed to go slowly with him, not add to
the pressures, but rather sustain him in a quiet holding. Yet for whom? I
felt suddenly foolish, taken in by the patient and by me, even as I got absorbed in a network of branching ideas and feelings, threading here and
there in a tangle this linear description cannot capture—as I sanded away.

I became immersed in and emotionally gripped by the array of historical and dynamic symmetries I had allowed to take shape in my perception of us both.

Mr. B's loss of his father in his early 20s, while still caught up in adolescent tensions toward both parents, brought him even more intensely
into his too close entwinement with his loving-dependent mother. She
often had told how, at his birth, she had exulted, "Now I will never be
lonely again." I had lost my physician father in the great flu epidemic
shortly after my birth. For a long time, my mother grieved and was
sometimes depressed, yet overall she was a warm, lively, loving woman
who devoted herself to my sisters and me. I had learned a lot about how
to comfort and hover when mother was down (Olinick, 1969). At the
same time, I was fortunate in having frequent contact with a paternal
outdoorsman uncle, a journeyman carpenter and ingenious craftsman,
who summered with us and taught me much until his abrupt and permanent departure to the West Coast in my early adolescence. His leaving
complicated and deepened my relationship with my mother and added
fresh conflict to my sense of being special to her.

Mr. B had lost his father around the time of his own son's birth, and he
often lamented that boy and grandfather had had no chance to know each
other. Some 20 years earlier, my mother had died a few months before my
wife and I had our son, our only child. I grieved that she had not lived to
know him—a yearning linked to much earlier longings to have known my
own father. I remembered Mr. B's months-past dream, which should
readily have come back to me during the *Shogun* hour. (I retrieved it later
from my notes.) Mr. B had described the dream: "I had replaced Sonny
and was doing a risqué dance with Cher—her one breast exposed. Then
on a beach running north–south, walking with my son back and forth past
a lifeguard. He seemed to be trying to resuscitate a body on the sand. I

wanted to get in there and help, but felt I needed to take care of my son. Later we encountered bears with big teeth that frightened my little boy."

Mr. B had done little with the dream at that time, as was his wont, beyond commenting on his admiration for Cher and abashed uncertainty in thinking of "making it" with her. This part of the dream and his association had reminded me of his embarrassed recall, in our initial interview, of how his mother had offered him her breast to suckle when he was about six, then stopped him because "it tickled good." I reminded him of this at the time of the Cher dream, but he responded with only intellectualized contemplation of how wrong it was that she had done this and how hard it had become for him to keep his wife separated, in his head, from his mother as a desirable sex object now that his wife was twice a mother herself.

Still sanding away, I recalled that we had done nothing with the body-on-the-beach segment of the dream. This omission was especially startling to me, for I had long since come to look on beach imagery in dreams as an often reliable primary-process referent to the pull and mystery of mother's depths, to pregenital fusion and merger, as well as to oedipal wishes to see and explore mother's body—all this as glimpsed from the uncertain safety of identification with father's high ground to stand on.

I had rich personal reasons to be especially attuned to these multiple resonances of beach imagery; I had often been told how I had been born at our summer home when my mother lingered too long into the autumn and my father was off in his city practice. Ours was a small lake resort, a beckoning surround of woods and water in which my first 20 summers of most active and enduring relationships were rooted, and where I learned as well to deal with autumnal loneliness and the quiet pleasure of solitary foraging in still places.

What I recalled of Mr. B's beach dream coupled quickly with his imagery and mine of the hour that day.

I drifted back to old memories, some long with me and others only painfully dredged up in my analyses: hints of anger at a father who died for his patients, rather than live for us, and old wonderings of where my father really was—in the Northern Lights that drove the wild geese southward? in the bottom of our lake? What riches I could discover were I suddenly to find myself lying drained one morning. I had had latency phantasies of myself, people around me, buried alive. Why had my uncle left in anger? Fresh intensities in familiar old ideas surprised and puzzled me, now grown more than middle-aged.

Somewhere between closing up shop and showering for bed, it became clear to me that I was not doing at all well in handling a specific and painful tension in my family life during roughly the same time span Mr. B had been in analysis. Our son, now passing 20 and moving steadily toward new levels of independence and maturing, had removed himself rather abruptly from our household for advanced studies in medicine and women. Although I continued to support his spunky adaptiveness and quietly effective rebellion, I saw that it had become indeed hard work to be a good father in the face of my envy of his youth and the wide horizons opened to him, and my anger at him and at my wife for what his move had taken from me in triggering my wife's mourning and depression around the empty nest. I had not been facing up to the intensity of my anger toward those I most deeply cared for. I had become enmeshed in a tangle of identifications and displacements I had created between my son, Mr. B, and me. Son to father, son to father and mother, father to son of wife-mother, had me in a whole webwork of love and rage, envy and guilt. My domestic tensions had rekindled in me old conflicts of competition, hurt, and anger at being deserted and shut out, yet needing reactively to stand by, rescue, and make up so that contact and love might be restored. I had displaced these onto my patient through the trivial and substantial likenesses and symmetries I had shaped between us. I had responded with a definite shift to a more reserved, quietly contained and cautious stance, a more watchfully contemplative mode quite familiar to me as part of an almost lifelong adaptation when under stress—but not my optimal analyzing stance and not, I think, my usual stance toward living.

The realizations of that evening were neither dramatic nor shaking and did not lead to sudden changes in my family relationships. I found that I gradually grew more aware of and comfortable about my anger and the shaping of more realistic and less idealizing perceptions of my family and me than those I had been attempting to preserve.

With Mr. B, I quickly returned to a freer and more active stance. For example, in the hour after what I have described, he launched into pained self-recriminations about his shortcomings as husband and father—maybe he or they would be better off if he were to remove himself from the scene. He could not find anything else to say and fell silent and very still. As I had attempted only once before, I pointed out to him that he had lowered himself onto the couch, just a few moments earlier, with his arms raised in his idiosyncratic gesture. This time I added: could he, in his stillness, be saying he should just be dead and buried? Mr. B gave a tense little jerk, paused at length, and then glumly said he would have to think about it. I remarked, "And meanwhile be flat and empty here with me—a way of being dead?" He reddened a little and said, "I don't like it when you get to me. I do watch what I say and try to keep things quiet and peaceful between us." He moved on to somewhat familiar ground, but this time with growing animation and intensity: his adolescent years, when he avoided contact with his father and wanted more active interplay but felt too loyal to his mother and also vaguely anxious. Then his father had sickened and died, and it was too late. Yes, he did feel he wanted more from me, but he was wary and afraid of letting down his guard, and of being let down by my not responding. His voice conveyed more feeling than had before been evident.

Two days later, he remarked, "Something is different here—don't know—is it you, or is it me? I feel more relaxed, like more room to move in—and you don't seem so removed. I think I've been afraid of you, of your making some kind of move toward me if I made any move—this has me going in both directions—and you're just sitting there. It is something in me [long pause] . . . this frees me up . . . but a little shaky and sad—I just don't know."

Mr. B and I were into the beginning of a slow but effective movement into an eventually affectively intense reworking of his father's final year. We were dealing for the first time with Mr. B's grieving and, behind it, his guilt, hostility, love, and competitiveness toward his father and excessive attachment to his mother, which became the work of his later analysis. Our work together on his peculiar gesture was a useful component of coming to understand Mr. B's conflict over beseeching love and intimacy versus fearing shameful dependency, as he became more comfortable in letting me engage him about it and be close to him about more of his withheld conflicts in a fashion that he, and I, had earlier been too anxious and distanced to tolerate.

Discussion

I think it is evident from this vignette that the necessary analytic work Mr. B and I had to do had been slowed down by the cautious and passive distancing modes of the patient, reinforced by the increasingly similar stance I took in responding with my own conflicts.

In the tangle of tensions that Mr. B brought to our work, I quickly found likeness and symmetry between us. His rich range of conflicts about his son, wife, mother, deceased father, and himself—as well as his being close to my son's age—allowed me the opportunity and liability to respond regressively. I was in a heightened readiness to do so in my struggle to ward off my own painful conflicts involving my wife, son, and me. These set off in me resonances of very old problems I thought my two analyses had long since settled. My overly cautious behavior, my too passive hovering in the first year of analytic work, rationalized as concern for his vulnerability, covered my overidentification with him as the grieving orphan. It masked my conflicted anger and competitiveness toward him/son and supported my falling back into old defensive/ adaptive ways to be removed from the swirl of anger, hurt, and needing that was alive in both of us.

How to understand the uncanny episode of the similar and simultaneous phantasies shaped by us and between us becomes a matter for absorbing but inconclusive conjecture—conjecture that would direct us to matters lying in the roots of empathy and identification as well as at the heart of shared analytic work.

That the event heralded the emergence of gut-level fresh awareness for me and then for the patient, gradually shaping into mutative insights as we struggled toward a closer working—of this I carry considerable conviction. That the concurrence of our separate "buried alive" imagery was uncanny and shocking lay only in my experiencing of it, of course. The doppelgänger resonances it held for me allow me some confidence that the event marked my first awareness, not yet in consciousness, of the swirl of likenesses I had built up about us—the beginning of the web of understanding and insights fashioned later in my workshop.

I was barely able, at that moment of startled awareness, to hear in the patient's voice a new quality of pleading and reaching out to me, and my response to him was modestly adequate. This second concurrence could be considered an indication that both of us were moving closer to addressing the conflicts that had been shaping our interactions. Yet were those freshly altered qualities in his voice that spoke, or were they in my ear that heard? It surely was the latter. If the former and therefore in both, it could have been that the patient, like me, could now make this move, having needed and used the preceding period of shared and safe frustration to build up the transference actualization of past relationships with fathers living, now dead. What we had created between us, during those months, could be viewed as the living reality in which both of us worked through strong resistances against grappling with our separate mordant concerns, now intertwined. The patient's small responsiveness in the hour allowed me no closure on this.

I have a deeper conviction that the insights I sanded my way to that evening were part of and party to the reshaping of my behaviors with the patient in the next hour and thereafter. Certainly they were reflected in the specific content of the two interventions I have cited. Although these were more abrupt and confrontational than I would in retrospect have wished, I do regard them as being on-target. And whatever their cogency, they conveyed a shift in me that the patient perceived and could react to. I see in his response, with its stresses, "I don't like it when you get to me. I do watch what I say," a heightened awareness of his defensiveness and acknowledgment of its purpose; in these I see the kind of self-observation preceding insight that Hatcher (1973) wrote about. Mr. B's later remark of that hour, about wanting more from me than he was getting but being afraid to admit this, extended this self-knowledge while allowing me to be part of it. His comment from the subsequent hour, about noting some change toward liveliness in or between us, carried some small increment of insight in his recognizing his fear/wish of prompting me to move toward him.

This, then, is how I see insight derived from analytic work being accomplished: from bits and pieces of experiential self-recognition gained, at times for both parties, in the immediacy of the actual relationship between the analytic pair, acquiring shape, meaning, and eventual articulation over analytic time.

I am not asserting that it is optimal that the analyst become so caught up, as I was, in his own regressive transferences. I would endorse a quieter working of the analyst's share of the analyzing instrument, as Poland (1988) described—and can make my claim to analytic work accomplished in relative equanimity. Yet there is something to be acknowledged about the power and impact of such events—perhaps the vividness and intensity reached by one or both participants, something that carries considerable therapeutic potential, when impasses can be lived through and resolved.

The ponderous phrase often used to designate such times and moments, the "actualized transference," is accurate enough, as this vignette attests for both the patient and me. Yet it does not capture the complementary and necessary component of what is experienced in these same moments by both patient and analyst as something crucially different from the old expectations both brought to the encounter. For Mr. B and for me, this fresh experiencing involved finding, in self and other, an opening and a way to transcend the limitations we had jointly enacted, to make the needed contact in optimal closeness that allowed the shared intimacy necessary to analytic work.

Mr. B had to live out his old psychic realities with me in order to find them no longer valid and inevitable. Then he could face and see differently those painful experiences and phantasies of his past that were shaping his current view of himself in his world. Such sequences as these allow me some conviction about the truism, earlier stated, that mutative insight requires the working over and discounting of previously acquired self-knowledge—that new insight is built on and out of the stuff of the past.

Mr. B did not conspicuously live out the second and correlated truism about states of anxiety and loss often encountered in the abandonment of past expectations: anxiety expressed as fear of being too far out, at risk of being exposed and vulnerable, attacked or lost, and grieving manifested as loss and inner emptiness over the giving up of old and accustomed ways of maintaining a safe surround. He only hinted at these: "shaky and sad." Subsequently, as he could gradually hang on to his insights and gains, he experienced and worked with both anxiety and loss, along with pleasure and expansion, in his changed ways of seeking.

To pursue these truisms from my side of this piece of troubled analytic work, it is evident that my need to regain an optimal analytic stance shaped into insights as I reworked and altered old concerns and aspirations about myself as husband and father—and analyst. I had displaced these onto the relationship with Mr. B in a fashion made easy by his experiencing of parent loss and his struggles to deny his aggression. This is not a gloss on the fact that my regressive experiencing of my troubled past and present in this way fell short of Fliess's (1942) ideal of only trial sampling.

The anxiety and startle that were my part of the uncanny experience stand as testimony to my reluctance to recognize the fresh truths behind my defensive distancing. My subsequent feelings—a rueful acceptance once again of the imperfectibility of my analytic capacities, and sadness and unsettledness in the further relinquishing of idealizations about self and family—I would construe as substantial evidence of the abandonment of previous self-perceptions for the eventual relief and freedom of the new.

Although some few may do their work in sustained equanimity, I think it is the lot of most of us to fluctuate (Olinick et al., 1973) as we struggle for fit and relevance. Our deeper motivations for self-searching after our efforts have faltered are, to my best knowing, those same and primary reasons for why we are analysts in the first place (McLaughlin, 1961). These have to do with needing to counter and repair old and unwanted urges, aggressive and sexual, toward our primary others, extended through life as a reaching out to and caring for the later others we must keep finding. In finding them, we seek to find ourselves. And invariably we do, for better and for worse.

That I was fortunate on this occasion to find ways to work usefully on this constriction of my analytic span, without conscious intent or direction, attests to the perennial value of some kind of self-analyzing commitment carrying us through our years, however fragile and unsure our fresh knowings may prove to be.

I have no quarrel with those who emphasize the limits and uncertainty of self-analysis. I assert, however, that an acceptance of the instability of our best analytic competence, and an openness, however rueful, to look for and work with the falterings that must be, can allow us a greater range and depth in seeing what we need to see.

CHAPTER 7

Is Self-Analysis Possible?

Working analysts commonly expect that their patients will acquire an ongoing capacity for self-analysis. Yet we seem chronically uneasy about the authenticity of our own self-analytic discoveries; we are wary of openly claiming these as analytic and write sparingly about our experiences in self-analysis.

For some analysts, self-analytic work is indeed an inescapable, expectable, and desirable part of their living, whether experienced as deliberately sought (Calder, 1979; Sonnenburg, 1991) or as fortuitous (Gardner, 1983; Beiser, 1984; Jacobs, 1986; chaps. 6 and 11, this volume).

From this second position, I address some questions central to the matter of self-analysis. What pressures in and around the analyst urge him to introspective inquiry? What is the nature of the self-analytic experience and of the circumstances in which the work takes place? How can we weigh the significance of self-analytic endeavors for the analyst in his work and in the other important relationships in his life and distinguish their effect from the profusion of changes inherent in the vicissitudes of the life cycle?

Motivations for Self-Analysis

I have picked for my focus just one sector: the ongoing impact on the analyst of his or her clinical work with patients.

It is my premise that work with patients, especially when patients stretch and burden us, powerfully impels us to introspection in our reach for adaptive changes in our theoretical view and technical approach. In other words, I see our clinical work as the compelling motive—especially for those analysts whose need to do therapeutic work with others derives from adaptive and reparative urgencies learned in mastering troubled relations with primary others of their childhood. Such a therapeutic investment fosters the deep involvement necessary for significant analytic work. It carries, however, the liability for the revival of conflict in the face of fresh provocation.

By saying this, I suppose I could be wide of the mark for those whose reasons for being an analyst, a therapist, lie elsewhere—perhaps, like Freud, more in the direction of exploration and discovery. Yet there is much that our strange calling demands of each of us, in our cave-dweller mode of restricted range and mobility, that points to an altruism of dynamic significance. How else are we to account for our willing acceptance of a working lifetime of muted affective and motoric outlet so that those few others we bring close to us might attain just those freedoms we have put aside? And how else to account for the inner turbulence and struggles that can take place in us as we live out the hours and years of being the working analyst whose accomplishments are dependent on achievements not our own?

In my years of analyst watching, my respect has grown for the integrity and tenacity of the need, in each of us, to wrestle with our impediments to doing our best work on behalf of the patient. Although the pain of lapse and shortfall may have its narcissistic base in prompting us to do better, our dogged return to the engagement with the patient reveals the strength of our need to relate to and help an other. And it is our rueful readiness to look to our own part in shaping the complications in the analytic venture that points to the deeply personal roots of responsibility felt and taken.

I am inclined to place the power of analytic work with patients to impel self-inquiry above even the poignancies of marriage and children. In familial relationships, we are less aim inhibited than in analysis, and, rightly or otherwise, we allow our personal needs a far greater legitimacy of claim to fulfillment and a more forceful voice in the compromises of intimate relating.

As I live longer with the bits and pieces of self-observation and self-understanding that have been my lot, and that of others known to me, I am comfortable about thinking of the work entailed in attaining these insights as self-analysis, particularly when some subsequent enhancement of self-understanding is discernible.

I feel that there are meaningful, experience-near indicators that we can discover and apply in judging the cogency of self-analytic moments. I dwell on these clinical criteria a little later.

As for insight itself, a concept central to most definitions of self-analysis, I regard it in its broadest sense as any fresh perception of oneself (*Webster's,* 1952). A bit more narrowly considered, the sort of insight essential to our work is mutative insight, the fresh perception of self, conscious or otherwise, that accompanies a developmental increment in the patient's psychic organization in consequence of analytic work (Moore and Fine, 1990, p. 99). Such mutative work is necessarily done in struggles to replace or alter old perceptions of self and other, now replayed in new variations in the very different context of the analytic relationship. In these intensities, the patient can come to experience more of himself and others in evolved and discriminating ways not previously available to him. Without such intensity to bring his intrapsychic conflicts to light, the patient is likely to experience little psychic change, and few felt insights. In my experience, this affectively driven process holds equally for the analyst.

As a frame for exploring self-analytic sorties, let me first sketch what I have noticed to be a familiar sequence in the unfolding of an analyst's perception of himself and his patient under the impact of analytic work over time. Oversimplified, this march carries from the comfort, when at a loss, of first behaving like one's own analyst; to the confusion of finding likenesses to oneself in each patient; and then to the recognition and acceptance of the unmergible differences between self and patient (McLaughlin, 1993a).

Here drawing mainly on my own experiences in this journey of discovery of patient and self, I highlight the demands for self-scrutiny that each step makes on us.

The Shaping of a Vintage 1950s Analyst

The training of the late 1940s required that we work from a position of cool detachment, confident in the fidelity of our unconscious attunement to our patient that would yield us the accurate decoding of the patient's manifest concerns. We were to trust our intuition, buttressed by the theoretical formulations provided us, to lead us to the exact interventions that would guide the patient through the morass of his infantile misconceptions. One result of these serene expectations was that, when faced with clinical situations outside the span of my supervised experience, I came up short. In such moments, I was most likely to steady myself by drawing automatically on how my analyst had dealt with me. For me, this meant much well-intended silence broken by throat clearing (as a sign of life still extant behind the couch) and then a gently intended *yes?* as signal or plea to the patient for more data. This could be helpful, but too often it led to impasses that left my patient and me adrift in improvisations.

A happenstance that moved me to seek a second analysis in my seasoning years was the large number of physicians in my analytic caseload. All men, they comprised a mixture of psychiatrists and other medical brothers with backgrounds often similar to mine. The trial identifications that Fliess (1942) would have had us make came easily but did not so easily go. Being receptively close to my physician patients was at times to be in a hall of mirrors. What we came gradually to recognize in ourselves were, in the lexicon of the times, conflicted nurturing maternal identifications anchoring a renunciation of direct satisfaction of one's own needs, except as attainable through service to others. Notably, these defenses against phallic-aggressive wishes tended to include an inhibition, sometimes massive, of intellectual strivings and other self-effacements consonant with the image of the Old Family Doctor and with the particulars of the Hippocratic oath as well (McLaughlin, 1961).

All this and more that each physician-patient brought to our work kept stirring resonances in me of matters of my own that I had thought comfortably resolved through my own analyses. At times, I was unable to sort out which dynamic shadings belonged to the patient and which to me, and I was concerned about the validity of the dynamics I was discovering in my patients. Was I really understanding what lay in them, or was I reading my own organizings into them?

The Impact of Likenesses: A Confusion of Voices

From these early times, one instance in particular now stands out. I was working with two analysands, both psychiatrists, one in a training analysis. Each was struggling to express and deal with yearnings for a beloved woman lost to him in his past. One had lost his mother to her protracted dementing illness and death when he was a latency child; the other, his wife through her sudden death from a cerebral vascular catastrophe during the early years of their marriage. Neither, for different reasons, had been able to mourn, to make peace with his loss and hurt over having been left, or to resolve his remorse over his part in shaping the loss. Both were caught up in these tensions, and both reproached me for not doing more to comfort and resolve their distress.

I felt burdened and at a loss. I had been with my own mother in her dying hours at her summer place about a year earlier.

During an hour with my training analysand, I made an incredible gaffe. I was caught up in noting new tones of distress in his otherwise familiar recounting of having been a 10-year-old immersed in his boy's world, only peripherally mindful of his mother's deterioration, and his wondering now why his father had not reached out across the distance between them to help him see what was happening. I felt he was ready for a formulation that I had been holding back for quite a while. I spoke to him of his need to defend himself against his anxiety and anger about his mother's slow desertion of him, which had led him to squelch his distress and direct his anger at his drunkard father. As support for my interpretation, I spoke of a dream from a recent hour depicting an empty Eskimo kayak bobbing helplessly in turbulent rapids and surviving only because its decking held out the white water.

The trouble was that this dream belonged to my other patient. I realized this as I finished speaking; I sat in a silence of shared shock. In our working through of the consequences of my mistake, three points stand out. First, by acknowledging my gaffe, I meant it when I made my apologies and stated that my confusion of the two surely involved something in me that I would work to identify and resolve. Second, I had a vague inner perception that there was some sense in my involving the candidate analysand rather than his counterpart in my misadventure. I had been put off and dissatisfied for some time with the obduracy of his distancing idealization of me. Yet I had seen him as not yet capable of being confronted with his disavowed aggression, and I had felt bogged down. Third, the qualities of my immediate distress during our charged silence were familiar: chagrin and anxious vigilance, the flush of foot-in-mouth shame, and misery over having done some irreparable harm. I had long known this flood of affects as central to my most painful experiences of misdeeds and blunders in childhood and adolescence. Through much prior analytic work, this affective state had largely attenuated to a signal cluster that I had come to recognize as a call for more self-inquiry. On this occasion, however, the impact was full and shaking.

In my own analytic hours, I had been obliquely reproaching my second analyst for helping me so little to get in touch with the grieving for my mother that she and I agreed was surely there and must be tapped. I came now to sense how necessary it was that I avoid full awareness of my mixture of need and vengeful distancing, now from my analyst and then from my mother, feeding into my habitual resort to solitary coping. I experienced the recognition that I had become caught up in strong resonances of likeness to both patients, especially to the one who suffered my slip. I had brought us into the replaying of unresolved son–mother entanglements, made static by uncompleted mourning. Who had shamefully and hurtfully neglected, rejected, deserted, or abandoned whom, and who ought to feel shame and remorse toward whom, were shifting uncertainties alive in each of us. These transference configurations had become animated in and between us in the intensities of the analytic relationship. In each of us, these conflicts were further magnified by paternal absence, and a consequent lack of the presence and support of one parent by which the vicissitudes of ambivalence in relationship to the other can be mitigated. This lack of the father I saw as contributing to the strong sense of responsibility for the well-being of others that could be identified in the patients and myself, as a way of countering guilt and concern over aggression in self and other.

It was in this fluid shifting of transference-laden mother–son identifications that I merged the three of us in my enactment. Prompted to come to grips in my own analysis with my own hung-up mourning, I could see my gaffe as an aggressive act against my patient, whose candidacy furthered my sense of likeness between us. In this context, my enacting my confusion of likenesses struck me as a kind of self-inflicted wounding and expiation, a compromise expression of my wishes to punish and to help, to reproach and to seek the forgiving rapprochement of shared understanding.

In the years after my second analysis, I became accustomed to dwelling in my off-hours on events with patients that had left me uneasy and unsettled. Working on the impediments that befell me—signaled by sleepiness, boredom, excessive intervening, or steering—brought me to moments of self-recognition of the disturbing likeness between patient and analyst and to fresh perspectives on my old history. Such gropings were not deliberate but were arrived at as, immersed in the serenity of accustomed doing, I puttered in garden or workshop. I learned to welcome these reflections and the dreams that drifted in on their heels, for together they somehow lighted up an awareness about an aspect of me that now made a mesh or match with my patient in our likeness and difference.

The Impact of Differences

What also flushed me out of my refuge in the illusion of detached objectivity was my daily encounters with some patients who seemed very different from me and beyond my comprehension. Here were persons who just could not tolerate being dealt with from a distance and through minimal communicative contact. They monitored with anxious vigilance my ways of trying to relate to them. All were liable to rapid decompensation in the analytic setting and disruptive behaviors outside—taking refuge in regressive withdrawal and somatic and emotional distress in response to my behaviors they experienced as slighting, preemptive, intrusive, or abandoning.

I was dismayed and puzzled by their reactions to interventions that I considered on target and tactful, and to my silences, which struck me as humanely intended. It took me longer than I wished, and more iatrogenic pain inflicted than I care to recall, before I could hear more in those negative responses than defensive avoidance and transference-driven resistances against a truth.

Varied cues and signals, in addition to the cluster already described, have triggered continuing self-explorations. I agree with Poland (1992) that heightened psychic tension in the analyst is the immediate driving force impelling him to self-scrutiny.

What usually has moved me is some degree of uneasiness while I am at work with a patient. It builds up gradually and often out of my full awareness, until I catch myself in some form of withdrawal or therapeutically intended steering, or get caught up in a more obviously regressive enactment. The resulting signals of distress press me to off-hours reflection.

Clinical Vignette: Mrs. P

Here is one of the many cases that have put their weight behind my on-going need for self-appraisal and change (see chap. 11). In the 1970s, Mrs. P underwent analysis for help with her long-standing isolation, bouts of depression, and chronic inability to find satisfaction in her life. Over the first year of our work, I had grown weary in my effort to reach her through her incessant and ambiguous circumstantiality as she de-tailed her hopeless failures as wife and mother. When I intervened—more accurately, had to interrupt to seek the point of her tortured ac-count, to identify her affective states, or to explore her obvious distress in allowing me to engage her—Mrs. P abruptly fell silent or drowned us both in her self-depreciation. In so doing, her thought processes transiently became fragmented.

When I tried my tactful best to explore her obsessive indecisiveness, to link it to her growing up with a work-absorbed mother and ever criti-cal father, she invalidated these interventions with contrary new ver-sions that destroyed the significance I had so carefully distilled. After such impasses, the patient reported worsened depression and binge eat-ing. I felt stuck in my inability to help her see, and shaken in my sense of my own competence to see. I was worried for her, for us, and could hear the rising edge of assertiveness in my interventions, made after my lengthy silences spent amassing more data that I hoped might eventually be persuasive. These were clear and compelling indicators that I myself had fallen into a regressed level of transference, signaling a stalemate that was mine to resolve.

Luckily, I became aware of a mannerism unusual for me: repeatedly removing my bifocals during such hours to gaze blankly at the blur of my patient on the couch and to enjoy, for moments on end, the soft merging of color masses (flowers) on my coffee table. The latter gave me a sense of peaceful detachment that I was reluctant to leave in order to observe Mrs. P once more through corrective lenses that did not help me see what I needed to know. Soon after, I heard an unusual intensity as I recounted to new friends an old story of how, when I was nine, my childhood visual impairment had finally been discovered by my golfing uncle when I turned out to be a hopelessly inept caddy—of how, once behind my glasses, I sighted with delight and expansion a world of immense reach and clarity.

Something fresh fell into place with my linking the storytelling and the ritual with my glasses. During my workshop reveries over subsequent weeks, a darker side of those times drifted into focus, one I had only touched on in my previous analyses. I recalled what it had been like to be semiblind and not know it—to have been comfortable enough in the family acceptance of my accustomed bumblings but to have known times of pain and despair, with shamed bewilderment over what was wrong with my knowing and doing that clearly was so different from the prowess of the others in the clamor of my family. I had accepted my inept lot and turned to books and their words to find an authority of meaning that my uncertain visual perceptions could not grasp. The puzzlement and uncertainty of those times drove my need, once I had my glasses, to be accurate and quick to see and say and do it right. These personal strivings found a comfortable fit in the job description of the competent analyst that my late 1940s training enjoined me to attain. As my work with Mrs. P made clear, I was prone, under her unswerving challenge to my sense of competence, to fall into an exaggerated use of this minimal analytic stance of authoritative knowing.

What I gradually came to see clearly enough was that Mrs. P's ways of evoking my efforts to reach out to her, then wiping them out with repudiation and altered contexts, had tapped into my old pain of uncertain groping and failing to know—that, moved by Mrs. P's very similar distress over asserting any sureness of knowing, I had fallen into defensive transference behaviors of excessive assertiveness or silent withdrawal as ways of being rid of the burden of her/our problem. In the enigmatic ways that self-analysis sometimes works, perhaps this time, in the mirroring of likenesses among differences that breached my defenses, I had come upon fresh sidestreams of familiar transferences and was able to feel the surprise of new understanding about old concerns I had thought well enough settled.

What gradually ensued between Mrs. P and me were mainly quiet differences in how things were said between us: on my side a greater freedom to float ideas and impressions in a tentative, nondeclamatory fashion, once the old imperatives to say it right could be put aside. And perhaps most important, once I discovered and attenuated my old pain of not knowing, I really could hear better the nuances of Mrs. P's manifold distress. It was easier to find more evocative ways to acknowledge the legitimacy of her pain that she

could not yet risk speaking about, and to grasp better the dynamic nature of her impaired verbal expressiveness.

From Mrs. P's side, her response to my shift showed up rather
swiftly, initially in a modest easing of anxiety and greater freedom to
challenge and check out my offerings and then in a cautiously offered,
repetitious, and grudging, "I knew that all the time," as acknowledgment
and dismissal of my offerings. She thus allowed me glimpses of the
shame-driven fear and stubborn withholding that lay behind her habitually not saying what she often knew or felt. Especially noteworthy was
that her falling into episodes of confusion and fragmented thinking
gradually diminished. Her preferred style became for a long time that of
disagreeing with whatever I said, then restating these ideas quite articu-
lately in her own words, deepening and extending those ideas in directions of her own that were important for me to acknowledge. It took
much longer for her to volunteer that she had quickly noted my
changed stance and had tracked it vigilantly for lapse or traps. By this
time, she was deeply engaged in confronting both of us with the enormity
of feeling herself utterly worthless and unlovable in my eyes.

Verification of Self-Analytic Experience

That sketchy clinical sample touches on the cluster of data I have come
to rely on in trying to assess the authenticity and carrying power of my
self-analytic encounters. I describe them here in the order of their happening and my getting a focus on them.

First is the inner experiencing of mutative insight, the uncertain mean-
der from inner tension and groping to a more relaxed and fuller comprehension that plays itself out in varying degrees of pace and emotional
impact. In this instance, I almost literally had to blind myself before I
could grope for the connections between the plight the patient and I were
in , my symptomatic behavior with my glasses, and the recital of a bit of
family lore. This oft-told tale then seemed gradually to light up, its familiar
dimensions still there, but their meaning and affective charge vastly trans-
formed and amplified, as when a hologram shifts or sets and lighting are
changed on the open stage. This sense of freshly seeing into old aspects of
myself came in an almost leisurely fashion over several weeks, along with
renewed energy and quiet pleasure.

I detail this gradual opening of awareness to contrast it with more intense flares of self-seeing that have occasionally been my lot. These tend to occur after jolting, even uncanny, experiences during an analytic hour. A typical instance is that triggered by the dream misassignment I described. There, the sense of sudden illumination was itself startling, and there was an intense exhilaration in feeling able, for a lingering moment, to see to far reaches of one's inner life—rather like experiencing bursts of heat-lightning that light up a familiar summer landscape with eery clarity before flickering into a darkness crackling with the tension of an imminent storm. These sensory and emotional qualities seem to me to point to the lifting of old repressions, with the consequences only later to be weighed as either ephemeral or durable and expanding.

Second is the nature of the effects that the fresh self-observation has on my ways of working with a particular patient, both in the short range and over the long haul, and then with my patients in general. In the work with Mrs. P, my sense of an expanded range of seeing and saying, which I have come to trust as a harbinger of a mutative insight, developed quickly. Among the later self-awareness that came over weeks and months was the rueful recognition of how my investment in my seeing and saying amounted to not listening to Mrs. P, not hearing her point of view, shutting off from understanding, and actualizing her worst expectations. I felt the regret myself that I had defaulted on my commitment to hearing my patient in order to ward off a revival of an old state of inadequacy, shame, and hopelessness too resonant with the misery that Mrs. P lived with constantly.

Third is the impact on the patient, as reflected in Mrs. P's emotional and behavioral responses to my altered stance and as acknowledged in her expressed awareness of the change. Mrs. P found what she needed to help her become more articulate, to reveal more of her hidden concerns, and to have less need to regress to helplessness. Eventually, she revealed how she had immediately perceived the change but had monitored it warily for a long time to be sure that it was "real."

Fourth is the discernible consequences of cumulative change, wrought by self-analytic moments, on how I am perceived by patients, family, colleagues, and others, and whether these accord with my own perceptions. Here the data are the most problematic, and the most vulnerable to wishful skewing. One large change in my analytic stance, evolving from years of work with patients in the range Mrs. P exemplifies, has been a commitment to acknowledging and working within the reality view of the patient. The collaborative enhancements of doing so have gradually led me to prefer this as a basic way of relating to all my patients, and to people in general. I take some affirmation of the durability of this attitude from the feedback I get from former patients who have returned for further analytic work. They are explicit about the ways in which they experience deeper levels of feeling reached and understood, and they see me as more consistently there for them. And so it is with other long-term relationships: family, friends, consultees, colleagues. From my side, I know that I convey more my appreciation of the strength and pain in others and try harder to avoid adding to the pain.

Another index of the impact of prolonged work with patients, and a reflection of the ongoing self-inquiry the work has stimulated, lies in the gradual but substantial shift in my analytic perspective. Exploring the potential of analysis from within the psychic reality of the patient has been a major preoccupation of my years as a clinical analyst. Reflecting a further shaping of my analytic identity, this commitment continues to embody the assets and liabilities of my healing bent and obviously calls for ongoing self-scrutiny in its own right. In addition, as I have learned this approach and have tried to convey it to those who consult with me, I find its technical challenges difficult and exciting and inevitably defining of one's limits of competence and need for the help of self-scrutiny.

The Consultative Experience as Stimulus for Self-Analysis

Here is yet another powerful adjuvant to the self-analytic bent: the stimulation inherent in the consultative process when the analyst knows he needs help with his work and is strongly motivated to seek it.

I have benefited from considerable consultation about my clinical work over these many years. None has brought me into so close and illuminating contact with my motives for my ways of working as has the consultation I have sought in my need to minimize my own point of view in order to analyze from the patient's perspective. Here I have had recourse to the outstanding proponent of this clinical approach, and whose work I have followed closely for more than 10 years. Schwaber (1983, 1986, 1992) has been a pioneer in exploring how much analytic work can be achieved through a committed focus on both the psychic reality of the patient and the nuances of all the behaviors of the analyst that have become so central to that reality. Schwaber has provided a specific technical base and rigorous mode of working by which to seek the patient's view, both conscious and undiscovered, of any aspect of his life and to recognize the dynamic logic of his perspective.

In consulting about my ongoing work with a patient similar to Mrs. P, I came repeatedly upon the many ways in which I lapsed from this mode of inquiry. In one typical instance, it became clear that I had not picked up enough on the patient's signals of distress over my leaving her for a vacation. I accepted too readily the mask of her sturdy self-sufficiency, and her voiced delight in anticipating her freedom. After several repetitions of this theme in varied contexts, I felt some of my signal concern and a need to address my oversight. I came to see a different perspective on my habitual preference for keeping all farewells and partings brief— that I often tended to close off separations, leaving and being left, with various disavowals and distancings. One favorite device was to get busy in some solitary activity that gave me pleasure. I had long ago retrieved memories of my childhood distress over my mother's absences, her leave-takings and somber states when I was very young, and had worked through much of what these had meant to me. But I had obviously found no need to connect those loss experiences with an adaptation I still valued, so ego syntonic as to leave me with a blind spot of personal values too aligned with the patient's defenses.

In such instances, at stake was not just an exercise in improving technical competence. The flow of the clinical data following my lapses clearly pointed to the patient's sagging into worsened depression, alienation, and hopelessness.

Working so closely to engage all levels of the patient's psychic reality seems inevitably to open the analyst to a heightened appreciation of the patient's affective intensities and to intensify the depth of his own emotional involvement. The impact of seeing and tracking my contribution to these repetitive enactments, up close and in living intensity, indeed had a cumulative and tensional impact that led me to some self-inquiry. The enlarged perspective that gradually lighted up was not surprising; I saw better that what was hindering my hearing the patient's pain had to do with my own old and reliable defensive postures. My nonresponsiveness to her masked distress over being left was very similar to my closing off my own sensitivities to partings, and my tacit support of her busy doings was a reflection of my own preferred solutions. My not exploring her blithe indifference allowed me to stay away from her shame and hurt over being so little and unimportant to me and to the mother of her early years, so like my own.

Transference Sanctuaries

We come now to a consideration of the circumstances in which self-analysis takes place once the stimulus of the clinical occasion has been felt. I emphasize this particular aspect of self-analysis, as it has been vital for me and for others who have written about their experiences. In fact, I consider its inclusion in accounts of such experiences to be another component of the validating context that I have come to rely on in assessing self-analytic efforts.

This enhancement has to do with the surround or circumstances in which analysts generate their insights. It seems significant that none of these special contexts is deliberately sought or contrived. Usually some private haven or safe place has been come upon without conscious intent; it has been selected for personal dynamic reasons that are vital to the self-analytic enterprise. Here the preconscious can hold sway while familiar routines are played out. Calder (1979) spoke of the "laboratory" of his bathroom, where he did his shaving and contemplated the "sharp winces" of self-critical remembering. Ticho (1967) told of other analysts' preferred settings, such as a bed, a warm bath, or comfortable travel; others have told me of the evocative power of the fishing skiff, trout stream, or park bench. What seems essential in this limitless listing is the relaxation and freedom for contemplation to be found in desultory minding while anchored in some routine physical activity reenforced by familiar sights, sounds, and smells. I have come to think of these specially sought circumstances as "transference sanctuaries."

Shop and yard are the sanctuaries I still seek. I shuttle back and forth between the two into very odd hours, and I have learned to trust that I will, without deliberate effort, see ways through the thickets of a patient or paper. As I focus on the immediate woodworking task at hand, I address our tangles with a kind of peripheral awareness, a sidewise looking. Gradually becoming aware of these unobtrusive rituals led me to an appreciation of their importance to my inner balancings.

In my early years after my physician-father's death from influenza six weeks following my birth, his brother was the single most meaningful male in my life. Uncle John spent the summer months of my first 12 years living at our summer place, his son like an older brother to me. Over those years, Uncle John improved the grounds and cottage in which my mother spent all the remaining summers of her life. Here lay her link to the husband she never stopped mourning, and my link to the father I knew through her.

My cousin and I often worked alongside my uncle as he did his improvisational carpentering and plumbing, planting and digging, repairing and building.

The smells and tastes of newly cut grass and spaded earth, the pungency of sawed wood, the heft and odor of hand tools—all were part of the nourishment and beckoning provided by a man who was there and available, a man who made me welcome in his world and handed me the tools for being in it. I have never lost my pleasure in and sense of replenishment from being actively caught up in the pursuits of workshop and yard.

I feel sure that these reliable surrounds and ritual doings have provided me with the rich ambience of what were the most sustaining and enhancing relationships of my first 12 years. In these settings, I tap into the most positive aspects of my memories of and identifications with the mother and uncle who meant so much to me.

It makes sense that, when I sought to do my very best in the intellectual-professional world of my idealized father, I needed the retreat and reassurance of drawing on evocations of the mother and uncle I had known. In these sanctuaries, I could be in touch with the complexities of my mother's feminine nurturing and my uncle's essential masculinity. There I could be reassured by what had sustained me in my parent's world, so full of daunting intimations of a father I could never know.

From all this comes a generalization I have some conviction about. In the familiar safety of these known places and rituals, these transference sanctuaries, we draw on transitional phenomena akin to those experienced in the analytic situation, yet richer in basic sensory qualities. We tap into latent traces of our positive experiences with one or both parental figures and draw once more on their nurturing and releasing aspects, which had helped us find our earlier way, to gain affirmation and strength to face our present and assimilate our unwanted, conflictual past.

So it is that, moved by urgencies in our patients and ourselves, we seek these special places and contexts wherein we may find the sustenance we must have to return in self-inquiry to the never finished task of repairing our troubled past, And in so doing, we come upon what we need to sustain the patient's quest.

WHAT WAS SOUGHT

Nonverbal Communication

CHAPTER 8

The Play of Transference
Some Reflections on Enactment in the Psychoanalytic Situation

Freud's (1914) renunciation of actual involvement between analyst and patient, including denying to the patient his usual visual access and cuing, has steered our science and technical craft to a focused reliance on the speaking and hearing of words and their music. The yield to all of us from the disciplined restrictions of the "talking cure" has been rich, indeed, over the past 100 years, and there is no end to the unfolding range and complexity of the instrument. We appreciate the enactive power that words and silence acquire when action is forsworn and words become tool and weapon in the regression of the analytic process. Words—how and when they are said or withheld in the psychoanalytic situation—do indeed become sticks or stones to splint or crack psychic bones.

Yet, while we do our best to attend to the patient's verbal productions, we are steadily immersed in a quiet hubbub of behavioral activities integral to the analytic situation. Hour by hour, patient and analyst are awash in a steady flow of nonverbal information: body rumblings, postural stirrings, alterations in voice timbre and rhythm, the quality of silence itself.

It is to the physical activities available to the patient otherwise immobile on the couch that I attend here: his sometimes conspicuous and idiosyncratic mannerisms and gestures occasionally noted in the analytic situation, along with those unobtrusive and repetitive small gestures that go along as steady background accompaniment to his verbal productions.

Paying attention to these couch behaviors is hardly novel. Since Dora (Freud, 1905) fingered her reticule, the analytic literature has been enlivened by excellent observation and inference. In the main, these have identified conspicuous and idiosyncratic behaviors and traced out their symbolic and expressive links to unconscious sexual and aggressive strivings and identifications based on early object relations. Feldman's (1959) engaging compendium, for example, provides a wealth of analytically informed anecdote and lore on common mannerisms of speech and gesture in Western culture.

Of those observing within the analytic situation, Deutsch (1947, 1952) provided the most extensively documented early data. He used stick-figure "posture grams" to capture all the preferred postures of 17 patients on the couch. He then aligned these with verbal content themes over many analytic hours. The impressive range and sweep of his observations, connecting different postures and relations of body parts to key figures and dynamic conflicts in the patients' verbal productions, captured much of what I have observed and provide as my clinical base. Gostynski (1951), detailing the behaviors of a female patient, noted particularly her hand gestures and thumb play, over considerable analytic time and therapeutic progress. He followed and described the temporal link between these conspicuous gestural behaviors and the patient's changing preoccupation with oedipal conflicts over penis envy, scoptophilia, and sexual rivalry with both parents. Needles (1959) provided an overview of gesticulation as a general discharge phenomenon occurring when emotional stress, as in the analytic situation, prompts a regression from differentiated speech back to its developmental precursors of motor movement and other primary-process behavior.

This older emphasis on the regressive and primitive significance of the nonverbal components of human communication has, as part of the traditional view of primary process, come under increasing challenge by a more developmentally centered viewpoint that would acknowledge a continuing place and contribution for primary-process modes in all aspects of human behavior throughout life (Noy, 1969; McLaughlin, 1978). Freedman (1977) explicitly articulated this alternative perspective:

> That physical activity serves as a nutriment, as a building block for schema formation has been widely held. . . . That activity continues to assert a sustaining influence in the encoding organization of thought throughout life has been much less documented. It is

contended here that body acts, as kinesic experience, provide the kind of support which is essential for secondary process [p. 111].

Mahl (1977), providing analytic documentation of this contention, followed certain conspicuous and repetitive postural behaviors of his patient and noted their temporal relation to later verbalized dynamic and historical themes. He concluded that the motor act preceding the verbalization facilitates and makes possible the subsequent putting-into-words.

It is this perspective that I support and extend: that the nonverbal behaviors of a patient significantly enrich and extend into experiential dimensions both what the patient is able to say to the analyst and what the analyst is able to perceive and resonate to as he listens; and that the enrichment is not just a primitive remnant of the infantile past but constitutes an integral and essential component of the full communicative capacities available to both parties in the analytic work.

A more personal reason why I consider these nonverbal cues and accompaniment important undoubtedly reflects the particular capacities and limitations I bring to the analytic quest. I need to look while I listen. I know many who wish only to listen and who grant little significance to the levels of communication and observation that are the subject of this chapter. Yet the fact, inescapable for us all, is that we must deal with this flow of information. Both parties register and process these levels of knowing and telling, subliminally and in awareness, whether we wish to or not. Automatically in the doing, we draw on communicative capabilities we have worked hard to develop from earliest childhood and cannot easily put aside. Our gestural proclivities are older than our speech and are at least as rich in their power to convey basic affective intensities. What we register, process, and convey at these nonverbal levels inevitably does its share in giving shape and content to what is communicated verbally between patient and analyst.

Off-the-Couch Enactment

Let me, in proper analytic fashion, begin at the surface with an instance of off-the-couch behaviors of a sort that undoubtedly are familiar to you. How patient and analyst meet, greet, and part may initially reflect their habitual styles and conscious motives. Over analytic time, however, these behaviors take shape from and give substance to the transferences of both participants[1] and provide commentary about the state of the analytic relationship.

Case Vignette: Mr. A.   Mr. A in late latency had lost his father and had by the time of his entry into analysis, in his mid-30s, become a chronically depressed, inhibited, and joyless man with a solidly obsessional personality. Initially, he greeted me with a quick head nod and a passing glance as he plodded by with eyes averted and face expressionless. For a year or so, once on the couch, he remained absolutely immobile except for occasional shifts of hands and arms from a resting position on his chest down to his sides. He filled the hours with flat ruminations and affectless pronouncements that leadened the atmosphere. I came often to know new levels of boredom, irritation, and heavy emptiness. Then, after about a year, he began to engage my eyes as he walked past me, even swiveling his head as he went by. Although his face remained impassive, his eyes burned with an enormous intensity that struck me at different times as yearning, hunger, smoldering anger, and pleading. His couch behavior remained still and flat. I often felt sad and stuck as I sat behind him. I became reluctant to go to the office door to admit him and found it more and more difficult to attempt to get through his wall of drear.

One day, I finally noticed something that we were repeating between us: when I was silent for most of the hour, he tended to leave in silence with that fixed burning gaze. But when I pressed myself more actively to explore his ruminations and silence as defending against painful feelings, he made no response and gave no acknowledgment that I had even spoken, but then he was slow to leave and occasionally flashed me a brief, warm-eyed parting glance. After one or two such instances in which I felt some pleasure, I also had mounting surges of impatience—so little for so much effort! Then came recollections of hours I

---

[1]In speaking of the transference of both patient and analyst, I am expressing my theoretical preference for Freud's (1912b) broader view of transference as an indispensable component of the psychic reality of each of us. This view allows the psychoanalytic situation and process to be conceptualized as an experience in shared exploration in which the analyst uses his more developed transferential capacities to sound, with the patient, the latter's primitive depths of transference so that the patient may grow to a more evolved psychic reality.

had spent in childhood coaxing near-feral young cats from their hiding place beneath our summer house—my endless kneeling in the autumn leaves with bits of food for kittens then two-months abandoned by the summer people. Although I was praised for these efforts, often I would rather have been stalking rabbits around the deserted cottages with my rifle. I pondered these memories and gradually understood better how certain early losses of my own, and the necessity to hover near the grieving ones around me, were contributing to my more than trial identification with Mr. A as a victim of parent loss. These were not new insights: what was important was to make peace with the fresh intensities I had reached through a shared regression in difficult analytic work.

I began to bring Mr. A's off-the-couch behaviors into our work by repeatedly trying to help him become aware of them and to question what was going on inside him. His response was not dramatic, but over months of nudging and grudging he developed and sustained increasingly intense feelings about me, with muted recall of his anger and stifled grief at the time of his father's death. There emerged a stark picture, poignant for both of us, of the boy in this man, living out his angry reproach of his deserting father and preoccupied mother and enacting with passive ferocity his insistence on active reparation from me, whom he saw as dead and defaulting when I was too often too silent in the regression of the shared transference.

On-the-Couch Enactments

We now come to some instances of on-the-couch behaviors ranging from striking and idiosyncratic enactments to subtle gestural kinesics. But first I must dwell on my shaping of certain aspects of the analytic situation and on a particular study mode I have used to try to capture, then record, and now convey as much as I am able of the patient's kinesics as they are played out simultaneously with his verbal productions.

In my clinical practice, I have somehow managed to arrange my office furniture, in three of four different settings, so that I sit obliquely behind the patient and to his right. I have long known that I do a lot of my listening while looking ahead with unfocused vision. This allows me a persistent, low-level awareness of the patient's movements through my left field of peripheral vision. I also have long known that each patient settles quickly into what become habitual ways of lying on the couch, ways that often speak loudly of the patient's personal style, attitude, and character.

Something else became evident. I began to be dimly aware that some patients repeated patterns of movement, of changing postural gestalts, that were not steadily present but had become familiar. They were neither recognizable nor understandable, just familiar. Direct looking did not help much. They had something to do with how the patient shifted his body, particularly his arms and legs in relation to trunk, face, couch, and each other. As I was half-watching these as I listened to verbal content, I drew the obvious conclusion that the sense of patterning I was experiencing had to do with the unity, or simultaneity, of the verbal and nonverbal data.

I began to work on a form of note taking, jotting down the patient's utterances almost verbatim while scrawling above the words brief notations as to the position of both hands and arms, feet and legs, in relation to each other and to the rest of the body. For a while, I thought my choice of when to sample was a random one. But it became gradually evident that often I felt moved to take notes of verbal content and gestures when I had perceived a familiar pattern taking shape, that I was documenting something I partially recognized. There were limits, some serious, to the extent to which I could carry out this effort. It was not difficult, using a shorthand, to note the major changes, but it was difficult, though not impossible, to record the more subtle qualities of these movements (e.g., whether hand touched hand or face in sharp striking, gentle pat, or rough stroke). Getting the full notations of verbal and nonverbal data in close coordination was possible only when the patient was in a fairly steady state in which speech and gesture were so paced that I could keep up with them. Getting my own words down adequately was, as always, difficult, and I noticed that my interventions became more tersely put. What combined with this last to constitute an insurmountable obstacle was the handicap the process imposed on my accustomed modes of listening and intervening. I could easily become too busy to hover. I first curtailed the length of my sampling to a few minutes out of any session. Then I attempted unsuccessfully truly to randomize the sample taking. Finally I put the project aside.

Nonetheless, over about four years of intermittent noting of the couch behavior of patients, plus an occasional subsequent sampling to assess change over analytic time, I had looked at enough data to allow me a modest level of confidence about what I now describe here. But I make no claims to a rigorous and sufficiently full sampling of these activities such as to dignify this effort with the title of research.

Conspicuous On-the-Couch Enactment

Case Vignette: Mr. B. As described earlier, after only a few months in analysis, Mr. B, a young man, began a ritual of lowering himself onto the couch in an unusual manner. While sitting, he swung both feet onto the couch and remained momentarily upright. Then he raised both forearms to a horizontal extension at a right angle to his upper arms and with both hands stiffly outstretched in a kind of salute, palms vertical. While doing so, he slowly lowered his upper body backward onto the couch and pillow and lay for many seconds with forearms and hands now pointed skyward. Then, just as slowly, he lowered both arms to his sides and gently folded his hands, usually left on top of right, on his lower chest. He seemed utterly unaware of this ritual. In his steady verbalizations, he dwelled mainly on his struggles to be a good husband, father, and provider for his young family, and on his vigilant warding off of his highly emotional and insistently intrusive mother. He made occasional, flat-voiced references to memories of his outgoing father, a World War II hero who died from cancer during the patient's late adolescence. There was an odd quality to his baritone voice: his sentences often began or ended with a brief, high-pitched squeak, like a pinched-off cry.

On the couch, Mr. B could be still for hours on end, making only infrequent small gesticulations of either hand. Gradually, a very pronounced and reliable lateralization pattern became evident as his motility increased. When he spoke of his mother or of matters indicating his deep identification with her, or of his wife and beloved little daughter, his left hand took to the air above his chest and waved about. When he talked of his father, the latter's "macho" and alienating behavior, or his small son's provocatively aggressive stubbornness—and his own struggles to succeed, have a mistress, and show off in his work—his right hand and arm were busily at work on his chest and in the air.

The stiff-arm descent onto the couch remained prominent, meanwhile, through most of the first year. I noticed that there were also times when Mr. B resumed this gesture—holding both forearms vertically for minutes on end—while on the couch. Usually he spoke then of flatly recalled memories of his father's last year of illness and death. But often this strange posture accompanied tense accounts of faint-hearted attempts to fend off mother's pressures to keep him the close confidant to her girlish outpourings he had been in his early youth. Over time, I built up an internal conviction that Mr. B's postural quirk was a behavioral reflection of two phantasy themes: first, that in settling onto the couch he was lowering himself into the grave of his father, about whom he was struggling in transference enactment toward me of his passive yearnings and guilt over competitive aggression, and, second, that he literally felt stuck in and with his mother through his unresolved attachment and strong likenesses. Both seemed to be actualized in his dealings with me and with the couch.

One day, I asked Mr. B to reflect on his raised hands as he talked about his father. He professed to be unaware of possible associations, and he could not develop any even when I pressed him with questioning. I did not go further. Over the next few months, however, he made slow inroads into his defenses against his grief and longing for his father, and ultimately he did some active work of mourning. The peculiar break in his voice disappeared, as did the sinking-into-the-couch ritual, once his crying literally had been accomplished. His on-the-couch hands-up gesture remained in evidence over several years, during much work done in the maternal transference, until it became absorbed into and superseded by a back-and-forth hand interplay accompanying his gradual comfort in blending his identifications with both parents.

Inconspicuous On-the-Couch Enactment

Here is an example of less conspicuous, less idiosyncratically determined couch enactment, from a portion of an hour in Mr. A's analysis, annotated in the manner I have described, and occurring some eight months after the off-the-couch episode presented earlier.

Case Vignette: Mr. A. Mr. A continued to dwell in a depressed and ruminative fashion on his joyless marriage and his lack of satisfaction in all sectors, including the analysis, but he had begun to loosen a little and to make some connections between his wife, whom he saw as self-absorbed and offering very little to assuage his needs for love, his mother, and his younger sister. He portrayed his sister as an emotionally and intellectually very limited person to whom his widowed mother protectively continued to direct most of her interest, just as both parents had always done since her birth when he was four. He was getting closer to recognizing that he was expecting as little from me as he had from his disappointing parents, but he was not at all in touch with how his rage over this and his huge guilt had combined to immobilize him.

He began the hour in his basic and peculiarly inert posture, legs stretched out uncrossed, hands folded on chest:

> But since yesterday I'm so depressed I can do nothing . . . I try to write, and I get anxious . . . spent hours organizing my cellar . . . everything neat and sorted . . . father was a methodical man, mother and sister totally disorganized and sloppy . . . father's desk with its tidy cubbyholes, mother so scattered . . . yet she was the businesswoman [left hand comes up above chest and stiff fingers thrust repeatedly rightward across chest], a sharp businesswoman . . . while father was more organized [right hand thrusts suddenly into pants pocket] . . . he was a failure [left hand again comes up and thrusts to right] . . . father had artistic talents [left hand comes up to brush across forehead and eyes] and my sister had art talent [left hand dances above face, then back to left chest, palm down; then both hands clasp softly on the epigastrium] . . . I was always between my father and mother . . . I couldn't draw, nor could mother . . . father and sister could . . . I didn't like that linkage . . . wanted to be linked with my father [arms fold across chest, left hand strokes right arm] . . . caught in tug of war . . . mother wanting me to side with her [left hand moves momentarily away to left, back to fold with right; then, during pause, both hands come up behind head to lock in cradling fashion; tone becomes soliloquizing] . . . she's obnoxious with the grandchildren . . . puts down their father . . . it was mother who pressured father into buying property . . . he did it, and it became our source of income [right hand caresses right side of face and beard] . . . he didn't have much to go on [right hand goes down into pants pocket; left hand comes up to rest on mouth while patient talks] . . . when the original building was condemned, he didn't care . . . she made him rebuild . . . it saved us . . . gave us what we needed to keep going . . . thinking now of father's father . . . his house in the city [right hand thrusts out of pocket into air above chest to emphasize *city,* then down to caress right side of face] . . . a big man

sitting here at Passover . . . I was afraid of grandfather [right hand moves quickly to pocket] . . . yet he used to bounce me hard on his knee [right hand in air pumps vigorously upward to right] . . . a hard man . . . whereas father was softer [right hand moves back to right side of face, beard and mouth in sustained soft hover and stroking] . . . remember kissing him . . . his stubble . . . a memory, an imprint [hour is coming to close] . . . I think what goes on in here is that I am torn between wanting to reach out to you . . . my father [right arm moves outward to right in sustained reaching] . . . yet I feel stuck with [left arm and head move leftward to rest on back of couch; right arm returns to chest] . . . tied to my angry, stuck mother [left hand falls onto forehead while right hand returns to pocket].

This fragment represents a typically prosaic instance of background behavior. I am sure you have found it as tedious to follow as I find it to relate. This is not an accident of choice. The descriptive words, however apt, simply cannot capture the patterned vividness inherent in the simultaneity of action and words.

I have presented two samplings of low-key behavioral enactments, both occurring in men who had suffered father loss during adolescence or early adulthood, when they much needed father's active presence to extricate them from pregenital immersion in mother, to help them consolidate and affirm a masculine identity. Both were obsessional in character structure—Mr. B being a bit more hysterical and more in touch with his feelings. Both could be said to have achieved advanced levels of psychic structure, with oedipal-phase intrapsychic conflicts readily describable in structural terms. One could say that, from their words alone, they could be known. Yet linking the kinesic behaviors to verbal content does show how much richer and more alive the dynamics of intrapsychic conflict become—as opera or ballet can convey vastly more dramatic and compelling statements of human interaction than music alone, or even music in combination with words.

Lest my sampling seem too limited, let me describe one more clinical instance, this time of a young woman, Mrs. T, whose idiosyncratic kinesic patterning, though it did indeed stand for specific historical content from midchildhood, was fed by much earlier traumata from the rapprochement period during the second and third years of life. Mrs. T had entered analysis for help with crippling anxieties that threatened her job effectiveness and capacities as wife and potential mother.

Case Vignette: Mrs. T. During her early months, supine on the couch, Mrs. T repeatedly became acutely anxious and cut off her otherwise non-stop stream of commentary about the myriad ways in which she was "up-tight" and almost unable to function. When she stopped, she declared herself "stuck" and grew silent. She often drew both knees upward and then placed both feet flat on the couch. Finally, she extended both arms downward so as to allow her to hook both forefingers around the heels of her shoes—all this quite outside her awareness. Analytic work during this time was extremely difficult.

Mrs. T could be caught up in acute anxiety that "something might happen": I might attack and damage her genitally as she lay helpless, she might uncontrollably seduce me, her mother might catch her or us, and all would be lost. In near simultaneity, it could be exciting and over-whelmingly delightful to her were I just to go ahead and insist on her sexual compliance—she with no choice but to surrender and go away with me. Indeed, she often came close to enacting these phantasies in her real life with dominating men who made sexual overtures. She seemed to feel neither that she owned her body and her sexuality nor that she could be responsible for what happened in her personal and professional life.

Gradually, an important part of Mrs. T's history unfolded: from age six to 14 she had to be examined repeatedly for what was ultimately dis-covered to be a serious bladder ailment. Over and over, she was put up in stirrups in the doctor's office and catheterized. This was done chiefly by male physicians who showed her brusque kindliness but who pro-scribed any display of feeling on her part. She was to be a good girl and lie still. Our prolonged working on this series of exercises in passive en-durance, and their coloring her experiences on the couch, had to be done before she could relax enough to participate even gingerly in the analytic work. An earlier antecedent came to light: both her father and older brother were much given to tickling the patient when she was a toddler, sometimes bringing her to helplessness and incontinence.

Mrs. T's postural gestalt continued to be played out. It showed up in what emerged as another context: her nearly unshakable conviction that to be on her own, to dare to assert emotional and intellectual separate-ness from her mother, was tabooed by the mother, and now me, and was sure cause for abandonment. Very primitive levels of separation anxiety, along with shaky object constancy, lay behind the patient's resorting to her stirrup posture. Repeatedly, she invoked this self-immobilization just as she was wishing for, or daring to experience in relation to me, re-bellious thrusts toward autonomy, active sexuality, assertiveness, or pleasure in independent functioning. She gradually recalled a painful experience from when she was three years old: she had became lost in a department store and, panic-stricken, had wet herself. Her mother re-trieved her and told the clerks that she had allowed her child to wander off and then had hidden herself so that the little girl would learn not to venture away. This screen memory became the shaping role the patient assigned to me, insofar as she saw our work as fostering her growing independence.

Mrs. T begged piteously for my help in solving her anxiety or show-ing her how to handle her anger and ward off retaliation in the outside world. Yet, when I responded, she sometimes sprang in an instant from suppliance to sitting-up rage and threatened to kill me or herself. Often she grabbed some office object, an ashtray or small sculpture, and threatened to hurl it at me or run off with it. Early on, I was jolted to vigi-lance, ready to duck or ward off a flying object. Although able to remain outwardly impassive, I felt much irritation, uncertainty, and puzzlement over what kept going wrong. Meanwhile, I grew wary and cautious.

A fresh gesture now took center stage as Mrs. T lived out her epi-sodes of fury. In this gesture, she clutched, white-knuckled, her neck-lace or pendant, a brooch, or the collar of her blouse as she cried out her outrage either that I was ignoring her misery or that I did not understand her at all. From my side, I became aware, during my too vigilant listen-ing, of a painful tension in my hands and neck. (This was during several years of such complaints, which eventually proved to be carpal tunnel syndrome.) Often I had small hand-twinges when she was being quiet and ruminating or being silent just after I had intervened. Some of these twinges happened just before an outburst or before I was consciously aware that we were headed for a blowup. In after-hours pondering on these strenuous sessions, I ruefully likened my hand signals to the whis-pering baskets the Sioux Indians carried on their heads. Dangling from the rims were small silver-tipped thongs that tinkled softly as the Sioux walked their plains and woodlands. Lore has it that these Indians had learned to become hyperalert for attack after suddenly becoming aware that the familiar tinkle had stopped: their neck tension, which quieted the small sound, was a response to ominous sights and sounds they had not yet consciously registered. This sortie into cross-cultural anthropol-ogy was small comfort, to be sure.

That Mrs. T did not carry out her threats, however, was reassuring. Meanwhile, I had grown aware that I was being spooked into excessive helpfulness by my anger and need to deny it. I began to recognize behind her verbal assaults an outrage that my not responding meant my indifference or belittling; while my interventions, when they carried even a whiff of steering her or adding to her insights, were to her a taking over of her thinking and a refusal to allow her the freedom to act independently. When I remained attentively and reflectively responsive to her predicament, but did no more, she settled and resumed work on her own. We learned much more about a piece of history already cognitively known between us: at age two she had been sweet-talked by her mother into being a big girl willing to give up her milk bottle and herself throw it in the garbage can. When she sought to retrieve it that night, it was gone. She was desolate but too angry and estranged to ask for it back or to seek comfort from her mother. I developed a better feel of Mrs. T's behaviors as reflecting old attachments to transitional objects, and of myself as transitional and unstable in her perception, needed and feared, tantalizing and gratifying. Over time, she worked these pregenital concerns out to a considerable extent: she felt greater comfort and confidence in her autonomy and capacity for pleasure in work and motherhood. The eccentric kinesics largely faded from the scene, but traces remained with her throughout, as reflected behaviorally in a continuing need to fondle or clutch some item adorning her clothing, and in her need to be assured of the possibility of renewing contact with me should she get into trouble.

Discussion

From such data as these, I have become convinced that the nonverbal behaviors of my patients are rich in allusions to meaning, motivation, and history. Through a kind of apperceptive looking, for me an integral part of freely hovering attentiveness, patterns of gestural and postural behavior take shape that are as much a patient's distinctive signature as are the shapings of his speech and thought.

I find it clinically and descriptively useful to distinguish between those behaviors that strike the eye as unusual and idiosyncratic and the more ubiquitous, unobtrusive behaviors that generally go unnoticed. These differences, though not always separable, determine how I come to understand and make clinical use of them.

Eccentric behaviors literally jump out to meet the eye and be recognized. At times, their meaning seems immediately clear, as with Mrs. T's stirrup hold. Waiting for impressions of meaning to build up through repetition and context remains necessary for validation before seeking ways to intervene, unless the patient himself is aware of what he is doing. I used to wait for long periods when the behavior lay outside the patient's knowing. Working in a tentative and questioning mode, I think it is possible to raise such matters without detriment to analytic work. Writing sensitively on this subject, Anthi (1983) showed how work on the idiosyncratic behaviors of his patients provided the basis for analytic understanding of body image formation and the preverbal base for symptom formation. In general, it is easier to engage the patient's interest in his idiosyncratic instances than in the background kinesics such as those exhibited by Mr. A and Mrs. T. I think this is because of the dramatic and miming nature of the larger movements—they have more the quality of play and playacting to them and are like dream imagery that both patient and analyst can explore and play with in a collaborative and creative fashion. I have occasionally found myself miming or internally imaging myself in the gesture, as in Mr. B's hand-arm position as he lowered himself onto the couch. Doing this leaves me with a richer affective-kinesthetic sense of knowing that movement—and the patient.

A patient's subdued behaviors, his fairly steady background kinesics, have a different impact. The changes and shifts in these positions seem trivial and random until watched over analytic time and in the context of the patient's words. Gradually, even his complete inertness, on one hand, and agitated frenetics, on the other, inescapably take on meaning. I knew for a long time that I was being informed by these behaviors, yet it was not until I had lived with my untidy notational study that I could grasp a little better the nature of the informational cues embedded in these quiet kinesics.

Idiosyncratic gestures are generally connected with special historical antecedents or particular dynamic conflict constellations, the essence of which can be visibly captured in their aptness. Background gestures speak more of intrapsychic conflict and of memories now an integral part of character and overall personality, yet still closely connected with the early object relations that helped to shape these conflicts over developmental time. I am suggesting that, in these background kinesics, one can glimpse the enactment of still active and important struggles of ambivalence over clinging and freedom, over merger and separation, over dominance and submission—child–parent relationships still being alluded to and dramatized even in patients whose well-evolved personality structure permits satisfactory application of the tripartite model.

I am persuaded in this direction by the consistency most of my patients show in linking a particular side, usually their right hand-arm, to spoken content related to themselves as active doer, to father, and, over time, to me in terms of masculinity, assertiveness, and dominance—and the other side to content connected with mother, femaleness, passivity, homosexuality, the analytic couch, and themselves as passive, the ones done to. Two exceptions remain vivid in my mind. The first was a right-handed man with active bisexual interests and given in all his relationships to reenacting an extreme anal stubborn link to his (enematizing) mother. This man gestured only with his left hand when talking of himself, his mother, and his sorties into business and sex. The other exception was a right-handed young mother, a professional woman, crippled by indecisiveness and fearful of disapproval. When talking about herself early in her analysis, she could not gesture with one hand without immediately using the other, and she showed no detectable preference for either. Yet her references to her mother were consistently flagged by left-hand movements. Clearly, each patient shows his own assignment of object meaning in this lateralizing way and is consistent within the pattern.

I am not prepared to assert that this claim to ubiquity is confirmed by my sampling. That I do not sit directly behind my patients (they lie to my left on a couch with its back to their left) may skew my data in a fashion that is at least reinforcing of right–left discrimination. What I can be reasonably sure of is that each of my patients, on my couch, tends to use his own lateralizing preferences in a fashion I have come to rely on to inform the work I do.

Deserving mention are other and more subtle patternings, of which the play of hands is a main instance—which hand covers, clutches, strokes, or picks at which, the hands' comings and goings in relation to each other, to the face and head, and particularly to their most favored resting place on the upper abdomen and lower chest. For the patients I have mentioned here, and indeed for most of my patients, this portion of the trunk is the most sought locus and meeting place for the hands, particularly the left hand, to rest. This very often is the case when these patients yearn for safe passivity, dependency, and old closeness, or retreat from independence and aggressiveness. It is probably no accident that this is so, for this bodily region is the locus to which so many poets and patients assign their emptiness, their grief, their sinking feelings and twilight yearnings—as well as pleasurable feelings of satisfaction and well-being.

This hand play, in the gestalt that includes head and trunk and the space immediately surrounding, is capable of expressing in wide range both dyadic and triadic relationships, and in these their full richness of pregenital, oedipal, and later intrapsychic conflict. Mrs. T's stirrup posture captured the immobilizing defenses she had marshaled to hold back her oedipal and adolescent urges to sexual contact and masturbatory play, as these had taken their particular shaping over years of urologic manipulations at the hands of male doctors she feared to yearn for. Her regression to immobility, with fingers clenching heels, held her in foundered bondage to a masochistic mother she feared to abandon for the exciting world of father and brother. Her blouse clutching and her trinket grabbing and discarding, in synchrony with powerful emotional intensities in both of us, were a compelling demonstration, at first for me and eventually for both of us, of the primitive uses of transitional-object dynamics brought to light in the maternal transference.

In Mr. A's instance, the continuing interweaving of dyadic and triadic conflict found quieter though still dramatic enactment in his background kinesics. Consistently, his right hand and the rightward space around his face and upper body stood for self, father, grandfather, and eventually me in our various states of weakness and strength as he experienced us in his inner life. Mr. A's left hand, and the couch it clutched, were connected with not only the oppressive mother image smothering and inhibiting him but also the protective, succoring mother who could rise up to point and stab in harsh criticism at the passive father, the right hand buried and out of sight in a dark pocket. This same right hand dove into Mr. A's pants pocket when he talked of his fear of his active grandfather; his hand then hovered softly around the right aspect of his face, beard, and lips when he spoke of his father's softness, hugs, and stubble.

I emphasize a point that these unexceptional vignettes may have made obvious: the simultaneity of spoken words and gestural accompaniment provides abundant affirmation of the prominent role of intrapsychic conflict in even ordinary behavior. Mrs. T cries out her need for freedom and autonomy while her hands clutch her blouse or trinket and her knees push tensely into the back of the couch. Mr. A's right hand reaches for closeness and likeness with his father and me while his left hand clutches the couch behind him. Mr. B asserts vigorously his wish to remain outside and free of the powerful envelopment he ascribes to his mother, and both his forearms go stiffly vertical in his coffin–caught–surrender posture. The intensity and poignancy of conflict are conveyed with an immediacy that words alone, with the exception of those relatively infrequently antithetic words voiced in the analytic dialogue (McLaughlin, 1984), cannot approximate. Adding to the impact of these moments are those equally countless others when background gestures quietly affirm and reinforce verbal content.

Most of this kinesic background usually lies beyond the conscious awareness of the patient. I have found only limited usefulness in bringing background kinesics to the patient's attention, and not for reasons of resistance. At most, a patient may relate some quality of affect to a particular gesture brought to his attention. For example, some patients remark that their resting of heel on toe—so that the upper foot, usually the right, points diagonally in the air from its perch atop the lower—looks lively or cocky. I, too, see this gesture as jaunty and playful, and often I observed it in evidence when the patient seemed comfortable feeling himself to be the admired and secure phallic extension of me in either or both parental transferences—and yet the patient carried the matter no further and quickly seemed to lose interest. Recognition and development of meaning here lay in the eye of the beholder—as is so often the case when we try to decipher what we come upon in the analytic process.

There must be important reasons that this is so. I feel that these small behaviors, these background kinesics, provide glimpses of a wealth of memories of a childhood time before speech is acquired, when relating and being are in the matrix of body contact between mother and child, and separation toward the sense of self and other finds support in the magic of transitional phenomena and the omnipotent claims of gesture.

Psychoanalysis, from its beginnings with Freud and then Ferenczi, has acknowledged the important communicative and nurturant functions, for the developing infant, of body contact and nonverbal interaction with caretakers. In his early conceptions of primary-process thinking and behavior, Freud (1900) asserted that the motoric and kinesthetic components are forerunners of the verbal communicative capacities of the growing child. In writing about early psychic development, Ferenczi (1919) noted the importance and magic of gesture and the close functional linkage and interchangeability of limb and body movements and the act of thinking itself. Since then, psychoanalysts generally have been comfortable with the concept that human thought and communication are a blend of three representational components. The infant's earliest mode is an enactive, sensorimotor–visceral–affective aggregate; his later or almost simultaneous imaging capabilities are visual, tactile, gustatory, auditory, and the like; and his verbal-lexical mode is superimposed toward eventual dominance (among many, Bruner, 1964; Horowitz, 1978), with the gradual acquisition of speaking and writing. Shapiro (1979) drew on data from psychoanalysis, kinesics, and linguistics to provide an organizing overview of the relations among the motor, affective, and verbal components of the communicative process over development and within the changing dimensions of primary and secondary process. Infant observers have had a wealth of insights into the primary capacities of the neonate to instigate and stimulate communicative interaction with a mother similarly charged with the urge for dialogue at a variety of nonverbal levels (Bullowa, 1979).

The specific role that hand and body parts have in this interaction has likewise been well examined, beginning perhaps with Hoffer (1949), who gave a central ego-organizing place to the infant's hand-to-mouth world explorings: how his touching, groping hands are extensions and organizers, *pari passu* with visual and auditory intake, for the mouth as the beginning and center of the child's developing ego. Hoffer recognized early on what has become a commonplace for us now: that the child's early ego is, as Freud (1923) said, first and foremost a body ego, and his world is built on extending his primary experiencing of his own body and that of the mother. Freedman (1977) furthered this thrust by detailing the close and necessary link between the infant's unfolding capabilities for hand expressiveness and exploration and his developing sense of self.

Another reach-of-the-hand capability is the act of pointing, which moves the child (and his observers) into the world of gestures as he grows during his first 20 months of life (Bullowa, 1979). Murphy and Messer (1979) emphasized the psychoanalytically obvious point that these hand-pointing and gaze-directing proclivities, so finely tuned between mother and baby by the end of the second year, become subsumed and overlaid by naming and other speech variants but are not lost.

Although the role of play and playfulness is of huge importance in all this, in its early forms it has been accorded little observational and analytic attention. In our field, Winnicott has probably been the most seminal, beginning with his noting the magical and real qualities of the psychological space the very young child gains as he begins to separate from his mother. Winnicott's (1953) conception of the transitional object and its phenomena as an instrument for claiming and filling this space, somewhere between illusion and reality, has provided the less imaginative among us a privileged window into the special realm of illusion, as it helps us all to realize ourselves in the world about us. His early catalogue of transitional phenomena includes "perhaps a bundle of wool or the corner of a blanket or eiderdown, or a word of a tune, or a *mannerism*" (p. 91, italics added).

I emphasize *mannerism* to strengthen the claim that gesture is, from the beginnings of internal psychic life, central to the growth and communication of that inner richness. Again, child observers have documented what we already know: that mothers initiate, and are willing to repeat endlessly, intuitively selected sequences of ritual encounters with their newborns. They tend to develop, over the first two years or so, initially body contact "games" (e.g., hugging, nuzzling, fondling) and then the sort of hand-centered games (e.g., "creepmouse," "little pigs to market") that put high focus on fingers and hands as mime, intermixed throughout with the handling and presenting of objects within the infant's visual scan, accompanied always by the music of verbal commentary.

As I see it, then, a child's earliest and most continuing (if he is lucky) developmental interactions, out of which emerge much of the shape and tune of his personality and basic expectations and adaptations, are made up of countless experiential shapings of endlessly played out nonverbal interactions—even long after verbal capabilities are acquired. I see these nonverbal levels as carrying and conveying, in authentic and affectively relevant ways we know intuitively to watch for and give weight to, import and significance on a par with or beyond those attributable to the verbal carrier in our analytic and other human dialogue.

We must grope through the sediment of time, habit, and social embedding to contact these meanings, quite lost to the patient. In the often subliminal flash and fleeting of these small gestures, we are in touch—I feel but cannot be sure—with the traces of times when touching and being touched were of the essence of knowing, when our world of doing and being was finding its map through playful explorings with hands as probe, first puppet, mime, and toy. Hand in hand, hand to heart, to mouth—these small doings lead us to the limitless knowing and telling that lie in holding and being held, in the unity of beholder and beheld.

CHAPTER 9

The Search for Meaning in the Unsaid Seen

The relevance of infant observation studies for what transpires in the adult analytic situation has been debated for as long as such studies have been reported. Briefly put, the arguments against relevance have clustered around two main contentions. From within adult analysis, a position has been taken that only those data that arise within the analytic situation, as these are stirred by the analytic relationship, are pertinent to the internal dynamics of the adult patient. From within both child analysis and child observation, a position has been asserted that the many discontinuities and accretions of change, which have been noted in human development, rule out the notion of straight-line extrapolations from infant to adult behavior.

Yet these caveats have not kept many of us, whether we do our peering and pondering behind the couch or beside the cradle, from drawing on the findings from the other field with the hope of enhancing our own knowing. In this our need is to be build bridges. Some of us build bridges to extend the healer's search for the furthering of our patient; others reach out for the pleasure of affirmation and acceptance of what we think we have found; for some, there is exhilaration in having expanded a range of knowing through links with outside others; others use bridges to support the joy of the joust and to empower the assertion of superior knowing.

However these motivations may be blended in us, they press us inescapably toward the familiar liability of observer-participant bias. In the two fields that share our focus today, this observer bias has historically slanted us toward adultomorphizing by child observers, and infantomorphizing by adult analysts.

139

As someone who has done analytic work with adult patients for more than 40 years, I continue to struggle with still evolving and conflicting views about what infant observational studies mean to me, and what contribution and complication they make to the understandings that the patient and I evolve between us.

General Significance for the Analyst

I am comfortable in my conviction that some of the data provided over these years by both child analysts and observers of the infant and toddler have had a useful impact on me as a working analyst. These observations have broadened my span of apprehension of the dynamic possibilities of meaning latent in my adult patients' behaviors and mine. They have thrown fresh light on the technical modes and precepts on which I try to base my analytic approaches. When these observations have confirmed my experience, I have had the pleasure of affirmation. When they have been at variance, I have been disquieted, challenged to rethink familiar expectations, and then I have struggled to test and assimilate their new perspective. Either way, they have added to the general chartings by which I hope to be more comfortable in my uncertainty. I see this array of inner models, or templates, to be the generic knowing that all of us accumulate over the years, through the channels of training, the lore of others, and our own experience.

This last, my own clinical experience, has been both lodestar and trade wind for my shifting course, for what I actually have lived through with each patient has afforded me the most telling measure by which to test the aptness, for me, of those mappings provided by all the other sources. Although I may appreciate and value the contributions of others, and wish to be alert to the possibility of encountering what they describe, I seem best to assimilate these into my work when they click into and throw fresh light on matters I had come upon and had struggled with but had not perceived in such a way before. I think I am describing here just another manifestation of the workings of transference in its basic significance.

It has been developmentally necessary for each of us, I suspect, to log considerable clinical exposure in order to wear down our hard spots (i.e., the lore and prescriptions of our training) so that we might become comfortable about what we retained or laid aside; we needed even more experiential time to reduce the dumb spots of plain ignorance of what we had not yet encountered, and hoped to anticipate through the lore and knowledge offered by others, as a way to enhance our discriminative capacities.

Yet it is this same steeping in clinical experience that can render our fondest convictions, our most hard-won knowing, liable to the blind spots of our personal psychic limitations and conflicts. It is then that we lapse into idiosyncratic perceptions of our patient and are apt to impose our understanding on him, or fall back on some ritual of training or the lore of others as generic sanction for some less than optimal enactment.

It is from this position of liability that all of us must assess whatever we think or feel we come to know about a particular patient, or feel we may import from the outside.

As we work to uncover and to recover, and have used the metaphor of the archeological dig to dignify our grubbing, we are especially vulnerable to the discoveries of infant observation—to us something akin to field reports about pristine primitive cultures. These perennially beguile us with fresh possibilities for the understanding of beginnings that we adult analysts cannot directly reach.

An example of this impact of imported lore on a piece of analytic work lies in the work of Margaret Mahler and her colleagues (1975). Their contributions came more or less to my attention at a time in the 1970s when I was engrossed with a project of my own that had to do with analytic looking. This project developed out of a particular bent and limitation that I brought to my analytic encounters. Hearing words was not enough. I needed to see, and respond to, the various behaviors of my patients as they lay on the couch. Here I was different from those analysts who preferred to sit completely behind their patient and gaze at a blank wall, so that they might attend better to their visual imagery. Having only limited capacities for such internal visualization, I found that I had to rely a great deal on what I could see as I listened and specifically could register in my peripheral vision as I sat behind my patient and obliquely to the right. It only gradually dawned on me, as I listened and observed in this way, that my unfocused looking was very much of a piece with my hovering listening—a synergy that enhanced my apperceptive grasp. Without trying, I began to be aware of repetitions and patternings, in some of my patients, that were shaped by the simultaneity of verbal utterances and their gestural, postural accompaniment. These patterns became familiar but often were neither recognizable nor understandable.

In the mid-1970s, I began the four-year effort to take notes regarding my patients' utterances while I made crude notations about the positions and movements of hands and arms, feet and legs. I recorded the changes of these body parts in relation to one another and to the rest of the body in as close synchrony to the spoken words as I could manage. I tried to capture nuances such as *soft stroking* and *rough scratch, slow separations* and *vigorous sweeps* and *soars.* (Stern, 1985, gave us beautiful words for these: the "forcefulness of vitality affects.") I was able to follow these patterns of words and movements over considerable analytic time and note their repetitious nature. But the effort interfered too much with my accustomed ways of listening and responding, and I had to curtail my sampling efforts. I make no research claims for this piece of work, but I amassed enough data to permit me modest confidence about some of the dynamic cues embedded in my patients' nonverbal behavior, made comprehensible when brought into the context of their words.

This combining of verbal and nonverbal content took on even richer possibilities of significance when I learned about some fairly well-documented findings regarding cross-cultural consistencies in the assignment of specific meanings to rightness and leftness. Thus, rightness (of hand, side, adjacent space) refers to father, masculinity, goodness, and self as agent, whereas leftness connotes mother, femininity, evil, and homosexuality. I had noted that many of my patients made such right–left discriminations and that each of my patients exhibited some consistency in their preferences. Reviewing Deutsch's posturology papers of the 1940s (Deutsch, 1947), I found that his primary data supported the validity of this sorting.

Two general observations took shape over time. Some gestural-postural patterns were rather striking and idiosyncratic, at times so much so that they were not difficult eventually to bring to the attention of the patient. Then we could learn about their history and significance. Dynamic conflicts, often oedipally shaped yet hinting at earlier happenings, were often captured in these conspicuous behaviors, and their historical relevance conveyed in dramatic aptness.

To illustrate, I return to the case of Mr. B, introduced in chapter 8. With his coffin imagery, he showed remarkable consistency in the deathlike body patterns that seemed so deeply linked to his father. It will not startle you to learn that problems of mourning for his recently deceased father needed to be addressed. This patient also showed re-markable consistency in gesturing with his right hand when speaking of his father, his swaggering little son, or himself as agent and in gesturing with his left hand when speaking of his mother and his deeply conflicted identification with her as immobilized martyr or when speaking of his wife and beloved little daughter.

Far more of the nonverbal kinesic patterns that I observed were of a quieter background nature. Their relation to conflict and compromise was less readily evident, and these patterns did not generally yield spe-cific historical data, however carefully approached. Yet, when watched over time in conjunction with the words, and especially when right–left gestural sortings regarding gender and active–passive assignments hap-pened to reinforce the verbal subject matter, these inconspicuous be-haviors could be read as glimpses of still active concerns over tensions around clinging and distancing, dominance and submission, angry ten-sion and quiet contentment. Here I could envision early child–parent re-lationships still being alluded to and dramatized in well-evolved adult personalities. Some of Mahler's concepts, particularly those related to separation and rapprochement, came vividly alive for me as possibili-ties, articulated from an outside vantage point, that these very early dy-namics to which she had brought our attention might be relevant for what I saw alive and kicking in some of my adult patients. I still know no way to be certain about these matters. The patterning that can be shaped from my data takes its substance from the concatenation of action, words, and affective music. The totality can be impressive, particularly when repeatedly observed over analytic time, but it remains a web of circumstantial evidence.

At this point, we must remain uncertain as to whether these clinical data have demonstrated their relevance for the issues of separation, indi-viduation, and rapprochement that Mahler (1975) helped us see through her infant research. I think that the circumstantial evidence is rather com-pelling, given its fairly clear link to very early dynamic concerns. Yet the evidence is only a mosaic, a patterning of circumstantial evidence; there is no unbroken linearity that might be logically persuasive.

As an aside at this point, I acknowledge that another reason for pro-viding this material is to portray the changes that can be discerned in the background kinesics of analytic patients as analytic work pro-gresses. The changes that patients generally experience as they im-prove over analytic time are evidenced by such nonverbal shifts as a gradual relinquishing of initial constraint and prevailing immobility, achievement of evident relaxation and more freely displayed expressive motility. The initial background kinesics tend to decline in frequency as the underlying dynamic concerns are reduced through the analytic work; they may resurface occasionally as these concerns return for further working through. I have found this pattern of changes particularly in patients with a preponderance of inhibitory neurotic symptoms and obsessional characteral disposition.

Current Resonances Between
Adult Analysis and Infant Observation

In my effort to see more clearly the communicative meanings of my patients' nonverbal behavior, I have drawn mainly on the work of Emde, Stern, and Sander, from the observational field—I can only apologize to readers whose favorite sources are not acknowledged—and I draw on only some particular fragments of observations that strike me as relatable to my adult patients.

Emde (1988) addressed the discontinuity dilemma as the "central developmental paradox"—how to deal with the analytic clinician's sense of the continuity and durability, indeed the implacability, of stereotypic, maladaptive behavior over time, and with the developmentalist's lament over the lack of predictability of behavior across time (p. 24). In resolving this paradox, Emde drew on many perspectives: developmental biology; cell, individual, and population genetics; and the transactional view in current human developmental studies. It is evident that he too was making patterns and building bridges and that he was intent on amassing the strongest aggregate of data to support his span. Emde saw genetics as influencing the unfolding of behavior across the life span, in a notably persistent way around traits of emotionality, sociability, and shyness and activity (p. 26). Yet these genetic influences require transactional involvement with the environment for their joint shaping, with no two of us having the same experience, even in the same family. As Emde put it, the "findings of population genetics point to the overriding role of the specifically experienced environment. . . . In infancy such an environment is contained within the specifically experienced caregiver relationship" (p. 27). He noted that infant research does not support the old notion of "sensitive periods" for the laying down of infant behaviors.

Further, early experience does not seem to become special by setting patterns of individual behavior. The research, instead, points to the continuity of experience as being more predictive of behavioral outcome than is the occurrence of a particular form of early infant experience. What may be formative is not that infant behavior patterns are set in an enduring way but that infant–caregiver relationship patterns are set in an enduring way. These relational styles and patterns become internalized in progression into childhood; continuing as strong influences, they become activated in similar relational contexts throughout life (p. 28). I have found this manifesto exciting. For me, these views relate nicely to what I think of as adult "transference expectancies," those hopes and fears that each of us brings to every relationship. And they mesh closely with what I find to be powerful and continuing necessities in a patient like Mr. E to keep seeking to develop fulfilling relationships despite the accretion of scars during years of only partial fulfillment. Hoary concepts like the repetition compulsion take on lively potential, seen in this fashion.

Emde cited research pointing to an array of basic motives, rooted in the primary press for activity, that are at play in the infant—intentions quite removed from our older analytic notions about the primacy of the need to reduce drives and avoid tension, but central to the revisions formulated by Loewald (1960) almost 30 years earlier. Emde (1988) was convinced that these intentions are inborn tendencies—that they operate throughout life as part-aspects of developmental regulation in general and are "continual processes that orient and reorient one's position in an expanding world" (p. 31). Two of these intentions, effectance and mastery, are ways of seeking stimulation of all sensory modalities. They are the roots of a species-wide, hereditary, basic motivational system directed toward handling increasing complexities of relating.

Another basic, social fittedness, specially intrigues me. In Emde's (1988) terms, it is a propensity for generating experience in a structured social matrix; in Bowlby's (1969) terms, it is a propensity for attachment. It is manifested at birth in the infant's hardwired readiness to participate in human interactions involving eye contact and alert attentiveness to the face, voice, smell, and feel; in his responsivity to being held, rocked, and touched; and in his capacities for cross-modal perception, orientation, and social imitation.

This propensity is manifested on the adult side as parenting complementarities essential for the unfolding of this mutual fittedness:

supporting eye contact, slow and exaggerated speech and facial expression, increased musicality of tone, and behavioral synchrony beautifully meshed in time and qualities with those of the infant (Stern, 1977). Out of this wordless interplay arises, by six months, a joint visual referencing: mother or infant following the direction of the other's gaze, the potential for a visual reality shared by the pair.

Linked with this last is yet another basic motive, affective monitoring. Well explored by Stern, affective monitoring is a preadapted capacity in the mother, hardwired in the infant, for monitoring and guiding experience according to what is pleasurable and unpleasurable. From at least three months on, expression of emotions is consistently organized along these dimensions. Emde's (1988) special interests in this area led him to propose an "affective core of self experience . . . that gives continuity to our experience in spite of the many ways we change" (p. 32). Emde argued that this core is biological and its vital relations unchanging; that it guarantees continuity across ontogenetic development, as well as continuity and understanding across the races; and that it allows us to get in touch with the uniqueness of our (and others') experience.

This capacity obtains its nourishment in the emotional signaling between infant and caregiver, evident early in "social referencing." The exploring infant comes upon the unfamiliar and quickly looks to mother. When her face, voice, and manner signal fear or anger, the infant backs off; when she signals interest and pleasure, he approaches and explores. An important finding in this domain is that positive emotions are extremely important in development from earliest infancy and are organized relatively separately from negative ones. Although the negative emotions can swamp the positive ones, the latter offer strong incentives for social interaction, exploration, and learning. Both Emde and Stern identified pleasure and interest as the major indicators of affect attunement; Emde (1988) found that the presence or absence of these positive affects in the dyad is the most sensitive indicator of emotional availability.

From social referencing comes logically the developmental step toward morality, what Emde referred to as "early moral emotions." Research into the first three years addresses the central importance of internalization, that still enigmatic process whereby external cultural constraints, hopes, and expectations become part of the young child's inner melange of fears, as well as his or her hopes for fulfillment of fondest dreams. The toddler learns "rules" of reciprocity in communicating—rules that seem to be the forerunners of tact and fairness. He implicitly counts on the reliability of the reciprocals in how the Golden Rule is supposed to work. By 24 months, he is visually eager for affirming affective responses in his other, as he behaves to her expectations. He shows what looks like pride in the gleam of her pleasure. He is as quick to fall into what looks like shame when her gleam is glum and he knows he has done wrong: he gazes elsewhere, he acts limp, his bounce is gone.

This manifesting of shared feeling is a marker of the internalizing processes by which the positive parental responses that give joy and encouragement, not just those reactions by which the parent reproves or constrains, contribute to the infant's emerging and positive sense of "we-ness." Here the roots of a shared reality, an intersubjectivity, have taken early form—developments that feed the toddler's strengthening reach toward autonomy. Emde noted that the infant, by the end of the first year of life,

> uses emotional expressions in a process of negotiation with another person. One often sees that low intensity and blended signals are presented in order to begin a discourse of emotional signalling; in this process, emotional expressions have a purpose of eliciting a set of responses from the other. . . . [that] are goal-directed and are subjected to modification in the course of achieving a mutually desired or compromised end point [p. 37].

It is Emde's hypothesis that this early social referencing facilitates experiencing of the self, of the other, and of the self with other into the "we-ness" that becomes dramatically evident in Mahler et al.'s (1975) rapprochement phase.

Emde's formulations remind me of how important it has been to me, over many analytic years, to remain observant of the manner of coming and going of each of my patients. Most of these comings and goings fall into a fairly consistent pattern to which I contribute my own consistencies. Specifically, I accompany each patient to the door and keep looking at the person's face while he or she leaves. Over analytic time and change, the variations that we shape between us break or alter these patterns in ways that of course prove to be dynamically rich when placed in full context.

Here I want to focus specifically on the moment of parting at the door. Some patients head resolutely out the door and do not glance

back. Many consistently turn or look back to make and sustain eye contact after passing through the doorway. Some, once through the door,
invariably check back a second time, with a lingering gaze that suggests a
wide range and intensity of affect. I have found that these behaviors cannot reliably be generalized, and I usually have not been able easily to address them directly. When they can be got at, it has been because work
has been done around some context that prompts the patient to address
the matter.

For a very long interval, Mr. E ended sessions in unvarying fashion.
From the beginning of the analysis, he quickly took control of ending his
50 minutes by either announcing its finish or rising abruptly in silence
and then bolting headlong out the door, eyes straight ahead. Occasionally, as he passed me, he repeated the right-hand-to-face motion and
quick glance that were part of his arrival ritual.

Mr. E had become able to intimate to me that I made him tighten up
when I questioned him about specifics or tried to enlarge on his laconic
offerings. He hesitantly informed me that he would prefer that I say little
or nothing beyond acknowledging that I had heard him. This was generally the manner of psychotherapists, and he had come to feel safe in this
mode. I complied with his request for much of the first year, during
which I heard a lot about his cautious maneuvering through what he saw
as the minefields of both his corporate working world and his uneasy
dealings with his unpredictable wife, and I pieced together some of the
shape of the history and background already sketched here.

The obvious comfort Mr. E derived from my unquestioning compliance was reflected not only in his quiet idealization of me, and in his talking a little more freely, but also in a small shift that gradually became
evident in his manner of leaving. He stopped at the closed door, hand on
the knob, volunteered a brief comment about something he had dwelt
on in the hour, and then took flight. What he said often touched on
affectively revealing detail and context that went beyond what he had
tiptoed through during the hour. He did not return to or allude to these
addenda in subsequent sessions. Although very curious, I kept my
peace. It was in this time of altered contexts that Mr. E began to open up
about his choked anger toward his wife and his mother—now to hint
that he experienced my silence as failing to meet his need to be helped
more actively. Yet when I tried to revert to my more accustomed mode
of floating questions and surmises, Mr. E again fell into his earlier state
of aggrieved quiet and obvious tension. I was puzzled and watchful.

This was the uneasy state of our relating when we created our enactment of his bloody finger-ripping and my jarring intervention, on the heels of which Mr. E reverted to his earlier mode of quitting the hour.

It took several months of Mr. E's withdrawal and my efforts to explore and repair before he resumed the leaving mode I have just described. It was during his seconds before "takeoff" that he first provided glimpses of his pain and letdown and dropped hints about his muted rage and stubborn defiance. In each subsequent hour, I made no direct reference to these over-and-out remarks. Instead, I spoke recognitively of such matters as the necessity of his moving deeper into himself, and the power of his silences as reproach to me and protection of both of us. I also spoke of my chagrin and regret for having hurt him. Mr. E showed surprise and wariness. In all his years, he had never heard his mother once express regret for anything. In silence, he was lonely but safe. From this came another hit-and-run remark at the door: his reproach about the inadequacy of my acknowledging chagrin. This time, bringing his comment into the next hour, I told him of its strong impact on me: that I was struck by how right he was and how wrong I was for assuming that I had conveyed the regret and apology I truly felt about my not perceiving how it really was for him. It was in this context that he likened an authentic apology to Unguentine, a salve applied to the surface of the skin. I had some sense of having reached him a little. At the same time, I thought of an old and family-worn protest made in response to the perhaps too facile apologies of someone who had just been wounding: "Cut my head and give me a plaster!" The Irish have been known to hold a grudge.

So, too, it took me more analytic time and continued efforts to reach out and touch in nonjarring ways in order to sustain Mr. E's cautious venturing into more explicit speaking. He was ever vigilant and ready to pull in. I thought of anemones or, more familiar to me, the wood turtles and other touch-me-nots of my rural youth. Only later, when he had grown much bolder, did I think of snapping turtles.

In those times of timid sorties, Mr. E found speaking patterns, hesitant ways that made the goal of free association but a wistful dream. He began to float ideas and opinions out to me in little flat bursts, interspersed with silences. His thoughts had an either–or quality; they always involved opposites and were heaped with tentative qualifiers. He could keep these going for a while. When I said nothing, he gradually desisted and became silent and glum and then nonstop in leaving; when I responded to engage the substance of one burst, he gave voice to the opposite, but then might linger at the door; when I tried in any fashion to speak about both sides that I had just heard, he withdrew abruptly into prolonged silence, and his departure was quick. His shutdowns were more prolonged, and his swift exodus predictable, when I called attention to his bracketing mode or when I attempted to address the two sides of the content itself from the standpoint of conflict or ambivalence.

So, once more I settled, over what seemed like a long time, for responding to each burst with some small comment, sometimes just a grunt. Gradually, Mr. E began to combine these opposites into a single offering and, then, so very slowly, to venture a preference for one side of the matter. I would like to say more about our slow reaching and probing, but I can only touch on them here. Mr. E obviously adapted my mode to his rather different purposes. During these times, I had many silent associations—to bats, submarines and sonar, airports and artillery, weather watchers and radar. Luckily, Mr. E, as he grew more relaxed and could be comfortable when I spoke, told of seeing a videotaped movie, *Das Boot,* that had engrossed him, for he had from boyhood been fascinated by submarines. I, too, had such a longtime interest, from reading Jules Verne and Tom Swift to being aboard a troop ship crossing from New York to Rabat during the U-boat siege of World War II. Submarines provided a metaphor that we were able to use in many rich configurations. We had a common tongue for speaking of his hiding his vulnerabilities, as well as his "firepower," which frightened him. We had an idiom through which we could allude to his trying to locate and "fix" me without betraying his own position. These modes had become his habitual ways of relating to people of significance to him—for instance, his forever checking with business associates and superiors and his exhausting himself and others in getting multiple opinions to guide him to the safest course for a current project or undertaking for which he was responsible. We dwelt more and more on his almost lifelong close monitoring of his mother and sister—his testing with cautious words and vigilant scrutiny their smallest reactions. My inner perceptions of him grew vivid: a chronically anxious toddler, hungry for and never certain of secure affection, too often blindsided by sudden attack just as he had begun to savor the offering of what he needed. Smoldering with outrage he dare not show, Mr. E had learned to take what he could, while bobbing and weaving, sounding and scanning.

Much of what Emde, Stern, and others have described as the optimal parenting qualities essential to the infant's development had been patently lacking in Mr. E's instance, or had been given to him in bewildering admixtures of nurturing and sudden rejection. Rather neat parallels can be drawn between Mr. E's adult needs simply to be allowed to hear affirmation, and to be accepted as he was, and the infant's need for pleased or even joyous participation in his exuberance of being. Similarities can be drawn between Mr. E's needs to explore the permissible boundaries of his world of relationships in work and loving, and to be supported in the doing by dependable cues from his others, and the infant's needs to explore, first with mouth and hands, the immediate reaches of his body and mother's, and then to extend foraging into the infinity of his world, with his seeing, locomotion, and speaking, all dependably supported by affirming and beckoning primary others. But these others he did not have, or he had them only in unreliable ways that could have been magnified by his avoidance and cooling down. And his parents, well into his adult life, remained quite consistently like he had described them to be from his earliest memories.

So I have no sure way of knowing whether the adult behaviors of Mr. E are relatable to the time dimensions of the infantile pea-patch in which Emde, Stern, and others have been hoeing and cultivating. Some collateral data from my grubbings—such as Mr. E's having chronically to struggle against overeating, and his early-childhood suffering with respiratory allergies and with moderately severe atopic eczema on his arms, back, and face—may by inference allow us to think of early, preverbal traumata.

Here is the best that I have been able to do in building my portion of the bridge on which Mr. E and I might shakily join hands.

Infant researchers have shown us a lot about affect attunement and "checking in," about the infant's need for affirming emotional responsiveness from the mothering person. These researchers have pointed to what may result when these essentials are lacking. For instance, the accumulated rage and frustration of the too often betrayed child may make him dead or nonresponsive to some of the good stuff that might also come his way. This makes sense to me in terms of Mr. E and similar others.

Mr. E's cautious glance to check in with me visually when he was entering the room seemed aimed at identifying my affective attitude toward him, but he did not really engage me long enough to be sure of it.

On the couch and deprived of eye knowing, he attempted to locate me ideationally and affectively with his verbal bracketing. While waiting for my response, he sometimes began in brief bursts to scratch his cheek or neck, often with his right hand. He stopped when I spoke. When he found my words nonthreatening or affirming, he seemed to have found me—found me not wanting, and he need not want. His bodily relaxation was visible, and he massaged his face or neck gently, with either hand—or with both hands, once more on his epigastrium, linked together in mutual stroking. On leaving after such moments, he tended to linger longer at the door and, gradually, to tell me of his doings in an almost confiding way. When I tried to do more than he could tolerate, or when my voice began to match his flatness, he flattened out and fled, as I have described.

Such behaviors strongly suggest the persisting needs of the battered and angry child to check out his Other in the hope of finding dependable affirmation, so that he might relax and expand in the comfort of support and acceptance—or recede, disappear, when he could not find the assurance he wanted.

I have found that I tend to use formulations around affect attunement as fresh metaphors for guiding and justifying my analytic behaviors. The effect on me of recognizing their aptness has been very like what these "social-referencing" experiences are said to be for the child. I felt immensely affirmed in what I had found, in my own fashion, to be right, and then I felt renewed energy, excitement, and interest in further exploration and involvement with my patients.

These observations also "set into resonance" or, one might say, "evoked into companionship" what Spitz (1957), Winnicott (1965), Fraiberg (1980), and a host of clinical analysts since Ferenczi have asserted about the necessity of engagement. I became increasingly able to hear these voices. In response to their affirming my own sounds and soundings, I have found it easier to be a much more responsive analyst in as many ways as I can fathom—my "neutrality" now a stance in which I try to acknowledge the positives as well as the familiar negatives that make up the patient's affective being.

Yet, even in the affirming excitement of new knowledge, I find myself holding back a little as I ask: is this really so, for my adult patients and me? I remember too well my heady exhilaration, 40 years earlier, using all the lore about the translative power of primary process and riding, astride my conquistador's saddle of analytic certainty, the royal road to the treasures of the unconscious. I had my small share of therapeutic trophies back then, too. But I also had my share of saddle sores and croppers.

In speaking of my caveats, I am aware of having arrived, literally and figuratively, at a place and in a context in which these new observations of the engaged infant have, for quite a while, enlivened the exciting perspectives of intersubjectivity and self psychology. I know that I am playing catch-up with such authors as Beebe and Lachmann, Stolorow, among others, for I have been slow to acquaint myself with the rich literature that has been the harvest these two modern analytic perspectives have derived from aligning their observations with these studies of the engaged child.

Yet I keep thinking of the earlier analytic babies others have discovered in our adult patients—the polymorphous yearning and puzzled Little Hans of Freud's ken; the raging-biting/remorseful baby of Klein (1957); the dependent-respondent baby of Winnicott (1958); the attached baby of Bowlby (1969); and the psychosomatically stricken babies that were my special concern in the late 1940s—those babies who had to deal with what might be thought of as the negative of engagement, the aloneness of solitary sleep as well as the infinity of parentally imposed dispositions of times of hunger, restlessness, and discomfort.

I keep thinking of the biological complexities of the brain and of the deprivations and outrages that could release our reptilian fundament. Fanciful, to be sure, but there are components of drive theory to which I would like to cling a while longer, in obeisance no doubt to the Sphinxes and Bigfoot, but more immediately to acknowledge the biological, genetically prepared implacability of some forms of destructiveness I have encountered. In this, I seem unable or unwilling to put aside my medical perspective, which I want always to respect and suspect.

As a commonplace instance, I have come to expect that, when up against those extreme situations that stretch or burst the limits of my clinical capacities, I am most likely to fall back on notions of primitive or deviant organic-brain level functioning, as befits my medical-Freudian grounding. I have picked up my small share of undiagnosed brain tumors and thyroid and other hormonal dysfunctions and have resorted to prescribing psychotropic medications, with at times positive effects. These cases have been clinically gratifying, but I am willing to remain uneasy about these doings to the patient, lest they deflect from my primary commitment to doings *with* the patient.

My conception of the collaboration implicit in doing-with centers on the relativism of knowing. On this I base my conviction that seeking to understand the patient's reality view (for me, synonymous with psychic reality) is the primary task of the analyst. This conviction is itself based in my clinical experience of seeing how the patient's recognition of my seeking this level of understanding can touch, nurture, and release him or her in ways that lie at the heart of analytic healing and growth. I do not know how this works. The concept of empathy does not encompass it. But I see it work.

Observations by Emde, Stern, and many others have thrown some affirming light on this particular way of seeking attunement. My attempting rigorously to work in this seeking, questioning mode and my struggle toward ways to do it better have occupied my analytic interests. Working on and consulting on the specifics of my contributions to this form of collaborative seeking have brought me, over and over, to the realization of how fiendishly difficult it is to minimize the imposition of our own viewpoint, which so much embodies our preferred theory and personal experience. And these preferences in turn reflect our reality view as shaped by our past, and now focused on our patient.

I think you can hear some passion in how I speak of these matters. It has taken me longer than I wish it had for me to stand somewhere near Hoffman (1992) and others who have espoused what I think is designated as a constructivist position. In recent years I have been called a constructivist, more recently a Schwaberian—just as in past years I was seen as a classical and then a dubious Freudian. I do not know how others have lived with their designated categories, but I have felt simultaneously a mild pleasure in "So that's how I come across!" and a stronger protest in "No way! I see and shade too many things quite differently."

Behind these reactions lies an unwillingness to be categorized. In being labeled, I experience the unease and diminishing of not feeling truly understood. And then I hear echoes of patients' voices, evoked companions in many painful experiences.

This is why I need to emphasize truisms. I need to remind me, and you perhaps as well, never to become too committed to preferred ways. Whatever they may be, we cannot escape them, and we will always convey them to our patient, will always be asserting some suasive pressure, however subtly and considerately.

Yet I do believe that a questioning stance, from a position of genuinely not knowing the patient's idiosyncratic view, holds the most promise both for helping the patient and for reaching levels of analytic data that can convey more of the patient's internal life, less of the analyst's imposed knowing.

And, having stated this ponderous manifesto, I shall try to keep questioning my questioning.

CHAPTER 10

Touching Limits in the Analytic Dyad

In the intimacy of the analytic relationship, the violation of permissible boundaries remains a continuing and unsettled concern for analyst and patient. This is so whether touching is defined only as actual physical contact of whatever nature between the pair or includes those psychic equivalents of touching that are powerfully actualized in the analytic dialogue.

The topic of touching has always been complicated by its connections with the unsettled liabilities of physical intimacy, sexual and aggressive, between the analytic pair. The specter of this ultimate excess has made almost impossible a dispassionate assessment of the technical implications of lesser forms of physical contact. And the proscriptive power of our conventional taboos has often left us open to, and justified in, well-intended analytic behaviors that breached and traumatized the boundaries and necessities of our patient.

It is my hope in this chapter to scan a wide range of analytic touchings, from actual to symbolic, toward a more encompassing appraisal of their place and significance, for both parties, in legitimate analytic work.

The course of any analysis can be described as a mutual exploration of the communicative boundaries of one by the other in the intimacy of the analytic dyad, with the aim of both parties to reach the core of the other while protecting one's own. Each hopes to get what he or she needs through contact with the other and to avoid suffering its opposite. And what each of us needs from the other, whether on the couch or behind it, is at depth pretty much the same for both. We need to find in the other an affirming witness to the best that we hope we are, as well as an accepting and dependable respondent to those worst aspects of ourselves that we fear we are. We seek to test and find ourselves in the intimacy of the therapeutic relationship, to become known to and accepted by the other, in whose sum we may more fully assess ourselves.

A shift to spatial metaphors may help in this awkward formulation by allusion to the distance, or its lack, between any two of us, as the space in which this engagement will take place, for better and for worse. The metaphor allows us to picture another aspect of each of us, that inner and guarded space that Modell (1990) depicted for us as the private self and that Winnicott (1965) before him described as the true self. It is this true and private self that comprises the core, both good and bad, of what we feel ourselves to be. It is this private self that provides inner stability and nourishment. Yet it is also the hiding place for those most unwanted and troublesome aspects of what we fear we are and wish we were not. It is this aggregate that we zealously protect, keep mostly hidden, and cling to as our essence. It is what we bring to the other when we engage in the analytic dyad.

Staying in the spatial metaphor, we can envision each of us as having set up our alerting systems, our defenses, as far away from, or as close to, our private self as we need for comfort. We know how far flung and concrete these perimeters can be, from national boundaries to the walls of home, from our left front fender to the cut of our clothing and fingernails, from the mote in our eye to the flaw in our loving. In the therapeutic engagement, we know that no outreach is beyond the early warning radar of a particular patient and how little it takes at times to set ours jangling. If any good is to come from what the analyst does, he needs to subordinate the primacy of his own needs so that he never presumes to know the ground on which he treads or claims right of access to posted fields.

In seeking to touch, the analyst needs to be comfortable about his fears for the privacy of the self that he carries in him. Then he may be open to the deepest stirrings of the patient, as these touch comparable depths in himself. And he needs to be secure enough about his disciplined control of his own liabilities and assets as to be open to their testing and stretching under the challenge of clinical pressures.

Yet in reaching for these ideals, we inevitably falter, obstruct the patient's quest, or limit his reach to touch and authenticate those depths in himself that he needs to make peace with with the help of our shared knowing. As we thread our way through his brambles, we trip over the big feet of our self-interest, then stumble to stand on those same feet to resume the quest for the other. This awkward formulation of a tension inevitable to the effort of any two minds to meet lacks the spare elegance of Buber's (1923) distinctions between the I–It of the manipulating relationship and the I–Thou of mutuality, and yet it may speak more closely to the uncomfortable actualities of an often ambiguous reality we seek to know. Although this acknowledgment of an inherent interpersonal tension is now a commonplace in our field, it is far from the traditional stance prescribed for the analyst—a stance I happily assumed as I emerged from my training in the late 1940s and have sought ever since to alter in my own analytic perspective.

The prevailing view of analyst and patient at that time, and surviving to this day, tilted the exploratory focus to the patient as the object of inquiry by a knowing analyst working from a position of objectivity and emotional detachment. The analyst's promised comfort was that of a claimed superior grasp of reality up against the turmoil and demands of a patient beset with infantilisms and characteral deformations. This conception of the analyst's priviledged position at the same time imposed on him powerful constraints and ethical expectations that he not exploit the disadvantaged patient for his own sexual and aggressive satisfaction (Freud, 1911, 1912a, 1913, 1914, 1915a).

The tilt in this view shaped an analytic frame that prevails to this day, for better and for worse. This frame requires that the patient put aside most of his habitual and trusted modes of sensing and monitoring his boundaries and how he reacts to possible dangers. Assured of the safety provided by the disciplined and abstinent analyst, the patient is asked to relinquish the option to run or fight, to forgo the cues of physical touching, and to put aside the visual scanning of the face and body of the other that customarily provides cross-validation of what he is hearing. This analytic mode powerfully channels discourse, particularly for the patient, both backward into the body language of skin and gut, where the private self takes its base, and forward into the separateness and distance of verbal-auditory exchange, where the boundaries of the social self can never surely be set.

Small wonder, then, that boundaries are in doubt when words in analysis take on the muscular force and subtlety of fist and fingertip, when body movements and gurgles speak to be heard by ears that are schooled to hear words.

The traditional analytic stance shaped by this perspective has proved its power and utility, given an analyst and a patient capable of living up to its demands and constraints. This austere stance, at its height in the 1950s, became idealized in the myth of the fully analyzed analyst, and its expectations overzealously inculcated in many of us trained in the United States in the years immediately after World War II. I tried to convey the nature of what this situation was like for me and others around me (McLaughlin, 1993a). Ours may have been an unusual happenstance, but I doubt it. In his introduction to *The Spiritual Life of Children,* Robert Coles (1990) provided an account of the constraints of his training in psychiatry and psychoanalysis at an East Coast analytic center at the height of the heady certainty of the 1960s. Coles's account adds sound, substance, and continuity to what I found analysis to be like for me a decade earlier. A more objective and enduring instance is central to my concerns.

Until relatively recently, countertransference as term and concept carried invidious connotations of defects to be expunged—the telltale mark of an inadequate or incomplete personal analysis. As Tower (1956) noted in her protest of the 1950s, open discussion of the private, especially sexual, experiences of the analyst was almost impossible. Only slowly has it become possible, perhaps even respectable, to speak openly of the psychology of the analyst—an easement to which I have been privileged to add some share (McLaughlin, 1961, 1975, 1991).

Through these freedoms, we have become better able to draw on the counsel and support of colleagues. Consultation with peers is the most effective external guide and restraint to which we are likely to turn. I have found consultation particularly indispensable to my sortings in these matters of intimacy and limits. I believe that in my papers on the analyst's dynamics I have touched common chords of shared experience with any analyst trained at any time. I believe that struggles to overcome limitations on open searching and seeing—in my case, limitations set by a combination of what I was trained to know and my own internal constraints—are inevitable in our discipline. They are rites of passage, from which none of us is spared.

I have come to see that my hard spots (i.e., allegiances to givens taught to me) often provided justification for my blind spots of personal need and bias. They safeguarded the self-serving adaptations of the narcissistically tinged I–It mode that is part of our ordinary relating. At the same time, ethical constraints that warn of the disasters of sexual intimacy and aggressive excess were indeed helpful in those brink moments narrowly averted. I think that such moments are inevitable for young analysts still not seasoned in the work and perhaps not yet based in a satisfying personal emotional life. I know that the memory of such close calls can become a durable part of the analyst's early warning system.

Balanced against these self-serving motivations and obstacles lie, in each of us who needs to be a therapist, urges that led or drove us to our peculiar calling, with its altruistic demands for I–Thou relating and its constraints on satisfaction of personal strivings. In myself and in those I have been privileged to analyze or supervise, I see this press to do therapeutic work as deriving from a need to master unacceptable sexual, aggressive, and narcissistic urgencies directed initially at the primary others of our childhood. Over developmental time, our efforts at mastery evolved into character traits, both sublimative and reactive, of altruism and service to others—traits anchored in nurturing maternal identifications.

Such a therapeutic investment fosters the deep involvement necessary for significant work (McLaughlin, 1961). But such commitment carries the possibility for the revival of conflict in the therapist in the face of fresh clinical provocation. The work ego of the analyst (Fliess, 1942; Olinick, 1980) is built from these old strivings and their neurotic compromises, is reworked into new capacities shaped by personal analysis and the lore of training, and is based in identifications with and allegiances to one's own analyst and with other mentors. As a new psychic structure, this professional identity is susceptible to strain and breakdown under pressures both inside and outside the analytic situation (see chap. 4).

Over my years of analyst watching, my respect has grown for the intregrity and tenacity of the need, in so many of us, to wrestle with our impediments to doing our best work on behalf of the patient. Although the pain of lapse and shortfall has its narcissistic base in prompting us to do better, our dogged return to engagement with the patient speaks for the strength of our need to relate to and help another. And it is that rueful readiness to look to our own part in shaping the complications of the analytic venture that points to the deeply personal roots of responsibility felt and taken.

I have lingered in this background context of the dynamics of the healer to provide a richer context in which to address clinical matters involving the common thread of touching and being touched. Only some of these matters have to do with actual physical contact between patient and analyst. Mainly (and there is a word that neatly speaks of a hand pointing and touching in emphasis), I am talking about how the sensitivities of both parties are steadily deployed in a highly tactile fashion, groping to be in touch with and getting the feel of the allowable limits of the other in the effort to collaborate. Poland's (1975) definitive paper on the function of the analyst's tact alludes to much of the ground that I traverse here. Poland made clear that tact is the handmaiden of empathy: "Tact follows empathy. . . . Empathy might be considered to be on the sensory end of one source of insight. Tact is on the motor end." And he noted the etymology of what I am emphasizing: that the roots of tact lie in touching, for him in the touch of the mother sustaining contact with the child bent on separation.

The Challenge of Actual Physical Contact

Actual touching, actual physical contact, between therapist and patient is the subject of still unsettled debate in the psychotherapies in general. The manifest issue of the ultimate possibility of overt sexual involvement continues to be so emotionally charged as to make it still difficult to explore the technical assets and liabilities of other levels of physical contact.

Within psychoanalysis, there is by now a well-documented history of our group need for some of our time-honored injunctions against sexual and aggressive excess. These are as necessary as ever, insofar as they provide ethical constraints against our most self-motivated and potentially destructive impulses. It is unfortunate, however, that the prohibitions against these extremes became absolutes that encompassed the entirety of the analytic relationship. True, the yield of our reliance on the verbal carrier has been rich, but we have learned that for many it has limited the comfortable explorations of other levels of communication.

In the years of my greening, even a handshake was to be avoided, unless one was a bona fide European or was trying to be accommodating toward a patient who was. I do not recall how many volunteered handshakes I flappingly avoided or cut short without even watching for the consequences of my discourtesy. Some insistent patients persevered, and my hand was wrung and soon wrung back. I like handshakes, anyway. I have watched this ritual contact over the years and have become comfortable shaking hands with some before a session, or after, or both.

Handshakes come and go with some patients, stay consistent with others for the duration. The cue comes from the patient. Without making it a matter of conscious attention, I have somehow found it easy to remain in touch with the individual differences among my patients. I

know that I welcome a handshake and rely on its varying qualities to receive and convey valuable information, and I am certain that the patient
does the same. Sometimes these qualities receive our overt analytic attention, but often they do not. Try as I may, I cannot see that this form of
touching has obstructed the progress of the analysis. On the contrary, I
have had patients who, when terminating, have told me of the positive
aspects of my handshake. The handshake provided for them a surer
sense of knowing I was there and in what kind of contact before our longer relating through the oral–aural reaching could be relied on. It had
been helpful that the handshake was continued thereafter as another
way to check in times of doubt.

Touchings that occur while the patient is on the couch are more subtly textured. To begin with, the varied meanings of "patient on the
couch," for both patient and analyst, tend more readily to be suffused
with sexual and aggressive undercurrents. These need to be sounded,
never taken for granted or treated lightly. I live with, and constrain, the
impulse to reach out and touch the hand, the shoulder, the cheek of a patient who is in abject misery. My experience of fingers touching, of
hands holding, has gradually stretched to my being comfortable reaching out responsively at times to touch the hand reaching back toward me
for support, consolation, or my presence in the face of the patient's not
yet speakable yearnings.

I put these matters vaguely to suggest the powerful ambiguity of such
moments when the intentions of the patient and my own press to respond are yet to be named, let alone understood. As experience and aging have enhanced my span of ease, I have taken the position that I will
make finger or hand contact in match with what is proffered and without requiring that the appeal first be explored and its meaning understood. Having grown much more attuned to pregenital stirrings in my
patients and myself and having come to some peace about sexual matters, I much prefer to be available to respond to the turmoil around early
relational struggles that, more often than sexual or seductive urgencies,
drive such reaching out for hand-touch or holding. I find that this responsiveness facilitates, rather than hinders, the patient's consequent
analytic seeking. This stance has not prolonged or increased these interactions. To the contrary, the need, now satisfied, tends to subside as
fuller verbal contact becomes possible between us. When my response
has stirred some erotic feeling in my patient, these feelings still have
remained analyzable.

I know that, in stating things in this fashion, I am at odds with my peers who hold to the letter of complete physical abstinence. Casement (1982) argues persuasively the merits of this position. In my experience, the kind of abstinence he advocated has often led to what I see as iatrogenic wounding and unnecessary suffering (Pizer, 1992).

Admittedly, risk and uncertainty are always part of an analyst's responding to felt needs for sustenance and comfort. Where and in whom, indeed, is the need located? In seeking to find out, I still draw support from my ethical constraints, and direction from the ideal of my commitment to the patient's best interests. I do not wish to sound complacent about these matters, which earlier caused me much concern. There seems to be a rueful truth to the old analytic adage (its vintage attested to by its sexist phrasing) that "analysis is an old man's game."

One incident from my training years remains in memory as an early breaking of the touching barrier—one that helped me reconsider the generic taboo.

Clinical Vignette: Ms. A. I had to handle in ad hoc fashion a problem with a fragile patient until I could bring it to my supervisor. Ms. A was an intellectually gifted and chronically anxious young woman who, in her second year of our work, had hinted about having been sexually fondled as a three-year-old by her doting and alcoholic father. Having revealed this, she fell into a misery of intensified anxiety, prompted in part by what she later told me had been my too eager efforts to get her to tell me more. She withdrew into depression and self-recrimination for what she felt to be her betrayal of her father to me. She had twice that week, in the midst of bewailing her disloyalty, sat up on the couch and begun wordlessly and tearlessly to bang her head hard against the coarse grasscloth wall covering. The first time, she gradually heeded my urging her, from my chair, to try to stop and to talk. She stopped but did not talk. There was an abrasion on her forehead. The next day, speaking of the same topic, she resumed her head-banging, this time even more vigorously, and continued despite my verbal interventions. I left my chair to place my hand between her forehead and the wall and told her that I really had to try to keep her from harming herself. She pounded my palm with her head for a few seconds, then grasped my hand with both hers and fell back on the couch in convulsive sobbing. Several minutes went by before she released her grip. She got to her feet suddenly and fled. I could sense in neither of us any sexual stirring in the episode, but I wavered

between feeling right about what I had done for the patient and concerned that I had blown the analysis.

Fortunately, the next day I saw my supervisor, a scholarly man with
great Viennese grace. He listened to my tale and shook his head. He said
that he had never had to do that, but it did not seem too bad. I should give
some thought, however, about how to keep this from becoming libid-
inized through repetition. On the train back to my office, I reflected first
on how his counsel reminded me of confessions and absolutions I had
known: "Go now, and sin no more." But being also eminently wise, he
had added, "There is no way you can rationally assess this until you have
thoroughly tried to find out what it meant for your patient." The full implications of this counsel did not strike me for many years, when I arrived at a
conviction about the central importance of such inquiry into the personal
reality of the patient, as the basis for any piece of analytic work.

Ms. A in the next hour seemed to have returned to her usual cautious
constraint and perhaps was a little less guarded. And I was relieved to be
safely and correctly in my chair. She did no more head-banging and
could not be directly engaged in pursuing its meanings. She was able,
fortunately for both of us, to let me know that she felt that my coming
out of my usual silence to explore her relationship with her father was
making her intolerably anxious, and she feared she might go out of control. I toned down my conquistador yen to exploit what I had seen as a
weakening of her resistances. We came to work well together. My cautious reticence luckily suited hers, and we did no harm to each other as
she made her substantial gains.

Several years farther down the analytic road, Ms. A was able to tell me
that this enactment between us had been crucial to the furthering of her
analysis—that to feel her head touching my hand, and not the harsh wall
covering, as she banged on it, had been immensely reassuring to her.
Here, she had discovered, was a hand that did not try to manipulate her
or to poke fingers into her for its own reasons—a hand that did not stay
aloof and out of touch in aversion to her as untouchable. Its being tangi-
bly there and protecting her allowed her a dawning sense that I might
not take advantage of her were she to reveal her secrets. Sensing this
gave her the courage to risk telling me at the time how I had added to her
distress, despite her wariness of me as bent on pursuing my own ends.

During these same early years, others like Ms. A puzzled and concerned me with their acute sensitivity to my interventions, so evenly and
incisively delivered. When I had got it right, some in their apparent

gratitude and relief reached back to seek my hand or hugged me on leaving, but I aloof. Sometimes, for good analytic reasons, for the sake of
eliciting more data, I steadfastly put off responding in kind or answering
their questions. Certain patients responded with distress and anger, followed by regressive withdrawal. Some attacked me verbally. Others put
their own silence and distance between us and conspicuously acted out
their distress while away from me. Occasionally, on leaving in obvious
frustration, a patient would grab my hand or hug me in what felt to me a
mixture of defiance and appeal.

Here were two very different contexts for being hugged. I was surprised, puzzled, and uneasy over the relative flurry of activity breaking out
around me—turmoil that I regarded as the patient's resistive breaching of
my analytic rules and her sabotaging of our analytic potential.

These actings-in by my patients, moved by what seemed to be very different emotions and reasons, were most troubling to me in this time of my
seasoning. My refuge in my presumed detachment had been blown away.
Their actions had flushed me out of my illusion of safe distancing and
grabbed us too close for (my) comfort. Inside, I had to deal with the fresh
surges these immediacies added to the sexual and aggressive, pleasurable
and repulsive, feelings and impulses between us. I had anxiously been
handling these as best I could from the safety of my analytic chair and
was lucky to be able to hang on to the staying powers of those powerful
proscriptions of training to shore up my personal constraints.

My distress and uncertain sense of hold on my analytic capabilities
soon pressed me to my second personal analysis, with Charlotte Babcock. My work with her, so much more engaging and challenging than
had been the rather solitary foragings of my earlier effort, opened me to
my feminine side and to fresh perspectives on the different levels of my
sexual and aggressive loadings. I became far more accepting of the hungry need, resonant in me as well as in my patients, for the give-and-take
of mother–child physical closeness and the urgency in us toward action
to evade, assuage, or avenge the pain and rage consequent to their lack.

Through that second analysis, I came upon a comfort in resonating
to developmental nuances of need and caring that had not been
reached in my prior explorations of my masculinity. I am convinced
that this comfort added a gut-level understanding of the sort that
makes impulsion to action less obligatory for the analyst, and then for
the patient as well. Some of these patients have less of a need to hug, to
act on impulse, when I had my own tendencies better in hand and could

listen and respond differently to their urgencies, which previously would have struck me as provocatively sexual or aggressive. And in the realm of my personal life, I gained enhanced capacities for gratification in the intimacies of being husband and father.

In this double enhancement that I have just sketched lies an important truism, one vital to matters of analytic boundaries and ethical observances. It is so obvious as to deserve overstatement. It is this: the real and impressive enhancements that accrue, through personal analytic effort, to the analyst's work ego and capacities for living are at the same time vulnerable to lacks and losses that occur both within and aside from his analytic work. His optimal analytic capabilities are best secured when gratification and sustenance are by good fortune adequately available in the larger context of the analyst's life.

To return to the complexities of hugging and touching: as I grew more comfortable, I was able to observe that these brief encounters often did not seem to carry for some patients the levels of discomfort and sense of boundaries being violated that I earlier had been apprehensive about. Indeed, the attention of these patients seemed more anxiously centered on how my anxieties, or my comfort, had come through in my responses. These disparities intrigued me. They brought to the foreground the complexities of a proscription that seemed both bulwark and barrier.

I gradually found that being hugged or touched by patients of either sex became an experience I did not need to cut off, or prolong, during the playing out of its many levels of similar or different meaning both for patient and for me. One obvious finding worth reiterating is that the ease of the analyst in accepting the hugging while continuing to do analytic work largely determines the course and outcome of the enactment. I base this generalization on the fact that my hugging experiences have become episodic and infrequent, in each patient subsiding in consequence of analytic work done after the act.

A derivative but less obvious point is that, in my experience, the proscriptions and stoppings of such huggings, on which I had insisted in earlier years, did not subsequently produce the analytic yield or relief of distress that was supposed to be the sequela of well-managed frustration. What more reliably followed were misery and a stalemated loggerhead over the continuing demands of the patient. This generalization has held for me. I think each of us must cautiously test these loaded matters for himself or herself.

I am talking about being hugged, about an action manifestly initiated by the patient, for I am old-fashioned enough to forgo initiating any physical contact with my analytic patients except under the most socially casual or professionally emergent circumstances. As I have grown older, I have found it easier to assess my sense of need to initiate the hug in these infrequent instances, and to rely on a close following of the consequences as control and guide regarding our enactment.

My use of the term *enactment* rather than the conventional *acting-in* is intended to convey that the matter of being hugged is not transparent. From my perspective, action behaviors occurring in the analytic situation are codetermined by the dynamics of the two participants. When the patient is the apparent initiator of the action, as is usually implied in our designating the patient's behaviors as acting-in or acting-out, closer study of the context often reveals that some less than optimal prior behaviors of the analyst provided provocation, seductive or rejecting, for the patient's regression to nonverbal levels of responding, including the urgent need for the analyst's physical response. This sequence was remarked on long ago by Winnicott (1958), then by Kohut (1971), and later by Schwaber (1983). Schwaber (1992) demonstrated that the analyst's defensive failures to recognize and acknowledge the patient's signals of distress over some recent breakdown of optimal contact between them induce defensive and regressive reactions in the patient. My own contribution to the exploration of these happenings has been to seek to identify the dynamic concerns of both patient and analyst at the time the enactment took shape. When these are bilaterally explored, there can be seen a potentiating interplay of similar and complementary intrapsychic conflicts in each, now being played out by both in the interactional field of the dyad (McLaughlin, 1991).

Under these circumstances, some huggings exemplify, in almost diagrammatic sequence, how defensive behaviors of the analyst, as he wards off some felt encroachment into his psychic perimeter of safety, initiate in the patient distress over loss of safe contact with the boundaries of the analyst. If the analyst hears and responds to this distress, his first defaulting may be rectifiable and the patient restabilized. If not, the patient, in his or her unacknowledged pain, may regress further to the level of action and touching, and may be driven at least to hug. Should the analyst meet the hug with a stiff or aversive response, this second rejection can be devastating, experienced as indisputable proof of the patient's worst fears.

From this perspective, I relate two clinical instances involving touching, with touching now being raised to include the derivative level of seeing. This shift, from touching to seeing as a way of knowing, is a big developmental step for us as very small people—a step impelled by biosocial pressures. "Look but don't touch" moves us from a primary knowing of holding, tasting, touching, and smelling what is near to a knowing through the reach of seeing across distance. The yield is a gain of range, but a loss of tangible sureness. Yet seeing is as old as touching and, in the welter of the neonatal unfolding of our perceptual array, is presumed to be party to the intermodal fluidity of early infant development. This is a ponderous way of saying what our everyday imagery and metaphor show us to be true: that seeing and touching are closely linked with each other, and with the other sensory modalities.

Clinical Vignette: Mr. E. This patient came to me in the early 1970s, when as an analyst I was quite interested in augmenting my knowledge by tracking all I could of my patients' nonverbal behaviors as they lay talking on my couch and in seeing how best to relate these kinesic data to the verbal data (see chap. 8).

A slim, somber man, stiff in movement and cautious in manner, Mr. E rarely made eye contact with me as he came and went but kept me vigilantly in his peripheral vision as long as he could. Invariably, as he passed me, he wiped his face on the side nearest me. In the intensity of his half-gaze, I occasionally felt, as time wore on, some transient tingling of my facial skin. During the first year, he remained motionless on the couch and kept his hands clasped tightly on his upper abdomen. He talked in tense bursts. His brief phrases were difficult to hear, couched in generalities and bracketed by steady disclaimers and revisions. "Maybe" and "But I don't know" edited his commentary, and "It could be" and "Perhaps" were his coda to mine. My initial appraisal of him was that he was an intellectually gifted man, chronically anxious, inhibited in assertiveness, uncertain in self-esteem, and held back in his full unfolding by obsessional defenses. I have described Mr. E in greater detail elsewhere (McLaughlin, 1992).

Mr. E's overall immobility on the couch was broken by near incessant hand play. I cannot recall another patient whose constant touching of his hands held so rich a repertory of hand-to-hand combat, play, and lovemaking. I watched his bursts of vigorous picking at fingertips and nails tattered and deformed. I imagined many years of habitual cuticle tearing and nibbling. At lesser intensity, his fingers scratched, squeezed, tapped, and banged on the others, or at times gently smoothed and massaged their own or their counterparts. His thumbs had their own place in the action, tapping or twirling around each other, grabbing or nestling in the curled fingers of the same or the opposite hand, and often the target of attack or caress from the other hand. I had watched these hand behaviors, and their timing with the patient's verbal comments, long enough to have noted that the hand play of attack or caress was often linked to affectional, erotic, and sadistic concerns about his mother and sister and himself in intricate and consistent patternings.

I learned that Mr. E had grown up as the middle child of three; he had a sister three years older and a brother two years younger. Their parents had struggled to survive in separate professional careers that took them early and regularly away from home after the brother was born. My patient carried a blur of memories from his early years, of cleaning women and babysitters looking in on him and his siblings. He had sharper recall in his memories, some of these his earliest, of his turning, as did his brother, to his sister for attention.

Mr. E still felt grateful to his sister for what she provided, though her ways too closely resembled the mother's unreliable bursts of caring. In our work, he tended to merge mother and sister in his sortings of his past. He described both as being at times solicitous and doing for him, in ways that could be comforting, yet more often taking him over and doing to him while demanding his grateful compliance. Both were capricious and totally unpredictable in responding or ignoring. Either could turn on him with fury, slaps, and stomping off, when what he did offended them. He remembered being bewildered and upset, lost and helpless, then growing quiet and cautious.

Father, on the other hand, was portrayed as distant, absorbed in difficulties with business and wife, and unavailable to his sons in their coping with mother.

Dealing with me warily, Mr. E seemed to idealize me as a detached, benign presence, and to relax in the doing. He gradually became freer to hint that he perceived my silences as failing to meet his silent wishing that I help him deal better with his emerging rage toward mother, and now his wife. His thumb picking increased in tempo and prominence at this time. Able to speak more about his needs and frustrations felt in relation to both parents, and now timidly in relation to me, he became more anxious, and began openly to pick at the periungual skin of both thumbs with the thumb and index finger of the other hand. These attacks were at times literally bloody. The bloodshed prompted me to call direct attention, for the first time, to what he was doing. I did so partly out of concern for this self-injury and partly because I knew from my analytic explorations of my own adolescent cuticle picking and nail biting what rich dynamics of pent-up anger and sexual conflict could lie in this behavior. I had long ago been struck by my awareness that I had done my finger tearing at the boundary between self and Other, where I had the potential literally to caress or claw someone important to me. Here was a most significant datum that I only partly understood. I knew that my old behaviors spoke of my wishes to attack—warded against by guilt and the need not to destroy the one on whom I vitally depended. Last, I intervened because I assumed that the physical pain he must be experiencing was surely in his awareness.

I was wrong in my assumption. After hearing me ask him to take heed to his skin tearing, Mr. E showed shock and anxiety in his flushed face and bodily rigidity. He lay totally immobile and was unable to speak for the remainder of the hour. I attempted actively to intervene—to reflect on his apparent state and to explore with expressed regret how what I had said upset him so. He gave no immediate response. Several sessions were spent in my trying to find ways to address his mute distress. Gradually, Mr. E regrouped, and bits and pieces came out. He had been utterly unaware of his skin picking; he felt caught, shamed, rendered helpless, afraid he was about to be given an actual beating. He felt my words as suddenly grabbing him by his shirt collar and jerking him off his feet. Angry words in his face made his skin burn and itch in shame. He expected that I would abandon him and literally drop him in a helpless heap. He acknowledged that his cuticle picking was a habit from his early school years. He had nothing more to say at that point.

On my part, noting his shock and immobilization, I felt immediate distress in a pattern familiar to me from childhood experiences of misdeeds and blundering: chagrin and anxious vigilance, the flush of foot-in-the-mouth shame and misery over having done irreparable harm. My two analyses and further self-inquiry had largely attenuated this affective state to a signal cluster that I had come to know as a call for more self-analytic effort. In this instance with Mr. E, the signal was pretty high on my Richter scale. I know that I worked assiduously to reengage him, chiefly through seeking to learn more about the details of the distress I had occasioned in him. It was slow going.

After our enactment, Mr. E's thumb picking left the analytic scene for several months, though his thumbs, and fingers as well, bore mute witness to ongoing assault elsewhere. Only later did more history about these kinesics emerge, as he worked over his experiencing me as having let him down. He let me know how I had turned on him and changed inexplicably from the comforting helper he thought he had. His usual disclaimers and qualifiers became fewer as this piece of work was accomplished, and as he became more forthright in his speaking. He could not remember exactly when his nail biting and picking had begun. It had driven his mother to enraged screaming and face slapping in her helplessness to break him of the habit. He recalled gloves tied on his hands, foul-tasting stuff smeared on his fingers, and beatings given him by both parents. These memories were entangled in recollections of even earlier battles and chemical warfare around thumb sucking, which struggles mother apparently had won. This later struggle she could not win.

In the aftermath of trying to resolve what I saw as an enactment painful to both of us, I became better able to hear, and reflect to him on, his pride in his nearly lifelong angry, stubborn holding on to what he could that was his own in any relationship, often at the cost of mutuality and intimacy. Recognizing the playing out of this struggle between us opened the way to our freshly seeing his being chronically burdened by his fear of his own temper, his fear of worse retaliation, and his dread that he might not ever fully be able to love anyone. He pointed out to me how much better it would have been, during our enactment, if I had conveyed my regret over having hurt him. I thought I had done so, and at length, but Mr. E recalled that I had spoken only of my chagrin, which he felt had to do with my distress over my technical lapse, not an acknowledgment of hurt done to him. He said he would have experienced my direct apology as a soothing, "like having Unguentine spread on bad sunburn."

It is clear that I was much caught up in watching Mr. E's kinesics in their simultaneity with the rest of his communications. I had reacted to his self-inflicted skin injury and bleeding by attributing to them a greater intensity of destructiveness than the patient himself experienced. I had made an intervention aimed at stopping his self-directed assault, much as I had done years earlier in response to Ms. A's head-banging. My justifications for doing so on his behalf turned out to be more important to me than to Mr. E. He was long familiar with and indifferent to his miniscarification and bloodletting, to which his scars bore witness.

I did some self-analytic work on the meanings that this discrepancy in our perceptions held for me, and on the significance of my signal response to the prolonged regression I had evoked in Mr. E. The fresh light thrown on my personal conflicts of old sadomasochistic involvements with mother and sisters was considerable, but beyond encompassing within the boundaries of this paper.

One outcome important for me lay in my richer gut-level appreciation of my early ambivalence over my impulses to tear and bite with tooth and nail: my tears and fear when I had done so. The locus of compromise lay at the tactile boundary between self and other, where the expression of the ambivalent polarity of caressing love or clawing hate depends on the slightest curl of lip or fingertip. Only token damage, and not total destruction of self or other, would be realized.

I also emphasize another aspect of my intervention that Mr. E found so shocking. Through prior work with the action behaviors of all my patients, I had already come to base my clinical approach to nonverbal behaviors on a distinction between two sorts of kinesics and to develop technical preferences regarding how best to explore these. There were conspicuous nonverbal behaviors, often not far outside the patient's own awareness, that could eventually, with a little tact, be pointed to by me without disruption to the patient, and we could engage in their exploration.

On the other hand were small, inconspicuous kinesics that I had found to lie usually outside the patient's awareness. These small, background movements, being aside from his conscious concerns, were better left alone. Bringing them to his attention was too intrusive; he felt caught in a private act. It was best to look on these as silent counterpoint and commentary, as confirmation or contradiction of the verbal content of communication (see chap. 8).

This time, with Mr. E, I had overridden my own experience to question a habitual behavior that was small in his scheme of things but loomed large in mine. Consciously aiming to learn more about him (and me), I had to surmise that, at another level, I wanted neither of us to penetrate into what might be shared and untouchable motivations in us both.

Mr. E clearly felt immobilized, indeed pinned and scorched, by my questioning what he was doing as he picked and tore. It is conceivable that his raising the intensity of his attacks to a conspicuous level signaled his wishes to reveal to me both his mounting aggression and his anxious need for my intervening. Had I seen his behavior in this perspective, I am fairly sure I would have found a better way to bring the strife to his attention. Instead, I spoke in a manner that breached boundaries between us that he had cautiously begun to trust—boundaries that I had set at the outset of the analysis, when I had implicitly emphasized that we would focus on what verbally transpired between us in the associative enterprise. I added insult to injury (how right these old cliches turn out to be!) in not letting him know that I saw and regretted the hurt that I had done to him. At a more abstract level, I acted on my own perception of the patient's reality, out of my own defensive interests and purposes and in violation of his, and I did not know it until confronted by Mr. E's response.

The cumulative effect of recognizing iatrogenic woundings inflicted on patients by experiences very much like my experience with Mr. E— causing unnecessary hurt to patients often much more sensitive and less stable than Mr. E—drove me to recognize the relativistic nature of the analytic enterprise when perceived from the different reality views of the two participants. Mr. E's shock responses could not truly be understood from an analyst-centered designation of these as resistance and regressive evasion of the analytic process. I had no choice but to address the extent to which my assertion of my own viewpoint ignored the necessary exploration of the patient's experience and undermined his self-esteem (Kohut, 1971).

The technical necessities of (a) working to alter my stance so as to keep my perspective more closely attuned to the patient's reality view and (b) actively attempting to retrieve that position and repair the damage when I find that I have retreated from it have been major preoccupations for me over the years. I have become less sure of any generalities about our field, except that it is vital that the analyst not act on what he presumes to know, from his theory or experience, about his particular patient. From this position of presuming little and trying to become informed, I ask more questions, am not so long silent, and volunteer more ideas and observations in a tentative and nonassignative fashion. Tracking the patient's responses to my varied interventions provides clues to whether the patient feels touched in ways that offer him space and freedom to engage, or feels poked, clawed, or pinned by words that stick to and in him (McLaughlin, 1993a).

In this endeavor, I have drawn on Schwaber's (1983, 1986) exploration of the analytic yield of a committed focus on the psychic reality of the patient, in both its conscious and unconscious dimensions, and on the nuances of the patient's responses to the analyst's behaviors.

The commitment to seek the reality view of the patient inevitably brings the analyst into closer engagement with his own idiosyncratic convictions and to a sharper awareness of how his own dynamics and defensive needs can influence his responses and the theoretical preferences that support them.

The following clinical vignette reflects my gradual shift from a minimalist analytic stance to the more active exploratory mode entailed in analyzing from within the psychic reality of the patient. I hope that the vignette illustrates how this manner of working can widen and extend psychic boundaries, even in a patient whose profound obsessionality, coupled with my earlier ways of working, had previously limited optimal access to affective depth.

Clinical Vignette: Mr. O. Mr. O and I worked, more or less together, in an analysis that stretched over more years than either of us cared to contemplate. He had been in a long prior analysis elsewhere and had turned to me when he could no longer deny his intellectual awareness that he was still stuck in his avoidance of success in work and love. Aloof and poker-faced, he complacently declared that he had no access to strong feelings, either loving or aggressive, and that he lived his life as an emotional isolate, behind a façade of immersion in his business.

In the early years of this analysis, I worked essentially from the austere base of my analytic origins: striving industriously to provide expectant silences and interventions carefully chosen for their accuracy and objectivity. My best efforts became blunted by Mr. O's unresponsiveness. Denied the feedback and guide of emotionally tagged ideation, I had to draw on all that I knew of theory, lore, and previous experience involving obsessionality and narcissism. My obvious lack of impact led me often to withdraw in boredom—or to try to get to him and get some response or else call it quits. Meanwhile, Mr. O seemed always to hover above me, as though nonchalantly stretched out in the gondola of a timeless balloon, peering down incuriously on what lay beneath him. His singsong voice was devoid of affect as he recited his languid soliloquy about the thoughts that came unbidden and alien and about which he might or might not speak once he had digested them. In my overt behaviors, I often became more like Mr. O in my silence and inertness. I heard my voice flatten and become distanced, or declamatory and insistent, when I spoke my piece. For quite a time, Mr. O basked in the comfort of feeling we were moving along "in stride," when to me it seemed we were marching in place.

We ground along, he making small advances toward minute engagements with me in the work and half-acknowledged, half-hearted sorties toward involvement with others of both sexes.

As I gradually developed more confidence in the active modes of analytic working described earlier, I felt my way with Mr. O into more exploring and contributing modes that addressed him differently— modes in which I offered tentative thoughts about him and followed his point of view more closely. Although these shifts in me were gradual, he quickly noted them, at first with mild alarm: I was "out of my cage" and crowding him, behaving like a bad analyst. Yet he gave other signs that my altered ways might be reaching him. His nearly fixed postural immobility on the couch—crossed legs in full extension, arms tightly folded, eyes squeezed shut—began to give way to hand gesticulations and leg stretching, at times with his feet flat on the couch and knees flexed and spread wide. His old and persistent physical distress, attributed to a chronic peptic ulcer, receded and some genital potency appeared mysteriously after years of dormancy. All this was only grudgingly and elliptically acknowledged by Mr. O, with considerable evidence of both anxiety and pleasure in being "reached." His abiding indictment of his former analyst and then of me was that, by interpretations that would "penetrate my defenses with a force that I can feel," we had disappointed his yearning to be reached. He came to make this reproach less frequently.

During this interval, the patient's habitually desiccated thought processes underwent a notable change. Mr. O was intruded on by an alien thought he was anxious to reject but could not dismiss: that as a very young child he had been in some fashion genitally molested by his doting mother. I followed the twistings and turnings of his efforts to explore this unwanted idea and to demolish it—my stance being that, whatever its basis, there was something in the thought that had touched and clung to him. We both were aware that his preoccupation had emerged in the context of my moving to put myself more into the space between us. Both our felt present and his not yet tangible past were there between and in us, not yet fully acknowledged and explored.

At the beginning of an hour during this period, Mr. O entered my office and remarked in alarm that I had seemed to smile broadly, perhaps even grinned, as I greeted him from across the room. Quickly on the couch, he added that he thought he did not like it.

Mr. O: What was it about—what did you have in mind? I've had the thought recently you might like me. No possible basis for that thought. It just comes. Like you just keep coming on. You've been like that for quite a while. You ask more details—like after I had that preposterous thought about my mother molesting me—asking what I thought it would have been like for me to have my mother molest me . . . sounds, body feelings, pleasurable or not. Of course I have no idea. You know that I'm an innocent victim in what happened [said in an ironic way that might intimate an admission that by now he knows better but wishes to keep his security of not-knowing].

McLaughlin: I have been more active. We know that know-nothing helplessness has been your way to ward off any meaning for you in your past and present. And you just spoke of my bothering you with my big smile, maybe even a grin—a grin you could not help seeing before you got to the couch, closed your eyes, and was safe.

Mr. O: You say that, and your voice sounds—uh—maybe playful—like you're smiling right now. I don't like that! [Mr. O's knees, which were flexed to vertical and pressed together, here move leftward and firmly into the back of the couch, away from me, seated obliquely to his right rear.] I want to get away from your face, your smile! [voice rises in pitch and resonance, now drops] But what if I would like you to smile at me, could let myself . . . [pause of about 10 seconds].

McLaughlin: It's a thought you're having, of hearing a chuckle in my voice and seeing my smile, and not quite knowing what might happen if you were to like it. Better play it safe?

Mr. O: Well, look at my legs: pressed away against the couch like I was protecting from something. I must be afraid of something. But a feeling in my back . . . here [slightly raises right shoulder and hip to show me where he has placed his right hand, behind his lower ribs, rubbing] . . . like you had touched me as you smiled. Feels pretty good when I do it, but . . . [again a brief pause; knees relax in open position].

McLaughlin: Good feeling when you rub back there, but . . .?

Mr. O: [A strident note in his voice] My back's tightening up! I hear you like you're seeing something in my "but" that I don't see. No! My "butt"! I couldn't have said that! [Laughing uproariously] Those enemas she sweet-talked me into . . . was that her molesting? your molesting? [Voice drops, sounds earnest] Something not right about that connection. You sort of chuckled after I just laughed, and it's like that made me feel like I was sitting in your lap, my back there and you holding me, warm and good. Now I'm confused about this idea about enemas, about what's good or bad about all this, what's between you and me, me and my mother. My back feels stiff.

McLaughlin: Could you be saying that my comments come at you as though I'm after something? Then there's my chuckling, which is like holding you so you feel warm and safe. How to read these mixed signals?

Mr. O: That feels close, but I think it's more that I'm used to being afraid I'll be taken advantage of, and of not letting myself dare. This is different. I get these ideas of friendly stuff between us and don't know how far to risk getting into that. Then I feel you are pushing something at me, and I'd rather not know what I feel.

There is nothing very striking about this hour in terms of breakthroughs achieved or fine insights reached. Mr. O was showing and acknowledging a greater affective range, both verbally and in his nonverbal communication. He seemed to have responded positively to the cumulative effect of my closer engagement. I felt that this man, once so grimly remote and impassive, was becoming comfortable enough to acknowledge phantasies and ambivalent wishes for physical warmth and closeness, despite his fears of the intrusion and overwhelming stimulation of a closeness that before had only threatened him with its sexual implications.

His imagery and idiom, expressed in his own words and prompted by his anxious yearning, spoke to boundaries being stretched and fear of their yielding. My smile was seen across a distance as offering liking and good touching, but more likely as a predatory grasp. Mr. O experienced my question from behind him first as a warm touch on his back. He quickly translated this into a back-stiffening intrusion from the rear. Yet now he less rigidly defended against this "homosexual" idea, which he had previously intellectualized about. He both slipped and laughed at his slip—defensively, of course. But now, for this brief moment, he was able to hear my chuckle as harmonic counterpoint, a sound that felt to him as my holding him in the warmth and safety of my lap while we looked together at his conflicted wishes.

Discussion

I have tried to sketch, in an impressionistic fashion, the always-present sense of touching in the analytic relationship. Whether what is sought or feared within the dyad is a tangible, physical touching or a psychic-level touching of core or soul, analyst and patient are raptly involved. Often, the interfluidity of imagery makes it almost impossible to discern the differences.

To paraphrase what I stated at the outset, each of us has needs to make authentic contact with the "real" or "true" core of the other (enclosing these words in quotation marks acknowledges the ineffable heart of the matter) in order to be affirmed by that other in some essential good and to have unwanted aspects of ourselves accepted. I am using *good* and *unwanted* in a most nonspecific sense, both to acknowledge their idiosyncratic nature for each of us and to point to the primary origins of these feeling wishes in our early object relations, now transferred to our present other.

Historically, we have expected this need for the acceptance of the unwanted as parts of ourselves to be true for the patient. We have come to find it to be true for the analyst as well. Acknowledging this truth, we can be more ready to see how our needs suffuse all that we are and do in the work and how we must endlessly be self-observing to discipline and optimize these tendencies that are both our strength and our weakness.

Although my clinical samplings have ostensibly been about patients, it is evident that my finger has pointed to the analyst—to the facilitating and hampering of his best work in consequence of the melding of his trained indoctrination and personal attributes. My generalizations about touching and hugging speak to limitations in the analyst compounded of blindly accepted training lore and personal defensive adaptations.

In the instance of Ms. A, this combination for a while limited my apprehension of the crucial importance of metacommunications in analysis at levels other than those of the oral–aural axis.

For Mr. E, it is evident that my particular research interests in non-verbal behaviors coalesced with personal conflict around recognizing deeper meanings in the shared neuroticism of embattled fingertips. Together, these led me to shape a specific intervention in which I asserted my defensive compromises and disrupted a safe place in which Mr. E was cautiously revealing fresh information about his sadomasochistic levels of aggression. Whose fury and pain did I chose not to stay with? That they were not yet his forced me to recognize my part in the enactment.

The cumulative effect of recognizing what I strongly believe to be iatrogenically shaped deflections and injuries has taught me to work assiduously to learn and analyze from the viewpoint of both conscious and unconscious perceptual experiences of the patient (see chap. 4). The analyst's working closely to engage the patient's psychic reality at all its levels inevitably opens the analyst to a heightened appreciation of the patient's affective intensities and to a deeper appreciation of his own emotional resonances. It forces the analyst to see and wrestle with how his own needs, his own preferred ways of seeing and coping, inevitably become imposed on the patient's space and freedom.

The result is a continuing self-monitoring with the aim of a sharper perception of an inherent dialectic, inevitably encountered when two minds attempt to meet in shared intimacy—an awareness of the endless oscillations between the pair as to who may speak to whom, and about what, so that the outcome may be mutually experienced and acknowledged as authentic for both.

I have been struck and poignantly touched by how different the quality of the analytic relationship can become for analyst and patient in the safer intimacy that this mode fosters. I hope that some of these qualities are evident in the closing vignette of Mr. O, who in his own words conveyed what he was feeling and telling about levels of our relating and boundary experiences that I could not anticipate. This small but common phenomenon, of the patient's finding his own way, provided for both of us a fine affirmation of the clinical power of working in this mode and of the cogency, the authenticity, of the insights generated when collaborative moments are realized.

I do not want to give the impression that this optimal state, similar to Isakower's (1963) "analyzing instrument" (Balter et al., 1980), flows unbrokenly from the analytic mode that I have described, for analyst lapses are inevitable and seldom go unregistered by the patient. I spend considerable time trying to work on and repair the consequences of my lapses. This necessary work can firm up the base for fresh undertakings—a possibility I have come to feel is enhanced by this analytic stance.

I also do not wish to overstate the analytic significance and moving power of these retrieved enactments. However, they do provide intensities that amplify the affective range of the patient, stir the transference resonances for both parties, and provide the experiential realness that enlivens the core of the analytic relationship. In the turmoil of these moments, the driving force of the analyst's reparative need to help the patient cope with the distress occasioned between them can, luck mingling with good judgment, be matched by the patient's own needs to help recover a state of good connection. This work of retrieval is more readily addressed when the ongoing analytic stance enhances a synergism by which both may transcend old expectations, and find expanded dimensions of themselves.

There is a healing touch in this that can reach to core levels of both members of the dyad. Herein lies the enduring motivation of many of us to persist in this work that we must do.

WHAT WAS THOUGHT
The Dialectics of Influence

CHAPTER 11

Dumb, Blind, and Hard
Can an Analyst Change His Spots?

The term *enactment* has crept into our analytic vocabulary in recent years without attention having been paid to what it signifies for us. Like other words borrowed from common discourse, it was already dense with multiple meanings and useful enough for a while in conveying what we needed to enlighten our informal analytic dialogue. Soon we shall have packed it with analytic meanings, only to come to the sad conclusion that we have a term utterly lacking in the precision that would satisfy those who like their theory neat.

So it is the purpose of this chapter to explore and debate the range of significance of the term while it is still relatively fresh and unencumbered, and to assess its value in furthering our clinical and theoretical pursuits.

Historical and Etymological Background

Although the word *enactment* has surely been in our analytic vocabulary and use for a long time, it is not in the subject index of the *Standard Edition* of Freud's works or in Fenichel's (1945) compendium. Guttman's (1980) *Concordance* has only one citation, to "On the Problem of Lay Analysis," wherein Freud (1926b) referred to the enactment of the Austrian "quackery law," using the term in its portentous sense of an act carrying the weight and controlling intent of a law.

Probably for Jacobs (1984) as it was for me when I made enactment the topic of a plenary address in 1985, I had only the sense of using a familiar term to speak of familiar things. And I did not there define it, except contextually—applying it generally to all manner of interaction

185

between patient and analyst, and specifically to the nonverbal gestural and postural components of patient communications (see chap. 8).

What meanings did *enactment* bring with it when we began to borrow it? Etymologically, it is a highly compacted trisyllabic word, each component of which reinforces the intensities in what it means to act.

According to *Webster's New International Dictionary* (2nd ed.), a key aspect is that the verb *act* is set between two modifiers. By itself, *act* carries a whole range of familiar meanings, from "do" to "act one's will by force" and "to exert power," all the way to "perform as an actor—play the part of—to simulate or dissimulate." Adding the prefix *en-* emphasizes *act* as noun and conveys "putting into or upon—to wrap in—make like—adding a more intensive force." The suffix *-ment* further intensifies the import and density of *act* as a noun.

So the word *enactment,* before we ever laid analytic claim to it, suggested an action with purpose and force raised to high impact and influence on the implicit other in the field of action. This implication of the other and of the intention of one to persuade or force the other is strengthened by the consistent inclusion in the definition of *act* of the idea of performing, playing a part, simulating, and dissimulating.

Enactment in Psychoanalytic Usage

Emphasis on the purposeful interplay of at least two parties makes the term *enactment* especially useful in focusing on the interactional aspects of the analytic relationship. As there is no agreement on or consistent use of the term among us, probably the best we can do is to declare our preferences and attempt to justify these as best we can on both clinical and theoretical grounds.

By attempting to articulate my own perspective on the meaning and usefulness of *enactment,* I am suggesting that we might agree to accept two complementary meanings: one very general, the other more specific. What I dwell on, though commonplace, is useful to review in these contexts.

General Ubiquity of Analytic Enactment

Enactment in a broad sense can be construed in all the behaviors of both parties in the analytic relationship. This is so because of the enormous intensification of the appeal or manipulative intent of our words and silences, normally present to some degree in all dialogue. The intensification occurs in the analytic situation for both parties because ordinary actions are forsworn and visual communication curtailed.

Given the potential for both parties' regression, induced by the deprivations inherent in the analytic situation, it is expectable that words, as the word *enactment* itself informs us, become acts, things—sticks and stones, hugs and holdings. This secondary process, cherished for its linearity and logic, becomes loaded with affective appeal and coercion, to be experienced by either or both parties as a significant act or incitement to action.

These charged words of the analytic dialogue are themselves embedded in and surcharged by a steady clamor of nonverbal communication between the pair, much of which is registered and processed, at times subliminally, by both parties. Each has learned from infancy, long before the words were there for the saying, how to appeal, coerce, clarify, and dissimulate through the signals of body language, gestures, facial expression, and vocal qualities. And both went on to add to, not relinquish, these wordless capacities to influence and be influenced as they also gradually learned the supple power and diplomacy of words.

To appreciate the imperatives that both members of the analytic dyad have in them and bring to the analytic work along with their full repertoire of evocative-coercive capabilities, it is helpful to draw on the perspective afforded by our concepts of transference. Especially useful is the broad view of transference as an inherent human tendency to impose the organizing of prior perception of experience on the present (Freud, 1925; Stern, 1977; see chap. 4) and thus as fundamental to shaping our psychic reality.

Put differently, whether we are analyst or patient, our deepest hopes for what we may find the world to be, as well as our worst fears of what it will be, reflect our transference expectancies as shaped by our developmental past. We busy ourselves through life with words and actions aimed at obtaining some response in self and other, in keeping with these expectancies. We are accustomed to expecting this to be so for the patient—that he brings the baggage of his expectations to the analytic relationship and tries his hardest to make them happen, keep them from happening, or find some compromise. As his words fail him—and they usually must before they eventually suffice—he increasingly intensifies his appeal and protest in nonverbal ways. In brief, he attempts to shape a happening, an enactment, in accord with his fears and hopes.

When the patient views his analyst's behavior as having fulfilled his own expectations, we are accustomed from our standpoint to designate his experience as the *transference actualization* (Sandler, 1976a), a phrase that nicely captures the patient's sense of the reality of his experience. It can also be viewed as an enactment in the general sense, because, from the viewpoint of the patient, it is a happening he experiences as an expectable repetition. If the patient's subsequent behaviors, based on his conviction that he has experienced the real thing, lead him to such further action as to strain or break the analyst's boundaries and capacities for doing analytic work, it is our custom to apply the somewhat pejorative label *acting-out*. This label is accurate enough, as far as it goes, but it falls short because it reflects only the unilateral perspective of the analyst and his chosen assignment of meaning from his assumed position of higher objectivity and uninvolvement. This shortcoming is equally evident in many of our conventional designations: *countertransference, acting-out,* and *projective identification,* among others.

What we have come to know about the shaping of the analyst, his work ego, and analytic competence has long required that we see ourselves in our work as indeed adequate at times, but liable to lapse and shortfall for many reasons. As we come to know the assets and limitations we brought to our choice of career, and the forces of conflict and compromise that shaped that choice, we see that we are not so different from our patients, except as our own analytic experience and training have helped us to evolve a little further in our development and adaptation through analytic ways of knowing. We realize that what we have been trained to do and what we have been molded to think both expand and constrain us and reflect our identifications made with and against those who educated us. We build on and take refuge in what they put before us.

When at work, we bumble, stumble, and get lost. We know we are into mixes of not yet knowing (our dumb spots), of not being free to know because of acquired biases and preference for theory and technique (our hard spots), and of having lost, for reasons of intrapsychic conflict, our hold on what we know or thought we knew (our blind spots).

Enactment as a Designation for Specific Shared Behaviors

From this view of the analyst as an involved and not invulnerable participant, I suggest that we use the term *analytic enactment* in a second and

more specifying fashion: to refer to events occurring within the dyad
that both parties experience as being the consequence of behavior in
the other.

It is obvious that the sources of the analyst's needs to enact (i.e., to retreat from or assert some pressure on the patient) can be any combination of dumb, hard, and blind spots, touched by the contributions of the
patient. The emphasis in this presentation is on the analyst's blind
spots—his regressions to less evolved perceptiveness in consequence
of the stirring in him of old and only partially mastered conflicts, now
given fresh and specific intensities by the particular qualities of the patient's dynamics and transference concerns. I see this focus on the analyst's blind spots as one that can encompass the many defensive factors
that contribute to selective ignorance (dumb spots) and theoretical-
technical preference (hard spots) in the analyst.

Implicit in this perspective of enactment in the clinical situation is the
expectation that close scrutiny of the interpersonal behaviors shaped
between the pair will provide clues and cues leading to latent intrapsychic conflicts and residues of prior object relations that one has
helped stir into resonance in the other, and between them actualized for
both. I hope the following clinical data exemplify this.

Clinical Vignette: Returning to the Case of Mrs. P. Mrs. P (see chap. 7)
began her analysis at a time when I was actively seeking technical alternatives to the accustomed ways of my analytic training and early aspirations, whereby I had come to expect that I was to accomplish my best
analytic work through an objectifying and assessing stance that allowed
me to see and convey to my patient my surer grasp of the reality of his situation. That stance I was to articulate with an interventive precision that
could be expected to promote mutative growth in my patients. Some of
the time and with some patients, this approach seemed effective; much
of the time, it did not. Mrs. P provided a plethora of the latter.

Mrs. P's running monologues about her chronic frustrations as wife,
mother, and career dropout were masterpieces of circumstantial ambiguity. She touched on painful times in her childhood and adolescent
years, but only in fleeting fragments. Her steady, flat intoning warded
off any but the most insistent interruption aimed at seeking to learn her
viewpoint or opinion about what she was talking about. At these interventions, she invariably became puzzled and unable to think, then
tensely silent and obviously anxious.

I could surmise from Mrs. P's history that her wary defensiveness and refusal to take a stated position or attitude were linked to her continuing frustration in reaching out to a distant and work-preoccupied mother and to a tension in fending off a sporadically attentive father whose genuine caring was expressed in an overriding style of critical solicitude and steering. Both parents had wanted this second child to be a boy. Instead, they had to settle for another little girl, whom they pushed along to grow up quickly and twin with an older, docile sister. What they ended up with was a quietly sullen rebel who held everybody at a distance for fear of showing shameful need and flaw—a woman who gave little of herself to anyone and expected or felt she deserved even less for herself. She had been a depressed, joyless underachiever for as long as she could remember, except for a brief time in latency when she displayed a flair of boyish athleticism.

In the early years of this prolonged analysis, none of my interventions seemed to help Mrs. P feel less morose, futile, and self-castigating. It was in this early phase of the work that repetitious behaviors quietly occurred between us. They illustrate what I see as crucial to the shared nature of psychoanalytic enactments.

Mrs. P had an unvarying "Yes, but . . ." response to my best interventions. Each response heralded a lengthy detailing of additional information offsetting or refuting what she had said earlier and on which my intervention had been based. I came to feel that her responses to my interventions not only destroyed the cogency of the points I had made, but buried their cognitive remains beneath a mound of negation.

Mrs. P's silences, topic shifts, and endless justifications for not understanding or agreeing were defensive modes I felt I could understand. Gradually, however, my curiosity and seeking to explore became dulled, as did my active wishes to help her to understand. In wasteland stretches of hours filled with repetitious recountings, I retreated to dogged silence and a heavy resolve to wait for better information. When occasionally I had a sense of finally seeing something useful and broke into her monologue to state my viewpoint, I did so with a declamatory insistence that bothered me even as I heard myself speaking. I knew I would soon hear her justifying counters presented in her flat and sullen monotone.

In a typical instance, I listened in long silence to an extended account of Mrs. P's obsessional seeking for just the right dresses for her toddler. I heard the pain behind her flat statements about wanting to give her little girl the right to choose her own clothing (implicit here was the desire that the girl not always be made to wear what mother wanted, as my patient said had been her own lot).

McLaughlin: [somewhat declaratively] So you want very much to be a good mother to [your daughter], not be the controlling mother you felt you had.

Mrs. P: Yes, but she really did give me choices. In fact, I could get anything I wanted because she'd never go with me. I'd pick what I wanted by myself, and it was never right—you've got it wrong. [voice briefly sharp, then suddenly flat] Let me tell you about my trouble with getting the walls painted . . .

McLaughlin: [voice more assertive] Your voice sounded angry then, and sounds angry now. Can you talk about what you are feeling?

Mrs. P: No . . . feel confused . . . you've mixed me all up . . . I don't feel anything except wish I could be comfortable. Things are getting worse at home . . . and here. I get afraid to say anything.

McLaughlin: What I'm doing somehow makes you worse.

Mrs. P: No, it's not you—I just can't think. It's the pot, I think, getting to me. . . . So much to worry about at home [rushes into tortured account of troubles with Mr. H, her decorator, who fails to give her what she wants, tries to get her to accept what he thinks she should have].

McLaughlin: [weary and somewhat irritated] You notice that you are talking of your decorator's forcing you to see things his way. I think you are experiencing me in this way—that I keep pressing you to consider matters I bring up.

Mrs. P: Where do you make that connection? I didn't say it quite that way about Mr. H. He's trying to do his job. I just get tired and begin to doubt my own instincts. Can't see any connection with what we were talking about earlier in the hour—what were we talking about at the beginning? I'm lost.

I too felt lost and baffled at moments like this. Even more bothersome was that I could expect soon to hear of the worsening of her depression and further retreat into binges of overeating, pot smoking, and uncontrolled outbursts of verbal rejection of one or the other of her preschool daughters. I worried about her sensitivity to whatever I said and about her potential for destructiveness toward herself and others she wished to love.

My distress for her and for my own helplessness to find ways to intervene effectively in the face of her stubborn provocativeness and volatility was ample warning to me that we were deeply involved in a stalemate that was mine to explore. Before I sketch the essentials of this exploration, let me turn briefly to an important question concerning the relationship between projective identification and psychoanalytic enactment.

Projective Identification and Psychoanalytic Enactment

The designation of *projective identification* could well apply to what was shaped between Mrs. P and me. Her behaviors left me repeatedly in a state of futility and bewilderment and doubting my capacities to see anything clearly about her or to articulate effectively. I took myself to task for my ineptitude and felt helpless and angry. These reactions of mine were implicitly very like the qualities of distress so central to her experience. And her behaviors effectively pressured me to experience these affects as my own with an intensity I found unusually painful.

This composite would agree well enough with one of the more balanced descriptions of projective identification I have found in the literature. Ogden (1979) identified the inciting phantasies and pressuring behaviors of patient as the eliciting cause of analysts' reactions that so mirror the patients'. Yet he emphasized that the analyst's responses are not "transplanted" but are his own, "elicited feelings—under pressure from— a different personality system with different strengths and weaknesses" (p. 360).

Ogden's is a more perceptive view of projective identification than that of others, like Bion (1959), who for so long depicted the analyst as a container for the projected thoughts and feelings of the patient. Yet, Ogden's (1979) viewpoint falls short by not acknowledging and exploring the specific inner experiences of the analyst—the wishes, affective states, and object representations as these transferential resonances are stirred in him in the course of what Kleinians choose to think of as projective identification.

I suspect that the cumulative effect of such traditional constructs as acting-out, projective identification, and countertransference has added to the blurring of our vision in perceiving and integrating the full significance of the analyst's contribution to the analytic work (see chap. 4). It is here that the term *enactment,* albeit another analyst-imposed concept, can help us in our discourse (while the term is still relatively unencumbered), and its emphasis on a conjoint process of attempted mutual influence and persuasion could be used to invite exploration of the contributions of both patient and analyst.

Further details of the work with Mrs. P may support this argument.

The Analyst's Contributions to Enactment

My protracted silences and assertive sorties in pressing my interventions in the first year of the work with Mrs. P were enactments of my making. I was distressed by their clear evidence of regressive trends in me in the presence of Mrs. P's unfocused circumstantiality and her reducing to fragments my best efforts to see and make sense.

From Mrs. P's viewpoint, her behaviors before and after my silences, so reminiscent of her mother's habitual unavailability and preoccupation with her own interests, were reasonable ways of warding off expected rejection or withdrawal from what she had to offer. And her defensiveness and obfuscation in response to my insistent interventions that overrode her defenses were as appropriate as were her old responses to her father's intrusiveness and shaming criticisms.

In chapter 7, I touched briefly on the meaning of my anxious tendency to remove my glasses during sessions with Mrs. P. I return now to the experience of this mannerism in more detail to illustrate the interrelatedness of the therapist's "blind" spot with a hardening of perspective and its complementarity with the patient's own conflicts.

Quite another side of these mannerisms drifted into focus over the weeks that followed with Mrs. P—recollections of what it had been like to be semiblind and not know it. I could see how it had been comfortable for me to have less expected of me in my accustomed bumblings. But, there had been a downside of defeat and failure in my inability to assert my knowing in the hubbub of my family. Older sisters, a male cousin, and I would have been through the everyday experiences we shared in fishing boat, berry patch, back road, and pasture. I, like the rest, had exciting recollections burning to be told. But my vague and uncertain recountings, vivid only to me, stood no chance in the forum of the family, full of sharp sightings and the keen words to express them. I was readily outtalked in any version of our shared doings. The correction of my efforts by sisters and cousin was frequent and often funny. In my impaired visual state, I had usually considered these as made not so much out of malice, but from the sheer delight of children asserting their sharpness of seeing. After I acquired my glasses, I could better recognize what was there of rivalry and put-down.

These inadequacies of seeing and knowing, while the others ahead of me were getting so good at them, gave me moments of pain and despair, and shamed bewilderment over what was lacking in me that was so blithely evident in the rest. I had turned in my nearsightedness even more to books and their words to find an authority of meaning that my own vague visual perceptions could not get quite right. Corrective lenses helped more than just my sightedness. Yet the puzzlement and uncertainty of the prior years left their traces in my continuing need to be accurate and quick in seeing and saying it right, now that I had the chance and the responsibility to do so.

Years later, functioning as an analyst in the manner of my training of the late 1940s was for me a natural extension of this bent: to seek and come upon the right interpretation or point of intervention, to articulate correctly my understanding of the patient and watch her reactions to my words. Obviously, my seeking to be right through a clear and accurate analytic vision was amplified by all my needs to be an analyst in the first place—mainly those centered on ambivalence toward close family members and compensatory needs to repair and enhance. As this clinical instance attests, I was vulnerable to excessive use of this basic analytic stance under times of particular threat to my sense of competence.

What I gradually came to see clearly enough and with fresh vividness was that my behavior with Mrs. P reflected my own needs and concerns, rooted in the vicissitudes of family relationships skewed for me in fairly specific ways by a visual defect (severe myopia and astigmatism), congenital or early acquired. I carried heightened sensitivities to extended attack on, or questioning of, my seeing and understanding. Mrs. P's particular ways of eliciting my efforts to reach out and provide understanding—and then turning them topsy-turvy with defensive repudiation, contradiction, and trivialization—brought me too close to my old pain of groping and failing. Anger and wary withdrawal into excessive silence as a defensive overuse of the classical analytic stance were signs that I was regressing from a more evolved and adaptive analytic position. The lensless blur was finally a cue.

What I experienced was so close to Mrs. P's distressful transference preoccupations as to place us for a while in a symmetry and simultaneity of wishes and fears, defensive postures, and affective tension. As I see it, ascribing all this to projective identification from patient to me would have blurred the perception of the very individual internal forces in me that had led us into common resonance. From my side, these intrapsychic pressures reflected the intensifying effects of the preceding months of effort to identify myself sufficiently with Mrs. P to be able to make contact with her pain and with the intrapsychic processes in her that occasioned it. In the necessary openness of doing so, I had fallen into transferences I obviously had not sufficiently worked through and mastered in this particular context.

Somehow, in the enigmatic ways that lucky pieces of self-analysis sometimes work, I was able to tap fresh sidestreams of familiar transference sources and was able to feel the surprise of new understanding about old concerns I had thought well settled. I find that, for me, this is often the way it is—that work with a specific patient brings into vivid focus an old conflict well known and dull in a generic sense, but now experienced in a particular variation that lights up yet another aspect to be recognized and settled as best I can.

I trust, though, that it is evident that this vignette, with its personal disclosures, is not intended as any new assertion of the value of self-analysis or as any claim for unusual capacities in me for doing the necessary work of self-correction that analytic work asks of each of us. Rather, the example is provided to exemplify the rich concordance and complementarity in the dynamic states found to have resonated in both patient and analyst when moments of enactment are explored adequately in both.

What gradually ensued between Mrs. P and me were mainly quiet differences in how things were said: on my part, fewer silences, and a greater freedom to say what I needed in a fashion that did not seem defensive or declamatory. With less need to be right, I could float ideas and questions in a tentative, exploring way that was less intrusive or preempting and provided in words much that Mrs. P could pick up or shoot down as she needed.

In a brief instance of the kind of exchange that came to signify our more effective and collaborative work over the next two years, Mrs. P launched into a long and familiar lament about how hard she was struggling to control her destructive tone and words of rejection toward her older daughter. As she went on, her voice grew high pitched and strained; with a squeak, it broke off into silence, as she scratched her head vigorously with her right hand.

McLaughlin: Sounds like you could be into more and more feeling?

Mrs. P: Why? Why do you say that? What do you hear?

McLaughlin: I think I hear your voice rising, getting more tense—maybe a hint of tears. Does it seem so to you?

Mrs. P: I don't know. You have a way of hearing things I don't. But it is true—I was hearing my voice going up. But I don't know why you'd connect that with tears—that's just your view of it. Why should it be tears, my tears?

McLaughlin: We could be hearing your voice differently. I thought I heard it break as you became silent and began to run your fingers hard through your hair. Made me think of strong feelings, maybe pain and anger, that you might not want to feel—or was I not hearing you right?

Mrs. P: [with sharp edge to voice] You like to be right, don't you! Oh, scratch that. [voice softer] I know you're trying not to force ideas on me, and I appreciate that—at least some of the time, when I can trust it. Right now, [voice loud and declamatory] I know you are critical. Right now I expect you to be critical, even before I say anything. I've said enough! Too much like father!

McLaughlin: Are you saying no more, or there could be real trouble?

Mrs. P: That's right! I don't mean I won't ever say, but right now I've said all I can say. I have to be sure.

As we parted, I had the impression that Mrs. P was less strained—that she had reacted with less defensiveness and some sense of relief in having her pain and anger recognized without yet having to risk acknowledging these feelings as her own.

Gradually, tentative, exploratory questioning became the main, but not exclusive, mode of our working together. When I could actively put into tentative, nonassigning words what Mrs. P's circumstantiality hinted at, she had words and ideas about the possible meanings of her experiences that she could discount, fend off, or cautiously acknowledge in a repetitious, grudging, "I knew that all the time, so what's new?" fashion. My diminished need to be right allowed us some access to the huge fear and stubborn withholding that lay behind her not saying what she consciously knew or felt, and then to her more affectively rich reworking of the transference origins of this defensive stance. Her style became one of disagreeing with the ways I had put things and then restating them in her fashion, which extended or deepened what I had put before her. I thought it significant that she could now experience my interventions, so tentatively put, as less intrusive and possibly helpful, in that she gradually showed less regression to tight helplessness in the hours and less bent to impulsive aggression outside.

Implications for Enactment

In the context of enactment, my altered ways of interacting to minimize unnecessary affront and wounding of the patient could be seen logically as the analyst's sharing in an enactment of the patient's transference hope to find understanding and not criticism, with the patient responding in a facilitating collaboration that extended her knowledge of herself. As we lack an adequate vocabulary to designate many of the positive events in analytic work, or to help us better to define what is essentially analytic in what we do, I regard such adjustments by the analyst to the patient's psychic reality, to her particular ways of experiencing the analyst, as indeed enactments of the sort usually attributed to analytic tact (Poland, 1975) or, in Sandler's (1976b) terms, instances of appropriate analytic role responsiveness.

As such corrections so often come about after the analyst recognizes that he and the patient have fallen into an obstructive interaction, the corrections can also be viewed as a restoration to a more evolved analytic stance of optimal neutrality and abstinence whereby such regressive enactments are avoided. The implications of this mode of close attunement to the patient's psychic reality can be applied to matters that lie beyond analytic tact and further than the responsibility of the analyst to repair his regressive lapses in technique.

While struggling to learn how I might work more effectively with patients like Mrs. P, for she was not that exceptional in her sensitivity to my
ways of responding, I came to sense the rich analytic potential and yield
that lay in steadily seeking out the patient's view of reality and doing all I
could to facilitate the patient's voicing his or her experiencing of that reality (see chap. 4). For me, this became the essential significance of Freud's
(1913) technical enjoinder that we begin at the surface, and it led me to
the tentative, questioning, and nondeclamatory mode already detailed.
Others have added understanding, in large increments, to this focus on
the patient's perceptions of his experience (Gray, 1973, 1982; Gill and
Hoffman, 1982; Schwaber, 1983, 1986). From their very different conceptual approaches, each of these authors has substantiated the value of a
way of working that seeks to avoid the imposition of theoretical presump-
tions or the assertion of personal bias and steering. I have been increasingly struck by the aptness of Schwaber's (1986) technical and conceptual
approach in furthering this quest through a mode of inquiry and listening
that seeks always to ascertain and acknowledge the patient's reality view as
reflected in his or her experiencing of the analyst's behaviors.

I emphasize the importance of this technical approach for enactment
in order to express essential agreement with Schwaber's observation
about many of the crises and complications in our analytic work—events
we have been accustomed to designating *acting-out* and may now designate
enactments. Schwaber saw these events as often being the patient's specific
responses to our earlier failures to seek and acknowledge the patient's
viewpoint of those of our behaviors that he or she has found distressing.
Schwaber noted the cumulative impact of the analyst's further failure to
respond and help to articulate the patient's distress. Her data are impressive in pointing to the analyst's lapses as reflecting countertransference issues of conflict and avoidance, along with defensive needs to adhere
excessively to theoretical-technical preferences.

The enactments that Mrs. P and I shaped demonstrate these points
well. When I was too long silent or too insistently declamatory, she gave
strong indication of not being understood or acknowledged. Her distress mounted as she became more needy, rageful, and depressed. For
quite a while, I took refuge in my silences and found comfort in my declamatory sureness, for these were analytic modes I saw as consonant
with my early training and technical knowledge.

We all can point to certain enactments that went on for some time before being uncovered and repaired by analyst and patient (see chap. 6).

In such instances, I had the strong impression that the period of tension and impasse and then the phase of discovery, reworking, and resolution combined to make for levels of affective intensity and an immediacy of actual experience that added appreciably to the clinical value of the experience for patient and analyst.

In the instance of Mrs. P, I did not have that conviction. Instead, I felt that the work could have moved into a more productive collaboration earlier had I not been impeded by both my idiosyncratic, regressive responses to her particular behaviors and the comfort I took in some of the stereotypes of my early training.

Although I have been able to go beyond some of the limiting aspects of the latter, I have ruefully rediscovered the old truth in the former: that the transference ghosts of the past are never entirely laid to rest. In the intensity of new work with qualities unique and not yet known, they return in fresh shape to revive shades of significance I had long forgotten I knew. Enactments are my expectable lot.

There is comfort in knowing that it is possible and restoring, most of the time, to turn back to the slip and shortfall—to rework these closely through the eyes of the patient. And there is satisfaction in finding those lucky moments when the reflections from the patient stir the glimmer in one's own eye that allows vision to be restored.

The concept of enactment acknowledges this two-sidedness of the analytic relationship. It can thus facilitate the analyst's recognition of and reflection on his own contributions and foster a more comfortable stance toward his lapses and their transference roots. Given such internal easements, self-analysis and seeking help from a colleague or group are more likely to occur, and their findings are more likely to be assimilated.

CHAPTER 12

Through the Glass Darkly
On Influencing and Being Influenced

The role of influence in the analytic relationship has bothered analysts since Freud first attempted to separate his new science from its beginnings in hypnosis. That he was unsuccessful then, as the rest of us have been as well, in disclaiming the power of influence has been our collective rue and challenge to this day.

I base what I have to say on three postulates. The first is the now accepted viewpoint that the effort to influence is inherent in, and indeed a driving motive for, all communicative activity. Those of a philosophical bent have been able to extend the reach of this notion across primitive cultures to all living organisms, including their cellular components, and thence to the astrophysical universe.

In our own field, child analysis and infant observational research have provided a convincing picture of the child as engaging, perhaps before but surely from birth and thereafter, in reciprocal communicative interaction with the mother. The behaviors of both, from wherever and whenever the start may be, speak eloquently of the urgency and power of the efforts of the one to evoke and shape the behaviors desired of the other. The back-and-forth sequencing and the simultaneity of this interplay during early development create what truly is a matrix of shared impetus and response—a mix so intersubjectively entwined as to blur any clarity over who separately wants (or does not want) what from whom.

My second postulate, which stands as corollary to the need of one to influence the other, also comes from this same swirl and confluence of shared and differing desires and needs in the infant–mother dyad. This second inevitability is that it is the conviction of the one that his or her behaviors are necessary responses to the behaviors of the other. Put differently, each experiences himself or herself as being influenced by the other, and his or her own reactions as being caused by that other.

Out of this same simultaneity and reciprocity comes yet another deep conviction of the then child, now adult. It is the third inevitability, the third of my postulates: that the one believes that his behaviors are the occasion and reason for the (re)actions of the other. That this is a paradoxical reversal of the second, to which I have just alluded, speaks to the primary-process nature and early developmental roots of both. I see this play of influence as inevitable and bilateral in the dyadic relationship, as evincing the primary forces impelling the analytic struggle. Its power is inescapable so long as one or both remain committed to trying to get what is desired from the other.

It is this fact of the bilateral need to affect the other that elicits from both the full range of their most evolved to most primitive adaptive efforts—hence, the full display of the transference potential in both. I hope to make a strong case for the proposition that we analysts do best when we openly and consistently acknowledge and monitor this ubiquity of mutual influence and the precariously advantaged position of the analyst, for then we may attempt better to minimize, modulate, and optimally direct the impingements of our influence.

My early struggles with the clinical constraints of my training in the early 1950s led me to focus on the psychology of the analyst and its impact on the patient–analyst interaction. We have, all of us, been so steeped in the influences of those before and around us that we, like artisans and artists, can claim only to have shaped our common materials in our idiosyncratic fashion. My particular preoccupation has been with the constant interplay of the analyst's transferences and those of his patient and the contribution that self-inquiry, self-analysis, can make to elucidating that interplay.

A central effort in my writing has been to articulate a more truly collaborative clinical stance of knowing less and seeking more to be informed of and understand regarding how each in the pair, patient *and* analyst, comes to perceive and comprehend things. For want of a better term for this technical emphasis, I think of it as analysis based in the psychic reality of the patient. Psychic reality embodies those primitive and preverbal aspects that Freud referred to as primary process yet includes all later acquisitions of perception and responses that come with the maturing of these primary modes and their entwinement with secondary-process capabilities.

I have come to a view of the psychic realities of patient and analyst in which it is a given that the past is indeed active in some fashion in the ongoing reality-view of each of us, in a complexity we call *transference,* as a consequence of the essentially conservative modes of survival of our psychophysical being. I cling to this emphasis on the centrality of transference the better to bolster my conviction that the analytic quest is more than storymaking carried out for the illusionary comfort of the two participants. It is a quest for the stuff that carries through and from the roots and trunks of our developmental past to give individual shape, color, and vitality to our unique experiential present.

This same conviction shapes my notion of the fundamental task of the analyst. It is that the analyst use his powers primarily to lead and guide the patient toward *how* rather than to *what*—how the patient can contemplate himself and others rather than what he will find when he does so.

I think that this specific deployment of the analyst's influence, toward how rather than what, guided Freud in his early discoveries, before his wondering gaze narrowed under the curse of creeping certainty about his discoveries. It was there initially in his invitation to the patient to associate freely. But invitation became insistence as the analyst's privileged position prevailed. The associative imperative emerged as a subtle pressure and demand by which analysis shaped the stereotype of the beckoning analyst and the resisting patient. Here was Freud's star and beacon by which to keep the analyst, along with the patient, fixed to their primary task.

In this renunciation of knowing why and what in favor of how lies what has been a significant shift in my analytic position. I still can see, beneath the manifest concerns that are the patient's "surface," many possible motives and dynamic configurations that my experience and lore have sensitized me to expect. These surmises are inevitably there in me, as cumulative shapings comprising my transference expectancies, my reality view. I would not want to be without the richness of context with which they inform my view.

Yet I find that these premises have little of the appeal they had when I presumed that it was my task to provide authoritative answers that would direct the patient away from his erroneous and infantile perspective. I have some confidence that this old stance, in my use, too often invalidated the patient's view and left him without this core sense of being believed. My conviction about this and my preference for the more subordinated analytic stance somehow convey to the patient the dynamic actuality of my third postulate about influence: that the one believes that his behaviors are the reason and occasion for the actions of the other.

We analysts have evolved our varying ways to handle this imposed invitation/obligation to associate. In enunciating a few of the proffered stances of various analytic perspectives, I shall caricature unpardonably, with no apology for the doing. My intent is to touch on differences in where the analyst places himself, and in his apportioning of influence between the patient and himself, as he addresses the analytic quest more or less in the context of the associative task.

When I think of those who have never swerved from the compass of free association, I think most immediately of Kris (1982) and Gray (1973). I can picture the stance of their analyst like this:

> I will sit beside you, perhaps as a music teacher might, and listen as you attempt to sing your song. When I comment, I shall do so mainly when I want to help you notice how you just soured or muffled your notes. Although I will keep an open mind to the reasons for the troubles you may encounter, I think that we will be able to demonstrate that you faltered as you began to grow critical of yourself. And later we may find that you had, just before that, begun to feel some ill will toward me that you were reluctant to disclose. And these matters, too, we can talk about. At all times, my single goal will be that you ultimately sing freely and to your fullest, and in your own key.

Here we might say that this analytic position aims to keep the analyst and patient looking at the effort to associate and to keep their attention focused alongside the axis of direct relating to one another. There are comfort and freedom for both in this stance, for the influence of the analyst is clearly directed toward the how—providing a protection of the patient from the analyst's natural propensity to drift into the what of the patient's outside life. This base comes to stand for their shared commitment to a definite task, a benchmark for rationality when direct relating inevitably becomes problematic.

The stance of Gill's (1982) analyst does not put primary emphasis on the patient's obligation to associate. Instead, it proposes:

> I will hear all you have to say, without criticism or response in kind. I will listen for, and ask you to consider, those clues in your discourse, whatever its manifest focus, that make allusion, obvious or subtle, to your sense of how you experience me in this relationship, and the feeling states stirred in you. My aim is to help you eventually to see and explore the manifold ways in which you find, in what I am and do, likenesses of those important to you in your developmental past, and differences between them and me, then and now, as well.

Here, we might say, the analyst actively places himself in the center of the affective-relational field and invites a shared attention to the consequences of his doing so.

My own stance, similar to Gill's but more closely aligned with that of Schwaber (1983), yet inevitably not identical with either, makes no strong stipulation that the patient associate freely. Its emphasis can be put like this:

> I will listen to whatever you may wish to say, with the intent to understand your meaning and viewpoint and with the least imposition of my own view or meaning I can manage. As I do not presume to know, I shall need often to question and to ask for illumination. I will be alert to and inquire about your nonverbal behaviors and shifts of affect, particularly as I listen for allusions to how you perceive and react to my behaviors. My aim there and always will be to help you articulate the validity and logic of how you see your world, and me in it. By looking at how you see me, I will try to help you see yourself, and I hope thereby to strengthen your capacities to find even more of yourself to authenticate and own.

Here, like the analyst in the mode of Kris and Gray, the analyst places himself alongside the patient in his function as observer. Metaphorically, however, he is somewhat behind, insofar as he waits to be informed rather than look for evidence of a particular intrapsychic constellation like, say, self-directed aggression. This analyst is alert to

verbal and behavioral clues that might indicate that the patient is reacting emotionally to internal content. Like Gill's analyst, he is particularly
alert to any references by the patient to the behaviors of the analyst.
Perhaps unlike Gill's analyst, he is less intent on deciphering implicit
allusions and putting these data before the patient as evidence of relational reference. Instead, he asks for and seeks to clarify the detailed
nature and quality of the patient's reading of the significance of his, the
analyst's, behaviors. He does so with the experientially supported expectation that this authentication of the patient's position strengthens
the patient's capacities to bring forth conflicted content and his own
recovery of developmental antecedents.

This stance reflects and supports a considerable shift in the power
gradient between patient and analyst—a shift that enhances the patient's place in the dyad at the relative subordination and redistribution
of the analyst's authority. In addition, this stance optimizes the invitation and opportunity for a deep and collaborative exploration of the patient's psychic life, in the patient's own idiom and from the patient's
own perspective. In these respects, I believe that this stance holds a potential to reach beyond the perspective offered by the analysts of Kris,
Gray, and Gill. This collaborative mode of looking with the patient at
what might be seen fosters a mutual receptivity in the work field between patient and analyst that allows both of us to say and hear much
more of each other's view than had been possible when my declamatory
style put me in the role of arbiter. The analyst will do this best insofar as
he or she can provide example and base and can serve experientially as a
model, flawed but trying, of exploratory openness to reflect, respond,
and be informed. In this, the patient can find the comfort and incentive
to explore his surface-to-depth personal view of the world and himself
through the shared refraction of another's gaze.

I have come to prefer, in both my analytic and consultative work, an
active style of tentative questioning and surmising in voicing my observations and ideas. I float these before the patient, rather than declaim
them in a way that he too easily can feel as fastening them to him. I do
not presume to know very much about most of what transpires between
us, including the meaning of our silences. I feel less burdened by the pre-
sumption that I must articulate my interventions just so, and I feel freer
to give voice to my own preconscious stirrings as tentative, sometimes
playful stuff that the patient can reject, play with, or revise. I do not wish
to suggest that this mode invariably surmounts all obstacles, reaches all

goals. What it can do is reduce unnecessary burdens of my shaping that make it more difficult for the patient and me to do our work, and it can allow access to content that neither of us could have anticipated.

The seeking mode requires that the analyst school himself to enter the patient's view—that he become accustomed to being in a perceptual state that is not his own. It is then that he most experiences a topsy-turvy unsettling that comes with renouncing one's own familiar outlook. Awash in fogs of ambiguity, he yearns to claim the guide and gleam of one's own knowing. But if he can remain steady, he is open to the surprise of fresh seeing, once he "gets it." I have put this last in quotation marks, for this is how I hear myself and others speak laconically of the affective richness that lies in finally grasping what the patient and analyst have been groping for. When the getting is done, it carries for both parties the excitement of having a hold on an authentic aspect of the patient's experience.

I wish to be clear that this search for the patient's psychic reality is not all that I find I must do. I consider the stance essential, at the beginning of the analytic relationship, in establishing the basis for what some think of as the therapeutic alliance. I consider it primary thereafter as well, as a matter of ensuring contact with the patient's surface, before the analyst feels right about bringing in agenda of his own.

My justification for assuming the right at times to assert my wisdom derives from a conviction, self-serving or otherwise, that goes like this. I am convinced that much of the incentive for mutative change, for moving on to new positions, lies, for all of us from childhood on, in the affirming and releasing challenge of the other who first proved the reliability of commitment to our cause. Here I emphasize the working of two separate minds so that I can make clear that the central focus on the patient's reality view does not mean seeking unbroken agreement and oneness in the dyad. The situation does not call for the abnegation of the analyst's use of his professional capacities and views, but rather for the active redeployment of these in the particular ways I have tried to convey.

The details of the clinical vignette that follows may capture some of what I have been trying to state in general terms.

Clinical Vignette: Mr. F. Mr. F. and I began our work in the early 1980s when I was finding my way into these modes of analytic listening. A successful businessman in his mid-40s, unmarried, Mr. F sought relief from low-level depression, fluctuant self-esteem, and inability to take pleasure from his work or to find comfort in his relationships with either sex. He dated various women with some pleasurable arousal but rarely attempted more than genital fondling. He preferred the anonymity and quick relief of men's-room sex with strangers and was emotionally close to no one.

Mr. F engaged me and the analytic task with well-mannered amiability mixed with bravado and contained wariness. It took several years of analysis for me to glimpse the chronic bleakness of his early years and to learn a little of how he had developed his façade of outward compliance and niceness. It was during those several years that I was finally able to get the feel of how he had pulled back into himself in pain and rage over the manifold ways in which his mother's lack of actively caring interest affected him. While still a preschooler, he had squelched his anger and outward show of aggression to the extent that, by adolescence, he could no longer feel his rage, or his sexual and tender feelings either. He rarely made contact with feeling states that he yet felt to be alive in the depths of his belly.

Mr. F surveyed his world with cold vigilance and opaque eyes, just as he had kept watchful score of the beneficiaries of parental preferences. For quite some time, I was unaware of his vigilance, for he smiled readily in greeting and leaving and kept dutifully still on the couch. Only when we became engaged in the struggles that I now describe did I become acquainted with the reptilian remoteness of his unblinking stare.

At times when Mr. F began to reveal his active bisexuality, he suddenly grew anxious and spun upward to a sitting position, from which he glared at me with slitted eyes for the rest of the session. He had to observe my face, see what really was there, for he could not trust my voice. He had to be sure that I was not about to do something bad to him. I found early on that, however gently expressed, any pressure to get him to resume lying down, or to tell me what he was experiencing, led to even more malevolent grimaces and spit-flying, gasping, inarticulate rage. These episodes slowly subsided into a dulled state that sometimes persisted for the remainder of the hour. For more than a year, he dismissed them as being as empty of content as his "fits," tantrums that he recalled having during his preschool years and that had persisted in diminishing frequency into the present. These episodes felt empty to me, too, insofar as I could not feel any force directed at me. I saw them initially as child-like tantrums, perhaps with a low-level temporal lobe instability that he had largely outgrown.

I was slow to engage these states, and he gradually let me know plaintively that I should somehow do more to help him during their turmoil.

They were the beginning of his many pleadings and attacks for what he saw as my reserved and indifferent stance, which left him abandoned and pressed me to rethink my reasons for my usually quiet stance and to comment and question more.

Gradually, Mr. F began to speak of fragments of what was going on in his head during his spells and their sequelae. While in a spell, he felt utterly like a small child, helpless and overwhelmed by bits and pieces of memories of endless guerrilla warfare with both parents around two major issues. That these matters might have been stirred by the quieter battles now staged with me seemed to me obvious, but he admitted nothing.

With his mother, it had been a power struggle over what he had to wear (rubber diapers for prolonged wetting) and receive (ongoing enemas for intractable constipation) until he was well into his sixth year of school. It was easy but not yet helpful to align this old struggle for the control or ownership of his sphincters with what was played out between us in manifold ways—as in his masterful hinting at and withholding of emotional signifiers and in his sudden rages, which would just as suddenly vanish as he made a slicing gesture to assign them to the inaccessible reaches of his lower abdomen. We worked in long frustration before he could call forth from behind his great divide muted glimpses of the hot anger and defiance that went with flatly recalled occasions in which he was repeatedly enticed into mother's reach with promises of food treats and snuggling. Once captured, he was swiftly enematized by mother and the maid. And there was Ex-Lax. They finally trained him, almost broke him.

Mr. F had turned to his reserved and chronically overworked father. First the boy flirted for attention, as his little sister had done, but then the father's shaming stopped him. He slavishly imitated his big brother, Ben, but made not a dent. When he was four years old, he attempted sex as best he could, in the fashion of his brothers, with a neighbor girl who was Ben's age and choice. They got away with it, perhaps were even chuckled over by their father. The boy was caught by his mother and turned over to his father for repeated thrashings, provoked by a stubborn refusal to desist. He finally did, and deadened.

In these same years, Mr. F shadowed his next older brother in their waking hours and snuggled close in their shared bed until well into their adolescence. Although their grown-up relating became perfunctory, Mr. F clung with gratitude and muted yearning to memories of their earlier relating in what he regarded as his only times of physical closeness and soft touching, and at least casual acceptance into the family of his years of growing up.

When we first met, Mr. F manifested shame and defiance when he touched briefly on his sexual preferences. Not until much later did he tell me that my lack of apparent rejection of him, and particularly my accepting his parting handshake, had allowed him some hope that I would not find him disgusting and untouchable. Over the ensuing years, he had been alert for indications that I was scornful of him and really wanted him to commit himself to heterosexuality.

In halting, groping fragments, he began to air in growing detail his fantasies and his lore about sexual matters, homosexual and heterosexual, at first ordinary, then obscenely perverse. I was jarred by his sudden alternations between anxious little boy and jaded de Sade in his manner of telling. I oscillated between hesitant fascination and feeling battered by the intensity of his lurid detailing. I felt propelled into greater intensities of sexual arousal and aversion in me than I was by then used to. With some 20 years of clinical seasoning in adult analysis, I thought I knew rather well what sexual content and context could turn me on or away or, more enigmatically, simply leave me unmoved.

For example, on the heterosexual side I found out early that I could expect to experience some amount of sexual interest, with at times genital excitement, when caught up in the appeal and challenge of certain women patients who embodied personal qualities and specific dynamic circumstances that could make them seem almost irresistible. Luckily, I had been in a first analysis, and then a second one, when these erotic intensities were most powerfully stirred in me. I was helped to find the understanding I needed to contain these near-misses (and myself) and to exchange intense oedipal tensions for fuller gratifications in my personal and marital relating. I am confident that these enhancements of my personal life allowed me the comfort of stronger defenses against acting on my impulses.

Of greater technical import, these easements allowed me the time and working space in which to solidify an analytic commitment to understanding, in preference to feeling impelled to act. Put in the classical terms of my training, I could rely on the sustaining power of aim-inhibited relating.

I was surprised, then, to feel unusual excitement as Mr. F, seeming to relax into a more revealing state, stepped up the intensity and volume of his fantasies about what sex with a safe and receptive woman could be like. I could sense myself straining to see what he was seeing, to feel what he was feeling, as though I were about to learn something unknown to me. And as his fantasies each time puddled into vagueness and confusion and he was beset with frightening images of the woman's sudden turning on him with ridicule or fury, I felt distress of my own and at times withdrew into silent ruminations of my own. I did not get what was going on until, after several "spells," Mr. F's fantasies took a sharp, sadomasochistic turn. Now he was both predator and victim vis-à-vis the woman of his dreams. He related these fantasies with a ferocity and relish that I had not seen before in him. I was at first repelled and chilled by the floridly gory details, and felt as though I barely recognized him. Where was the timid person I thought I knew?

This last twist somehow let me get it. I had been resonating to Mr. F's yearning fantasies with very similar wonderings of my own early adolescence. I, too, had had my share of frustration-driven sadistic twistings. We were both back there: he the anxious, ignorant one that I too had been, both of us reaching out in frightened fascination to mysteries beyond our ken. But when his fantasies exceeded mine at their worst, the spell of likeness was broken. I had to wrestle with renewed questions and confrontations about myself in relation to my mother and sisters, to swings of ambivalence that I had thought well-enough quieted. This heating up of old conflicts produced transient turbulence for the course of this particular piece of analytic work. I think it was the essentially familiar nature of these dynamic tensions that allowed me after a while to recover a comfortable stance.

The impact of Mr. F's homosexual preoccupations hit me quite differently.

I truly could sustain an adequate stance of inquiry into his casually described homosexual exploits until the threat of AIDS became a reality. Mr. F seemed oblivious to the risks of indiscriminate oral sex. I, to the contrary, was caught up in the deluge of confusing public and technical information of those times about matters of which I was quite ill informed. I felt a pressure to take an active medical stance, which I did.

Here we entered into a prolonged, quietly turbulent tensional state, triggered by my questioning of Mr. F regarding his awareness of the risks he faced. He let me know that he knew far more than I about the matter. I learned no more than that he knew enough to take precautions. It was clear to both of us that we had initiated a power struggle, one that I, hesitant in the face of my uncertainties, was slow to acknowledge and explore.

Mr. F increased both his homosexual cruising and his forays with women. Within the analysis, he began to flood the hours with both fantasies and depictions of actual encounters with both sexes. Professing to find petting with women far more exciting and gratifying of his wishes for closeness than sex with men, he went through a succession of brief and ill-fated affairs with ill-chosen women. His descriptions of these essentially masturbatory encounters highlighted his sadistic fantasies, poured onto me in relentless detail. Here he could half-acknowledge that, yes, he wished me to feel the helplessness and frustration he wanted these women to experience as he allowed them to have only a finger.

In the midst of these heterosexual misadventures, he switched suddenly to detailing his intensified homosexual encounters. I heard much about bleeding gums and cracked lips. He spoke, with what seemed to be anxious provocativeness, of a new-found ambivalent interest in offering himself for the first time for anal penetration, about which he had previously felt only disgust and avoidance. Soon he was telling me, with fervid fascination, of the latest lore, from both U.S. seacoasts, about the grotesque anal antics witnessed or talked about when he was cruising. Again switching suddenly, he spoke yearningly of his wish that we be sexually close and genitally comforting, as he vaguely recalled it had been like with his brother in the warmth of their shared bed.

What I experienced during these kaleidoscopic shifts and spins truly perplexed and disturbed me. Again, I thought that my prior analyses had given me comfortable enough access to my passive-erotic yearnings toward the uncles and cousins with whom I had close contact in my early years. And I had years earlier recovered some disturbing memories about an early Boy Scout camp experience: my frightened avoidance of the assistant scoutmaster, about whom other and older campers were whispering insinuations that I only vaguely understood. That he was later dropped from the troop made matters a little clearer, but not more comfortable.

With Mr. F, I first found myself fascinated and repelled by the graphic and literally bestial anal-sadistic descriptions of activities I had not previously heard of. It would be accurate to say that I felt the shock of having had shoved in my face the strange and unspeakable, as though I were being assaulted and overwhelmed. Then, with his abrupt switching over to his little-boy-genitally-comforted-by-older-brother yearnings, I was as suddenly in the safe cocoon of warm bed and nonthreatening arousal. It was the extreme contrast in these shocking and beckoning states proffered by the patient, threatening and seductive, that stirred my uneasiness and unbalance.

Outside the analytic hours, I became immersed in unbidden runs of recall and phantasy elaboration of the Boy Scout episode. These centered on anxiously ruminative foraging around whether I had been one of those successfully enticed into the scoutmaster's tent. Had I, the smallest and youngest of our country lot, been molested and gone amnesic? Why did I now keep coming back, at night in the warmth of my bed, to near sleep images and actual dreams of mud and manure, as in the cow pasture where our tents were scattered during that rainy week? Why was I so eager to be rescued by my mother and uncle when camp ended? These questions were driven by my distress and confusion during those hours with Mr. F when I faced what I could not recall ever having come upon before: both my fascinated aversion to the grossly sadomasochistic, and surges of positive curiosity and warmth about the reassuring nurturing and phallic pleasure of my patient's brother-to-brother evocations.

During this interval, I retreated to my earlier analytic mode of expectant silence. I temporarily found comfort in the distancing notion that I was dealing with Mr. F's wish to reproach and assault me for not gratifying his passive sexual needs, in the context of a mixed-parental transference.

Mr. F effectively shrugged off most of my well-chosen evidence about AIDS. I felt quite a tug in me to advise restraint and caution in his cruising encounters. I tried not to convey these urgencies, but, driven as they were by my own internal struggles of fascination and aversion in the face of the unknown, they were not concealable. In consequence, when Mr. F picked up on my going against the potential self-destructiveness of his homosexual cruising, I fed into his fears that I was attempting to interfere with or proscribe his genital activities. From this heat of the turmoil that we had stirred between us emerged a positive side that he could find in my concern and eventually could put into words: that my having at him showed that I was not indifferent to him or disgustedly turned away from him, as his father had been.

Meanwhile, I pushed myself to return to the active analytic mode I was learning to count on: trying to stay with and speak about the patient's content and his affective shifts in an effort to get close to him and to the meanings their imagistic and emotional qualities held for him. At this point, I saw that I was also trying, in counterphobic fashion, to help desensitize my anxiety.

We came to some shared perspectives. Yes, Mr. F wanted to shake and seduce me, out of vengefulness and a wish to have us break apart. But alongside that and as important, he was himself frightened of, yet unable to shake off, his sadomasochistic surges and his deep yearnings for a closeness he could never trust. Either, he feared, could drive me away forever.

In my own bursts of concurrent self-inquiry, taking place mostly out in the garden, and then extending into bedtime, I was unable to come up with any convincing fresh indications of actual encounters during my week in Boy Scout camp. But I recalled being told by my mother not to enter the house of a kindly bachelor neighbor because "he did bad things with young boys." She did not amplify, and I did not ask. In my anxious boyhood ignorance, I did not go far in my conscious fantasies. I surely said nothing about it to my male cousins, just as there was very little about sexual matters in general that I felt free to speak about until we were adults. The best that I could come upon in my current reveries was a fresh poignancy around my autoerotic phantasy life during the sexual isolation and ignorance of my adolescence, when my perceptions of mother's shaming aversion toward active sexuality of any sort most painfully oppressed me.

I came to a sense that my current turbulence was a revival, not of old actualities of shockings or soothings with either sex but, rather, of the intense and guilty phantasizing that I had resorted to in my early adolescent years. I had long known that the sadistic qualities in those phantasies had been fed by my rage at feeling so constrained. I retrieved memories of how my fantasies had fed on the specific reinforcement and lurid detailing I discovered in the adventure and murder magazines that were the pulp pornography of the early 1930s. I found a fresh intensity in my excitement and discovery when I furtively scanned copies discovered at the bottom of the pile at the barbershop, and especially in my arousal and anxious eagerness to learn more when I came upon a spicy mystery tucked away in my uncle's workshop. Here was a sort of masculine permission and direction, unspoken and to be kept hidden, that for better or worse gave me counter for and relief from maternal disapproval and scorn. Anger, easement, and regret were just part of the swirl of old and new feelings that came with seeing afresh the constraining of our respective sexual attitudes and freedoms that lay in the relationship between my mother, uncle, and me. This perspective somehow steadied and made easier my stumbling efforts to restore analytic contact with Mr. F.

He slowly accepted that I was trying to find the feel and texture of his viewpoint.

In the recurring enactments between us, he and we came upon the details of the layering of true and false selves made familiar in our lore by Winnicott (1958), Modell (1990), and others. Mr. F's façade as a docile, ever-compliant boy/man with painfully perfected social skills hid, even from himself, the rage and contempt with which by the age of four he had come to regard the world.

I close this clinical vignette with excerpts from two hours of the last year of our work, consecutive but with a five-day break occasioned by one of Mr. F's frequent business trips. The quoted material is as close to verbatim as I could excerpt from his steady stream of variations and elaborations.

In the hour preceding the break, Mr. F dwelt with enthusiasm on his increasing grasp of "my basic self, my gutsy kid-self that would never give in, even if it meant I had to hide all of my life. I love him! He's real, and he's mine! He's me!" His voice dropped in vigor and insistence. "Even as I say this, I'm fading, losing hold."

McLaughlin: Such strength and conviction in your voice, as you held him, and now sound sad and weak and giving him up?

Mr. F: [Half-sits up as he replies] Are you putting me on? You know we've just again been talking about how saying anything I really mean means I give it up. It's not mine. It's yours. It's nothing! [sinks back onto couch] But I know that's not really so—I could hear your voice. No teasing in it. I will hold on to this base self regardless! [pause of several moments] This is harder to say, to stick with. When I feel this me that seems real, I'm also feeling something about you that feels real. I'd like to say it feels good. But that would mean giving you something. And I can't give anything that's real, that's worthwhile. Something goes wrong [sounds perplexed, heavy].

McLaughlin: It's something more than turning good stuff over to me?

Mr. F: Yeah, but I don't think of words for it—don't want to. Makes me think of some stuff you were going on about a while back. When I was talking about how good it felt between little Ben [patient's lovable young nephew]

and me, you said something about the generosity of
loving back. I didn't get it. I know it's time to go now.
I'm going to try to hold on to this base feeling that I feel
I'm getting!

Bustling into the next hour, Mr. F was quick to inform me, "I've held on
to me all this time. Now I can tell you I wasn't giving it to you quite
straight. Underneath that base me is the real me." His voice grew deeper,
almost raspy. "I've hated and despised everyone most of my life—like
that was the only way I knew to feel, to stay safe, to not care. Like I'm
hating you right now!"

McLaughlin:	Your voice sounds heavy, harsh. This is your hatred now?
Mr. F:	I have to hate you! Yet I keep telling you, without really telling you, that it is only in here, with you, that I can really feel this real me. Why must I hate you? Is that all I am? I know by now you don't hate me, don't despise me like I've done to you. [on verge of rare tears] I'm remembering something you said to me, said years ago, about how you kept getting glimpses of a real person in me that I had to keep hiding. I thought you were nuts, or kidding. But I thought I heard feeling in your voice, maybe sadness. I think I felt love for you for that. I know I wanted to reach out and hug you. But you'd have seen that as my homosexual stuff. And I've been letting you know long enough how angry I have been that you told me you couldn't let me have sex with you—how that was your problem, not mine—but it's made me want to withhold everything from you.
McLaughlin:	That's still the way it stands?
Mr. F:	No, that's changing, too. I can feel you've had a lot of caring for me, respect for me, and say! I think I've got it—about that generosity of loving back. I have felt it with Ben. I'm feeling it now with you—that my loving you for your loving me makes me feel I do have something good to give back! It feels safe here. Will it be safe out there? I've been slow to get there, but I'm going to

give it my best try! [The hour is ending, and Mr. F is about to rise.]

McLaughlin: I'm proud for you!

He suddenly hugs me as he passes, his first hug, and I return it. There were two more such brief hugs by the time the work ended. We did some analytic work on them.

Hours like these marked the progress Mr. F made in the latter half of the work. He gave up cruising to enter into a sequence of intermittent yet satisfyingly intimate affairs with men of his own caliber, in cities connected with his business ventures. At home, he sought and sustained in sequence two fully sexual affairs with women, either of whom seemed qualified to afford him a compatible long-term relationship. Transference resonances, evident in all these encounters, were eventually openly admitted to and worked on. At the same time, Mr. F could not bring himself to make more permanent ties to either a man or a woman during the time of our work. Since termination, he has occasionally checked in with me to report his continuing enjoyment of his noncommitted bisexuality in relationships that tend to be mutually gratifying until the partner presses too insistently for an acknowledged commitment. Mr. F is then happy to move on.

Discussion

I see my overall stance of responsiveness to Mr. F as having helped him to locate, specify, and authenticate his reality view. One yield of my effort to enter his worldview lay in his experience of being believed about his very fundamental perceptions. Such affirmation is sometimes hard to come by in our usual familial relationships. Mr. F had had precious little of it, once he was beyond infancy. The supportive and releasing power of being perceived and believed, recurring in myriad configurations between us, evoked in him sufficient trust in how and why I work and growing confidence in his own capacities to see what before he had striven not to see. Then, gradually, he could reveal, to himself as well as to me, his hidden self, whose surges of genuine love and rage both delighted and frightened him; and eventually he could find value in the highly adapted social abilities of his façade self, which previously he scorned as his shameful submission to those he hated and needed.

And, as Mr. F's own words say clearly enough, when he could trust me enough to feel loved and believed in by me, he found in himself capacities to trust and claim his own positive as well as negative feelings toward himself and others.

In the transference states that I experienced during the turbulent periods described earlier, I felt caught up in a considerable span of gender confusion and sexual intensities. I was generally able to sustain my preferred analytic stance in the face of Mr. F's shifting pressures of seductive and aggressive attack, as long as these remained within the context of his transferences to me as his rejecting/seductive mother who had so tantalized and enraged him. Qualitative likenesses between us in these sectors intensified my being in touch with the urgencies and anger of the lonely, yearning, and hungrily curious small boy within us. And I could truly appreciate the high value he placed on his resolute autonomy.

Yet I obviously broke with him at times around quantitative differences between us. There were destructive and sadistic depths to his rage and vengefulness toward women—extremes that I could slowly become comfortable with, but not make touch with, in their likeness in me.

Similarly, yet more strikingly, I found myself initially shocked, alienated, and fascinated by the emerging passion of Mr. F's conflicted homosexuality. The intensities and specific detailing of his anal-sadistic intentions that emerged in the work, directed toward women, then men, and at me in both gender configurations, were startling. Their assaultiveness highlighted old issues of my own and magnified them for both of us by their utter contrast to the pathetic little victim of his earlier portrayal. I could not for a while restore my stance. It was during my destabilized state that I most perceptibly acted on my wish to put a halt to his risking, to quiet the sadomasochistic oscillations stirred in both of us.

It did help me to go back once more to the two unsettled bits of personal history around exposure to homosexual experiences. I was driven by my uneasiness over my strong affective involvement with Mr. F, both as the lonely, yearning little boy and as the latter-day de Sade. I could recapture fresh intensities of oral and genital sadistic impulses of my own toward my important women, blended with sexual tenderness and cherishing, that mounted in me up through adolescence. I scanned what I knew of my yearnings for my lost father, and uncles and cousins who came and went—this time I deliberately fantasized what oral–genital sex with them, in the manner of my patient's descriptions, might feel like. I could grasp some of what Mr. F felt was so pleasurable, but I could not feel drawn to be actually involved. I did imagine with some gusto that one satisfying component of being the fellator could come from the literal fulfillment of an infantile wish—the sensation of adult-mouth-fully-filled-with-phallus to that of infant-mouth-filled-with-nipple—but I could discover no experiential resonance.

What did come into fresh focus was how important to me had been my old and intermittent relationships with uncles and male cousins across my early years. We had been able, at times traveling to each other over distance, to develop enduring relationships that served as models for other rewarding friendships of my adult years. These friendships carry qualities of intimacy and depth that have been highly gratifying and, to my awareness, unstrained by homosexual or aggressively loaded components. I have to leave unresolved whether or not there remain unaccessed portions of my past that would speak oppositely.

My seeking, at the time of my work with Mr. F, did not bring out much that involved significant homosexual tensions. It did give me an amplified sense of how my many changes of winter residence and schools in my first 15 years had screened me from some of the possible consequences of unbroken youthful intimacies. I saw more vividly how this itinerancy had heightened my sense of comfort in my autonomy and reserve, while pressing me to evolve a considerable social adaptiveness in the face of continuing environmental change. Here was an approximation, on a lesser scale, of Mr. F's driven isolation and defensive façade of autonomy.

I had to conclude that it was my lot to develop under circumstances that maximized issues of intimacy and aggression in the maternal realm and minimized strongly conflicted actualities with paternal or male sibling figures. I had space and aloneness in which to consolidate my ways to modulate and set limits as I needed. One liability, of course, became that I had less experiential exposure to relational complexities with paternal or fraternal persons in a position to threaten me. Doing analysis, particularly in the classical modes that marked my training, offered me ample opportunity to play out the safety of this protected state, until its limitations and mine pressed me to extend beyond its confinements toward a deeper analytic intimacy. Put more succinctly, being experientially less prepared than I needed to be to relate to such persons as Mr. F, I was forced to extend and expand as best I could in my analytic encounters, to seek to be open to likenesses and differences between us around matters that I had not adequately assimilated.

The easements that I came to in this piece of self-scrutiny allowed me, and eventually Mr. F, more comfort to explore the perspective that I might have done something to make for tensions between us. He was initially repelled, wary, and anxious. That I might acknowledge having acted from a position of being wrong was utterly alien to his experience. I might be ensnaring him with sweet talk. Reiterated and played out over time, my stance influenced basic aspects of Mr. F's reality view—among them his coming to feel that his fierce defensiveness and phony façade were acceptable but no longer needed.

We both were often aware of and weighing the effect of our impact on the other. Our most enduring struggles played out around the matter of Mr. F's dangerous cruising. What eased the matter here was first his feeling safe enough to speak of his wish/fear of provoking me to banish him. In evident relief, he then made it quite clear that it was my dissembling that was making him both furious and anxious. I should be out in the open, where he could know what to do. I was able then to speak about the quandary of my wish to urge him to do the sensible thing, countered by my concern for his need for autonomy. The piece of collaborative work that ensued around this acknowledgment of mutual influence marked the beginning of his relinquishing the cruising.

Mr. F has remained resolute in his pleasure in the easements the analysis brought him. It is quite possible that, had he been confronted with an analyst whose homoerotic conflicts and resolutions more closely approximated his own, he might have been impelled by different intensities to seek different compromise solutions. Such intensities could well have pressed him to a fuller commitment to one or the other sex. For myself, I know that Mr. F challenged me to confront old heterosexual issues anew, to find new levels of comfort with my omnipresent dynamics of aggression and bisexuality. Especially did he challenge me to sample and assimilate immediacies of overt homosexuality at intensities I had not consciously known before. We both came out of this piece of analytic work with our own deep sense of having been changed by the impact of an intimacy with an other that was novel and disturbing, then acceptable and enhancing to us both. I suspect that this is an inevitable consequence of working in the intensities of the analytic dyad and, indeed for both, a major gratification that rewards the quest.

In this core experience is a moving power, by and for the two participants, that I do not fully fathom. A possible clue to a central ingredient may lie in the archaic quality of the belief, particularly when mutually acknowledged, that one can indeed be the cause of the behaviors of the other, that one can indeed have such significance as to evoke the behaviors of the other. This way of experiencing the interplay of mutual influence and power is prominent in the closeness of baby and mother (Stern, 1985). The utter absence of this belief in early development can stunt or kill a child or bring a mother to despair. It is a belief that pervades the entwinement of lovers and colors every intense relationship throughout life, including the analytic relationship.

Let us note here how different is the feel of this stance from our traditional position, so well captured in the older and defensive connotations of the term *countertransference*. As I have experienced it, the analyst's feeling and timely acknowledgment of the impact of the patient on him, and of the analyst's impact on the patient, can evoke in both parties powerful resonances of those oscillations of mutual influence and confluence that were central to our early relating. Such evocations lend particular intensities of immediacy and realness to the experiences of being touched and touching, seen and seeing, moved and moving, influenced and influencing in the analytic dyad.

When patients felt understood, or even when they just sensed that such understanding was what I was seeking for them, they often moved on to a fresh and surprising uncovering of significant fantasies and their historical antecedents. Quite on their own, each patient could fashion insightful retrievals and constructions that carried more conviction for both of us than the interpretations I might have devised. I wish emphatically to emphasize that working in this fashion is not an effort to be empathic. I hold to the conviction that the analyst's empathy rests most legitimately in his efforts to enhance his sense of resonance with the patient through intuitive openness. Its use is always to be questioned when the analyst tries to convey empathy through his words and other behaviors, for then he is most likely to be off on a thing of his own.

In seeking the fullness of the patient's view, the analyst is trying to grope for and foster an understanding of the patient's often deepest and never articulated seeing—to hear and resonate to the patient's words through close attention to the patient's idiom and affective shading. It allows the analyst to assert quiet pressure to provide the how of his inquiring view and slant, while asking for ongoing feedback of countering, altering, and additive input from the patient. This way may come across as empathic in that it acknowledges the patient as the ultimate teller of the tale and places the analyst more as the recognitive audience to the patient's creative effort, but it is a dedicated effort and struggle on the part of two separate and different minds to seek information, not to provide empathic responsiveness.

Much of this close attention paid to the reality view of the patient may seem to involve small matters, but, singly and cumulatively, these matters manage to amass a moving force in the working dyad. And such an influencing force, the deployment of which is most often ambiguously experienced, constitutes for me the essence of what analytic movement is about.

In summary, I emphasize once more the potential for mutative analytic progress in the working through of the experiences of mutual influence in this manner. Over time and bit by bit, the significance and value that each party finds in the words and actions of the other, the power and meaning of one for the other, the trust and belief in what is discovered between self and other, become experienced, articulated, and assimilated.

Putting the matter thusly suddenly brings to the fore the realization of a clinical observation alive in the background of my experience for now many years. The words of appreciation I have heard from my patients in their taking leave, like the parting words of the patients my colleagues have told me about, spoke very little or not at all of the analyst's towering intellect or analytic prowess. Instead, semiarticulate phrases allude to small analytic happenings, still resonant in these patients, that provided core perceptions of their having felt stood by, their pain and joy recognized, their personal value affirmed, something essential in them believed.

REFERENCES

Anthi, P. (1983), Reconstruction of preverbal experiences. *J. Amer. Psychoanal. Assn.,* 31:33–59.

Arlow, J. A. (1969), Fantasy, memory, and reality testing. *Psychoanal. Quart.,* 38:28–51.

_____ & Beres, D. (1974), Fantasy and identification in empathy. *Psychoanal. Quart.,* 43:26–50.

Aron, L. (1996), *A Meeting of Minds.* Hillsdale, NJ: The Analytic Press.

Balint, M. & Balint, A. (1939), On transference and counter-transference. In: *Primary Love and Psychoanalytic Technique.* London: Hogarth Press, 1952, pp. 213–220.

Balter, L., Lothane, Z. & Spencer, J. (1980), On the analyzing instrument. *Psychoanal. Quart.,* 49:474–504.

Baum, O. E. (1977), Countertransference and the vicissitudes in an analyst's development. *Psychoanal. Rev.,* 64:539–550.

Beiser, H. (1984), Example of self analysis. *J. Amer. Psychoanal. Assn.,* 32:3–12.

Benedek, T. (1953), Dynamics of the countertransference. *Bull. Menn. Clin.,* 17:201–208.

Beres, D. (1960), Perception, imagination, and reality. *Internat. J. Psycho-Anal.,* 41:327–334.

Bernfeld, S. (1941), The facts of observation in psychoanalysis. *J. Psychol.* 12:289–305.

Bion, W. (1959), *Experiences in Groups.* New York: Basic Books.

Bird, B. (1972), Notes on transference: Universal phenomenon and hardest part of analysis. *J. Amer. Psychoanal. Assn.,* 20:267–301.

Blau, A. (1946), *The Master Hand: A Study of the Origin and Meaning of Right and Left Sidedness and Its Relation to Personality and Language, Research Monogr. No. 5.* New York: American Orthopsychiatric Association.

Bollas, C. (1999), Dead mother, dead child. In: *The Mystery of Things.* London: Routledge, pp. 106–126.

Breuer, J. & Freud, S. (1893–1895), Studies on hysteria. *Standard Edition,* 2:1–309. London: Hogarth Press, 1955.

Britton, R. (1998), *Belief and Imagination: Explorations in Psychoanalysis.* London: New Library of Psychoanalysis.

Bruner, J. (1964), The course of cognitive growth. *Amer. Psychol.,* 19:1–15.

223

Buber, M. (1923), *I and Thou*, trans. W. Kaufman. New York: Touchstone, 1970.

Bullowa, M. (1979), Prelinguistic communication. In: *Before Speech*, ed. M. Bullowa. Cambridge, England: Cambridge University Press, pp. 1–43.

Burris, B. (1995), Classics revisited: Freud's papers on technique. *J. Amer. Psychoanal. Assn.*, 43:175–185.

Calder, K. (1979), An analyst's self-analysis. *J. Amer. Psychoanal. Assn.*, 28:5–20.

Calef, V. & Weinshel, E. M. (1985), Facts of observation in psychoanalysis by Siegfried Bernfeld. *Internat. Rev. Psycho-Anal.*, 12:341–352.

Casement, P. (1982), Pressure on the analyst for physical contact while reliving trauma. *Internat. Rev. Psycho-Anal.*, 9:279.

Cassirer, E. (1946), *Language and Myth*. New York: Harper & Row.

———— (1953), *The Philosophy of Symbolic Forms*. New Haven, CT: Yale University Press.

Chused, J. (1991), The evocative power of enactments. *J. Amer. Psychoanal. Assn.*, 39:615–640.

Coles, R. (1990), *The Spiritual Life of Children*. Boston: Houghton Mifflin.

Cooper, S. (1993), Interpretive fallibility and psychoanalytic dialogue. *J. Amer. Psychoanal. Assn.*, 41:95–126.

Cornell, W. F. (2000), Entering the gestural field: bringing somatic and subsymbolic processes into the psychoanalytic frame. Presented at meeting of Pittsburgh Psychoanalytic Society and Institute, November.

Crouch, S. (1990), Liner notes to compact disc, *Deep in the Shed*, Marcus Roberts. New York: BMG Music.

Dahl, H., Teller, V., Moss, D. & Trujillo, M. (1978), Countertransference examples of the syntactic expression of warded-off contents. *Psychoanal. Quart.*, 47:339–363.

Dean, E. S. (1957), Drowsiness as a symptom of countertransference. *Psychoanal. Quart.*, 26:246–247.

Deutsch, H. (1926), Okkulte Vorgänge während der Psychoanalyse Imago [Occult processes occurring during psychoanalysis]. *Imago*, 12:418–433.

———— (1947), Analysis of postural behaviors. *Psychoanal. Quart.*, 16:195–213.

———— (1952), Analytic posturology. *Psychoanal. Quart.*, 21:196–214.

Dickes, R. (1965), The defensive function of an altered state of consciousness: A hypnoid state. *J. Amer. Psychoanal. Assn.*, 13:356–403.

———— & Papernik, D. S. (1977), Defensive alterations of consciousness: Hypnoid states, sleep, and the dream. *J. Amer. Psychoanal. Assn.*, 25:635–654.

Domhoff, G. W. (1968), But why did they sit on the king's right in the first place? *Psychoanal. Rev.*, 56:586–596.

Eissler, K. (1953), The effect of the structure of the ego in psychoanalytic technique. *J. Amer. Psychoanal. Assn.*, 1:104–143.

Emde, R. (1988), Development terminable and interminable, I: Innate and motivational factors from infancy. *Internat. J. Psycho-Anal.*, 69:23–42.

Engelman, E. (1976), *Bergasse 19: Sigmund Freud's Home and Offices, Vienna, 1938*. New York: Basic Books.

English, O. S. & Pearson, G. (1937), *Common Neuroses of Children and Adults*. New York: Norton.

Erikson, E. H. (1950), *Childhood and Society*. New York: Norton.

———— (1954), The dream specimen of psychoanalysis. *J. Amer. Psychoanal. Assn.*, 2:5–56.

Fairbairn, W. R. D. (1954), *An Object-Relations Theory of the Personality*. New York: Basic Books.

Feldman, S. (1959), *Mannerisms of Speech and Gestures*. New York: International Universities Press.

Fenichel, O. (1941), *Problems of Psychoanalytic Technique*. New York: Psychoanalytic Quarterly.

———— (1945), *The Psychoanalytic Theory of Neurosis*. New York: Norton.

Ferenczi, S. (1909), Introjection and transference. In: *Sex in Psychoanalysis*. New York: Basic Books, 1950, pp. 35–93.

———— (1919), Thinking and muscle innervation. In: *Further Contributions to the Theory and Technique of Psychoanalysis*. New York: Basic Books, 1952, pp. 230–232.

———— (1950), *Sex in Psychoanalysis*. New York: Basic Books.

———— & Rank, O. (1924), *The Development of Psycho-Analysis*. New York: Nervous & Mental Disease, 1925.

Fliess, R. (1942), The metapsychology of the analyst. *Psychoanal. Quart.*, 11: 211–227.

Fraiberg, S. (1980), *Clinical Studies in Infant Mental Health*. New York: Basic Books.

Freedman, N. (1977), Hands, words and mind: On the structuralization of body movements during discourse and the capacity for verbal representation. In: *Communicative Structures and Psychic Structures*, ed. N. Freedman & S. Grand. New York: Plenum Press, pp. 109–132.

Freud, S. (1895), Project for a scientific psychology. *Standard Edition*, 1:295–397. London: Hogarth Press, 1966.

———— (1900), The interpretation of dreams. *Standard Edition*, 4:1–338; 5:339–625. London: Hogarth Press, 1953.

———— (1905), Fragment of an analysis of a case of hysteria. *Standard Edition*, 7:7–122. London: Hogarth Press, 1953.

———— (1910), The future prospects of psycho-analytic therapy. *Standard Edition*, 11:139–151. London: Hogarth Press, 1957.

———— (1911), The handling of dream-interpretation in psycho-analysis. *Standard Edition*, 12:89–96. London: Hogarth Press, 1958.

———— (1912a), The dynamics of transference. *Standard Edition*, 12:97–108. London: Hogarth Press, 1958.

———— (1912b), Recommendations to physicians practising psycho-analysis. *Standard Edition*, 12:109–120. London: Hogarth Press, 1958.

_____ (1913), On beginning the treatment (Further recommendations on the technique of psycho-analysis I). *Standard Edition,* 12:121–144. London: Hogarth Press, 1958.

_____ (1914), Remembering, repeating and working through (Further recommendations on the technique of psycho-analysis II). *Standard Edition,* 12:145–156. London: Hogarth Press, 1958.

_____ (1915a), Observations on transference-love (Further recommendations on the technique of psycho-analysis III). *Standard Edition,* 12:157–171. London: Hogarth Press, 1958.

_____ (1915b), The unconscious. *Standard Edition,* 14:166–215. London: Hogarth Press, 1957.

_____ (1920), Beyond the pleasure principle. *Standard Edition,* 18:7–64. London: Hogarth Press, 1955.

_____ (1923), The ego and the id. *Standard Edition,* 19:12–66. London: Hogarth Press, 1961.

_____ (1925), Negation. *Standard Edition,* 19:235–239. London: Hogarth Press, 1961.

_____ (1926a), Inhibitions, symptoms and anxiety. *Standard Edition,* 20:87–175. London: Hogarth Press, 1959.

_____ (1926b), The question of lay analysis: Conversations with an impartial person. *Standard Edition,* 20:183–250. London: Hogarth Press, 1959.

_____ (1926c), Postscript [to the question of lay analysis]. *Standard Edition,* 20:251–258. London: Hogarth Press, 1959.

_____ (1931), Female sexuality. *Standard Edition,* 21:225–243. London: Hogarth Press, 1961.

_____ (1933), New introductory lectures on psycho-analysis. *Standard Edition,* 22:5–182. London: Hogarth Press, 1964.

_____ (1937), Analysis terminable and interminable. *Standard Edition,* 23:216–253. London: Hogarth Press, 1964.

Friedman, L. (1978), Trends in the psychoanalytic theory of treatment. *Psychoanal. Quart.,* 47:524–567.

_____ (1980), Kohut: A book review essay. *Psychoanal. Quart.,* 49:393–422.

Fromm-Reichmann, F. (1939), Transference problems in schizophrenics. *Psychoanal. Quart.,* 8:412–426.

Gardner, M. R. (1983), *Self-Inquiry.* Boston: Atlantic/Little Brown.

Gill, M. M. (1979), Analysis of the transference. *J. Amer. Psychoanal. Assn.,* 27(Suppl.):263–288.

_____ (1982), *Analysis of Transference: Vol. I: Theory and Technique.* New York: International Universities Press.

_____ (1983), The interpersonal paradigm and the degree of the therapist's involvement. *Contemp. Psychoanal.,* 19:200–237.

_____ & Hoffman, I. Z. (1982), A method for studying the analysis of aspects of the patient's experience of the relationship in psychoanalysis and psychotherapy. *J. Amer. Psychoanal. Assn.,* 30:137–167.

Gitelson, M. (1952), The emotional position of the analyst in the psycho-analytic situation. *Internat. J. Psycho-Anal.,* 33:1–10.

_____ (1962), The curative factors in psycho-analysis. I. The first phase of psychoanalysis. *Internat. J. Psycho-Anal.,* 43:194–205.

Glover, E. (1927), Lectures on technique in psychoanalysis. 1. Introduction: The analytic situation. 2. The opening phase. *Internat. J. Psycho-Anal.,* 8: 311–338.

_____ (1931), The therapeutic effect of inexact interpretation. *Internat. J. Psycho-Anal.,* 12:397–408.

Goldberg, L. (1979), Remarks on transference–countertransference in psychotic states. *Internat. J. Psycho-Anal.,* 60:347–356.

Gostynski, E. (1951), A clinical contributor to the analysis of gestures. *Internat. J. Psycho-Anal.,* 32:310–318.

Gray, P. (1973), Psychoanalytic technique: Ego capacity to view intrapsychic activity. *J. Amer. Psychoanal. Assn.,* 21:474–494.

_____ (1982), Developmental lag in the evolution of psychoanalytic technique. *J. Amer. Psychoanal. Assn.,* 30:621–655.

Green, A. (1986), The dead mother. In: *On Private Madness.* London: Hogarth Press, pp. 142–173.

Greenson, R. R. (1953), On boredom. *J. Amer. Psychoanal. Assn.,* 1:7–21.

_____ (1960), Empathy and its vicissitudes. *Internat. J. Psycho-Anal.,* 41:418–424.

_____, rptr. (1961), Panel on the selection of candidates for psychoanalytic training. *J. Amer. Psychoanal. Assn.,* 9:135–145.

_____ (1967), *The Technique and Practice of Psychoanalysis, Volume 1.* New York: International Universities Press.

_____ (1971), The "real" relationship between the patient and the psychoanalyst. In: *Explorations in Psychoanalysis.* New York: International Universities Press, 1978, pp. 425–441.

_____ & Wexler, M. (1969), The non-transference relationship in the psychoanalytic situation. *Internat. J. Psycho-Anal.,* 50:27–39.

Guttman, S. (1980), *Concordance to the Standard Edition of the Complete Psychological Works of Sigmund Freud.* New York: International Universities Press.

Hacker, F. (1962), The discriminatory function of the ego. *Internat. J. Psycho-Anal.,* 43:395–405.

Hartmann, H. (1939), *Ego Psychology and the Problem of Adaptation.* New York: International Universities Press, 1958.

Hatcher, R. L. (1973), Insight and self-observation. *J. Amer. Psychoanal. Assn.,* 21:377–398.

Hoffer, W. (1949), Mouth, hand, and ego-integration. The *Psychoanalytic Study of the Child,* 3/4:49–56. New York: International Universities Press.

Hoffman, I. Z. (1992), Some practical implications of a social constructivist view of the psychoanalytic situation. *Psychoanal. Dial.,* 2:287–304.

Horowitz, M. (1978), *Image Formation and Cognition.* New York: Appleton-Century-Crofts.

Isakower, O. (1963), Minutes of faculty meeting, New York Psychoanalytic Insititute, November, New York City.

Jacobs, T. J. (1973), Posture, gesture, and movement in the analyst: Cues to interpretation and countertransference. *J. Amer. Psychoanal. Assn.,* 21:77–92.

———— (1986), On countertransference enactments. *J. Amer. Psychoanal. Assn.,* 34:289–307.

Johan, M., rptr. (1992), Enactments in psychoanalysis. *J. Amer. Psychoanal. Assn.,* 40:40–41.

Johnson, A. M. (1951), Some heterosexual transference and countertransference phenomena in the late analysis of the oedipus. Presented at meeting of Washington, DC Psychoanalytic Society, March.

Kern, J. (1978), Countertransference and spontaneous screens: An analyst studies his own visual images. *J. Amer. Psychoanal. Assn.,* 26:21–48.

Kernberg, O. F. (1965), Notes on countertransference. *J. Amer. Psychoanal. Assn.,* 13:38–57.

———— (1976), *Object Relations Theory and Clinical Psychoanalysis.* New York: Aronson.

———— (1979), Some implications of object relations theory for psychoanalytic technique. *J. Amer. Psychoanal. Assn.,* 27(Suppl.):207–239.

Kirsner, D. (2000), *Unfree Associations: Inside Psychoanalytic Institutes.* London: Process Press.

Kohut, H. (1971), *The Analysis of the Self: A Systematic Approach to the Psychoanalytic Treatment of Narcissistic Personality Disorders.* New York: International Universities Press.

Kramer, S. (1979), The technical significance and application of Mahler's separation-individuation theory. *J. Amer. Psychoanal. Assn.,* 27(Suppl.):241–262.

Kris, A. (1982), *Free Association: Method and Process.* New Haven, CT: Yale University Press.

Langer, S. (1942), *Philosophy in a New Key: A Study in the Symbolism of Reason, Rite, and Art.* Cambridge, MA: Harvard University Press, 1957.

Langs, R. (1976), *The Bi-Personal Field.* New York: Aronson.

Laplanche, J. & Pontalis, J.-B. (1968), Fantasy and the origins of sexuality. *Internat. J. Psycho-Anal.,* 49:1–18.

Little, M. (1951), Counter-transference and the patient's response to it. *Internat. J. Psycho-Anal.,* 32:32–40.

Loewald, H. W. (1951), Ego and reality. *Internat. J. Psycho-Anal.,* 32:10–18.

_____ (1960), On the therapeutic action of psychoanalysis. *Internat. J. Psycho-Anal.,* 41:16–33.

_____ (1962), Internalization, separation, mourning, and the superego. *Psychoanal. Quart.,* 31:483–504.

_____ (1978), Instinct theory, object relations, and psychic-structure formation. *J. Amer. Psychoanal. Assn.,* 26:493–506.

Loewenstein, R. M. (1969), An historical review of the theory of psychoanalytic technique. Abstracted by J. S. Beigler, *Bull. Phila. Assn. Psychoanal.,* 19:58–60.

Low, B. (1935), The psychological compensations of the analyst. *Internat. J. Psycho-Anal.,* 16:1–8.

Mahler, M., Pine, F. & Bergman, A. (1975), *The Psychological Birth of the Infant: Symbiosis and Individuation.* New York: Basic Books.

Matte-Blanco, I. (1975), *The Unconscious as Infinite Sets: An Essay in Bilogic.* London: Duckworth.

McLaughlin, J. (1961), The analyst and the Hippocratic oath. *J. Amer. Psychoanal. Assn.,* 9:106–120.

_____ (1973), The nonreporting training analyst, the analysis, and the institute. *J. Amer. Psychoanal. Assn.,* 21:697–712.

_____ (1975), The sleepy analyst: Some observations on states of consciousness in the analyst at work. *J. Amer. Psychoanal. Assn.,* 23:363–382.

_____ (1978), Primary and secondary process in the context of cerebral hemispheric specialization. *Psychoanal. Quart.,* 47:237–266.

_____ (1981), Transference, psychic reality and countertransference. *Psychoanal. Quart.,* 50:639–664.

_____ (1984), On antithetic and metathetic words in the analytic situation. *Psychoanal. Quart.,* 53:38–62.

_____ (1987), The play of transference: Some reflections on enactment in the psychoanalytic situation. *J. Amer. Psychoanal. Assn.,* 35:557–582.

_____ (1988), The analyst's insights. *Psychoanal. Quart.,* 57:370–389.

_____ (1989), The relevance of infant observational research for the analytic understanding of adult patients' nonverbal behaviors. In: *The Significance of Infant Observational Research for Children, Adolescents, and Adults,* ed. S. Dowling & A. Rothstein. Madison, CT: International Universities Press, pp. 109–122.

_____ (1991), Clinical and theoretical aspects of enactment. *J. Amer. Psychoanal. Assn.,* 39:595–614.

_____ (1992), Nonverbal behavior in the analytic situation: The search for meaning in non-verbal cues. In: *When the Body Speaks: Psychological Meanings in Kinetic Cues,* ed. S. Kramer & S. Akhtar. Northvale, NJ: Aronson, pp. 131–162.

_____ (1993a), Work with patients: The impetus for self-analysis. *Psychoanal. Inq.,* 13:365–389.

_____ (1993b), Work with patients and the experience of self-analysis. In: *Self-Analysis,* ed. J. Barron. Hillsdale, NJ: The Analytic Press, pp. 63–81.

_____ (1994a), Analytic impasse: The interplay of dyadic transferences. Presented at meeting of Karen Horney Psychoanalytic Institute and Center, March, New York City.

_____ (1994b), Modes of influence in psychoanalysis. Presented at meeting of American Psychoanalytic Association, December, New York City.

_____ (1995), Touching limits in the analytic dyad. *Psychoanal. Quart.*, 64:433–465.

_____ (2002), Book review: *The Shame Response to Rejection. J. Amer. Psychoanal. Assn.*, 50:1088–1090.

Menaker, E. (1942), The masochistic factor in the psychoanalytic situation. *Psychoanal. Quart.*, 11:171–186.

Modell, A. (1990), *Other Times, Other Realities.* Cambridge, MA: Harvard University Press.

Moore, B. E. & Fine, B. D., eds. (1967), *A Glossary of Psychoanalytic Terms and Concepts,* 2nd ed. New York: American Psychoanalytic Association, 1968.

_____ & _____ (1990), *Psychoanalytic Terms and Concepts.* Binghamton, NY: Vail-Ballou Press.

Mosher, P. W., ed. (1987), *Key Words and Author Index to Psychoanalytic Journals 1920–1986.* New York: American Psychoanalytic Association.

Murphy, C. & Messer, D. (1979), Mothers, infants and pointing: A study of gesture. In: *Studies in Mother–Infant Interaction,* ed. H. Schaffer. New York: Academic Press, pp. 354–581.

Needles, W. (1959), Gesticulation and speech. *Internat. J. Psycho-Anal.,* 40:291–294.

Norman, H. F., Blacker, K. H., Oremland, J. D. & Barrett, W. G. (1976), The fate of the transference neurosis after termination of a satisfactory analysis. *J. Amer. Psychoanal. Assn.,* 24:471–498.

Noy, P. (1969), A revision of the psychoanalytic theory of the primary process. *Internat. J. Psycho-Anal.,* 50:155–178.

Ogden, T. (1979), On projective identification. *Internat. J. Psycho-Anal.,* 60:357–374.

Olinick, S. L. (1969), On empathy, and regression in service of the other. *Brit. J. Med. Psychol.,* 42:41–49.

_____ (1980), *The Psychotherapeutic Instrument.* New York: Aronson.

_____ Poland, W. S., Grigg, K. A. & Granatir, W. L. (1973), The psychoanalytic work ego: Process and interpretation. *Internat. J. Psycho-Anal.,* 54:143–151.

Oremland, J. D., Blacker, K. H. & Haskell, F. N. (1975), Incompleteness in "successful" psychoanalyses: A follow-up study. *J. Amer. Psychoanal. Assn.,* 23: 819–844.

Orr, D. W. (1954), Transference and countertransference: A historical survey. *J. Amer. Psychoanal. Assn.,* 2:621–670.

Pfeffer, A. Z. (1959), A procedure for evaluating the results of psychoanalysis: A preliminary report. *J. Amer. Psychoanal. Assn.,* 7:418–444.

_____ (1961), Follow-up study of a satisfactory analysis. *J. Amer. Psychoanal. Assn.,* 9:698–718.

_____ (1963), The meaning of the analyst after analysis: A contribution to the theory of therapeutic results. *J. Amer. Psychoanal. Assn.,* 11:229–244.

Pizer, B. (1992), Discussion of "Touching Limits." Presented at meeting of Massachusetts Institute for Psychoanalysis, October, Cambridge.

Poland, W. S. (1975), Tact as a psychoanalytic function. *Internat. J. Psycho-Anal.,* 56:155–162.

_____ (1977), Pilgrimage: Action and tradition in self analysis. *Internat. J. Psycho-Anal.,* 41:474–504.

_____ (1988), Insight and the analytic dyad. *Psychoanal. Quart.,* 57:341–369.

_____ (1992), Self and other in self-analysis. Presented at meeting of American Psychological Association, April, Washington, DC.

Racker, H. (1957), The meanings and uses of countertransference. *Psychoanal. Quart.,* 26:303–357.

_____ (1958), Psychoanalytic technique and the analyst's unconscious masochism. *Psychoanal. Quart.,* 27:555–562.

Rangell, L. (1969), The intrapsychic process and its analysis—A recent line of thought and its current implications. *Internat. J. Psycho-Anal.,* 50:65–77.

_____ (1979), Contemporary issues in the theory of therapy. *J. Amer. Psychoanal. Assn.,* 27(Suppl.):81–112.

Reich, A. (1960), Further remarks on counter-transference. *Internat. J. Psycho-Anal.,* 41:389–395.

Reich, W. (1933), *Character-Analysis: Principles and Techniques for Psychoanalysts in Practice and in Training.* New York: Orgone Institute, 1945.

Richards, A., rptr. (1980), Panel on technical consequences of object relations theory. *J. Amer. Psychoanal. Assn.,* 28:623–636.

Ross, D. & Kapp, F. (1962), A technique for self-analysis of countertransference: Use of the psychoanalyst's visual images in response to patient's dreams. *J. Amer. Psychoanal. Assn.,* 10:643–657.

Rothstein, A. (1980), Toward a critique of the psychology of the self. *Psychoanal. Quart.,* 49:423–455.

Rycroft, C. (1962), Beyond the reality principle. *Internat. J. Psycho-Anal.,* 43:388–394.

Sampson, H. & Weiss, J. (1986), *The Psychoanalytic Process: Theory, Clinical Observation, and Empirical Research.* New York: Guilford Press.

Sander, L., rptr. (1980), New knowledge about the infant in current research: Implications for psychoanalysis. *J. Amer. Psychoanal. Assn.,* 28:181–198.

Sandler, J. (1976a), Actualization and object relationships. *J. Phila. Assn. Psychoanal.,* 3:59–70.

_____ (1976b), Countertransference and role responsiveness. *Internat. Rev. Psycho-Anal.,* 3:43–47.

Schachter, J. & Butts, H. (1968), Transference and countertransference in interracial analyses. *J. Amer. Psychoanal. Assn.,* 16:792–808.

Schilder, P. (1950), *The Image and Appearance of the Human Body*. New York: International Universities Press.

Schlessinger, N. & Robbins, F. (1974), Assessment and follow-up in psychoanalysis. *J. Amer. Psychoanal. Assn.*, 22:542–567.

_____ & _____ (1975), The psychoanalytic process: Recurrent patterns of conflict and changes in ego functions. *J. Amer. Psychoanal. Assn.*, 23:761–782.

Schur, M. (1966a), Some additional "day residue" of "the specimen dream of psychoanalysis." In: *Psychoanalysis: A General Psychology. Essays in Honor of Heinz Hartmann*, ed. R. M. Loewenstein, L. M. Newman, M. Schur & A. J. Solnit. New York: International Universities Press, pp. 45–84.

_____ (1966b), *The Id and the Regulatory Principles of Mental Functioning*. New York: International Universities Press.

Schwaber, E. (1983), Psychoanalytic listening and psychic reality. *Internat. Rev. Psycho-Anal.*, 10:379–392.

_____ (1986), Reconstruction and perceptual experience. *J. Amer. Psychoanal. Assn.*, 34:911–932.

_____ (1990), Interpretation and the therapeutic action of psychoanalysis. *Internat. J. Psycho-Anal.*, 71:229–240.

_____ (1992), Countertransference: The analyst's retreat from the patient's vantage point. *Internat. J. Psycho-Anal.*, 73:349–362.

Searles, H. F. (1959), The effort to drive the other person crazy—An element in the etiology and psychotherapy of schizophrenia. *Brit. J. Med. Psychol.*, 32:1–19.

Shane, M. (1980), Countertransference and the developmental orientation and approach. *Psychoanal. Contemp. Thought*, 3:195–212.

Shapiro, D. (1976), The analyst's own analysis. *J. Amer. Psychoanal. Assn.*, 24:15–42.

Shapiro, T. (1979), *Clinical Psycholinguistics*. New York: Plenum Press.

Smith, H. F. (1990), Talking and playing with babies: The role of ideologies of child-rearing. In: *Before Speech*, ed. M. Bullowa. Cambridge, England: Cambridge University Press, pp. 264–288.

Sonnenberg, S. (1991), The analyst's self-analysis and its impact on clinical work. *J. Amer. Psychoanal. Assn.*, 39:687–704.

Spitz, R. (1956), Countertransference: Comments on its varying role in the analytic situation. *J. Amer. Psychoanal. Assn.*, 4:256–265.

_____ (1957), *No and Yes*. New York: International Universities Press.

Stern, A. (1924), On the counter-transference in psychoanalysis. *Psychoanal. Rev.*, 11:166–174.

Stern, D. (1977), *The First Relationship: Infant and Mother*. Cambridge, MA: Harvard University Press.

_____ (1985), *The Interpersonal World of the Infant: A View from Psychoanalysis and Developmental Psychology*. New York: Basic Books.

Stone, L. (1961), *The Psychoanalytic Situation: An Examination of Its Development and Essential Nature*. New York: International Universities Press.

Strachey, J. (1934), The nature of the psychotherapeutic action of psycho-analysis. *Internat. J. Psycho-Anal.*, 15:127–159.

Szasz, T. S. (1963), The concept of transference. *Internat. J. Psycho-Anal.*, 44: 432–443.

Thomas, H. (1997), *The Shame Response to Rejection*. Sewickley, PA: Albanel.

Ticho, G. (1967), On self-analysis. *Internat. J. Psycho-Anal.*, 48:308–325.

_____ Chediak, C. & Iwasaki, T. (1971), Cultural aspects of transference and countertransference. *Bull. Menn. Clin.*, 35:313–334.

Tower, L. (1956), Countertransference. *J. Amer. Psychoanal. Assn.*, 4:224–265.

Tronick, E. & Gianino, A. (1986), Interactive mismatch and repair: Challenges to the coping infant. *Zero to Three: Bull. Natl. Ctr. Clin. Infant Programs*, 5:1–6.

Wallerstein, R. S. (1973), Psychoanalytic perspectives on the problem of reality. *J. Amer. Psychoanal. Assn.*, 21:5–33.

Webster's New International Dictionary of the English Language, 2nd ed. (1952). Springfield, MA: Merriam-Webster.

Weigert, E. (1952), Contribution to the problem of terminating psychoanalyses. *Psychoanal. Quart.*, 21:465–480.

Winnicott, D. W. (1949), Hate in the countertransference. In: *Collected Papers: Through Paediatrics to Psychoanalysis*. New York: Basic Books, 1958, pp. 194–203.

_____ (1953), Transitional objects and transitional phenomena. *Internat. J. Psycho-Anal.*, 34:89–97.

_____ (1958), *Collected Papers: Through Paediatrics to Psychoanalysis*. New York: Basic Books.

INDEX

235

James T. McLaughlin, M.D. received psychiatric training at the University of Pittsburgh School of Medicine and attended the Philadelphia Psychoanalytic Institute from 1945 to 1952. Subsequent to his graduation from the latter, he returned to Pittsburgh, where he established his private practice and helped create the intramural analytic institute at the University of Pittsburgh. Some 30 publications in major analytic journals and service on their editorial boards attest to his abiding interest in the evolution of psychoanalytic theory and technique. McLaughlin's writings have centered on psychosomatic medicine, nonverbal communication, and the intertwined psychologies of patient and therapist.

Trained in transactional analysis, body-centered psychotherapy, and psychoanalysis, **William F. Cornell, M.A.** is author of 30 journal articles and book chapters, many of which explore the interfaces among interpersonal, body-centered, and psychoanalytic modalities. He is coeditor of the *Transactional Analysis Journal* and of *From Transactions to Relations: The Emergence of Relational Paradigms in Transactional Analysis*.